W9-APW-804

POPULATION CHANGE AND BUILDING CYCLES

POPULATION CHANGE
AND BUILDING CYCLES

by *Burnham O. Campbell*

ASSISTANT PROFESSOR OF ECONOMICS

UNIVERSITY OF CALIFORNIA

Bureau of Economic and Business Research

UNIVERSITY OF ILLINOIS

URBANA, ILLINOIS

PREFACE

The research that led to this volume began some time ago with the intent of investigating the relationship between monetary policy and residential construction. It soon became clear that existing theories of the residential building cycle were incomplete or even misleading in their implications and did not provide a suitable starting point for analyzing the effect of monetary policy on residential construction. In particular, no existing model of the residential building cycle accounted for the influence of changes in the age composition of the population on the level and composition of housing demand.

The first two chapters are used to establish the rationale for an investigation of age composition and housing demand and to develop a model of the housing market that incorporates differences in the level and composition of housing demand between age classes as a parameter. Except for the last, the remaining chapters are concerned with the empirical analysis of the influence of population and age composition changes on past long swings in residential building in the United States and of the sources of past changes in age composition. The last chapter, which may prove most interesting to those readers directly involved in the housing industry, covers the probable effect on residential construction (in total and for rental and sales units) of the unprecedented changes in the size and age composition of the population that are presently occurring and that will take place in the next 20 years. It is an updated and expanded version of the projections first published in the *Illinois Business Review* ("Prospects for Homebuilding in the 1960's") in May, 1961.

Los Angeles, California
July, 1965

BURNHAM O. CAMPBELL

CONTENTS

LIST OF TABLES

LIST OF CHARTS

I. INTRODUCTION

There are several persuasive reasons for investigating the demographic determinants of residential construction and of the residential building cycle. First, recent interest in the problem of economic development has underlined the need for better understanding of the sources of economic growth and fluctuations in developed nations such as the United States. In this context, anyone attempting to explain long-run change in the United States cannot ignore the close relationships between past long swings in residential building and economic activity and growth in this nation. There is a growing realization that demographic change — in particular, immigration — has been significant in determining both the pattern of economic growth and the residential building cycle in the United States.

Second, there is justified concern mixed with premature optimism regarding the effect of population growth in the next two decades on residential construction. The tremendous growth about to take place in the population over 15 years of age has been well publicized. However, concentration on population totals has tended to obscure the equally tremendous changes — including an absolute decline in the number of people in some age groups — that will take place concurrently in the age composition of the population. Only by examining the influence of changes in age composition on residential building in the past can the import of such changes in the immediate future be understood.

Third, since World War II an inverse relationship has existed between residential construction and gross national product. Increasingly, economists seem to be taking this as evidence that residential construction can be added to the list of built-in stabilizers. The usual explanation of this development is that the government's mortgage insurance programs have made the demand for new dwelling units highly interest elastic, and interest rates tend to move with the level of income.[1]

---

[1] The contracyclical nature of the short cycle in residential construction is shown in Jack M. Guttentag, "The Short Cycle in Residential Construction, 1946-59," *American Economic Review*, Vol. 51, No. 3 (June, 1961), pp. 278-98. An explanation of this relationship based on the inverse relationship between the demand for residential mortgages and the general level of interest rates is given by Leo Grebler in *Housing Issues in Economic Stabilization Policy*, Occasional Paper No. 72 (New York: National Bureau of Economic Research, 1960).

1

However, before deciding that residential construction has been and will be systematically and inversely related to fluctuations in gross national product, several questions must be answered. For example, the effect of changing credit conditions on housing starts would have to be empirically determined. To accomplish this, the influence of the other determinants of housing demand on the total and tenure composition of residential construction must be isolated. In other words, a model relating the total and tenure type of housing starts to population changes and to the key nondemographic determinants of housing demand is required.

Although there have been several studies exploring in detail the relationship between income changes and residential construction, demographic variables beyond family formations or changes in the total population have been generally neglected in housing market models. Briefly stated, the goal of the present volume is to carry both the theoretical and the empirical analyses of the relationship between demographic change and housing demand beyond the consideration of the above aggregates.

Earlier Models

There have been several attempts to explain the national level of residential construction, ranging from loose verbal formulations of the major relationships to precise econometric models.[2] Most of these explanations have suffered from the same fault; they have ignored the problems of aggregation found in housing market analysis.

Changes in total population or in family formations have been related to the national output of dwelling units without consideration of the kind of unit demanded or the geographic composition of demand and of the housing stock. In some of these models the relationship between the population variable and residential construction has been a constant, and

[2] See, for example, the following discussions of the housing market: David Blank, Chester Rapkin, and Louis Winnick, *Housing Market Analysis,* Housing and Home Finance Agency (Washington: U.S. Government Printing Office, 1953); V L. Bassie, *Economic Forecasting* (New York: McGraw-Hill, 1958), Ch. 9 and App. C; Arthur F. Burns, "Long Cycles in Residential Construction" in *The Frontiers of Economic Knowledge,* National Bureau of Economic Research (Princeton: Princeton University Press, 1954), pp. 341-47; Leo Grebler, "The Housing Inventory: Analytic Concept and Quantitative Change," *American Economic Review,* Vol. 41, No. 2 (May, 1951), pp. 555-68; Ernest Fisher and Robert Fisher, *Urban Real Estate* (New York: Holt, 1954), Ch. 10; Sherman Maisel, "Variables Commonly Ignored in Housing Demand Analysis," *Land Economics,* Vol. 25, No. 3 (1949), pp. 260-74; G. W. McKinley and W. C. Freund, "Housing Outlook, 1954-55," *National Savings and Loan Journal,* Vol. 9, No. 2 (February, 1954); Lawrence Klein, *Economic Fluctuations in the United States,* 1921-1941 (New York: Wiley, 1950), pp. 89-95, 101-5, 130-32; and J. Mattila, *An Econometric Analysis of Construction,* Wisconsin Commerce Reports, Vol. 4, No. 1 (1955).

in others it has depended on the level or rate of change in income. A few models have given explicit recognition to the role of credit, and the verbal models and less formal equation systems have often introduced lags in the adjustment of production to changing market demand to explain the building cycle. All of the models have ignored the relationship between changing credit conditions and the supply of new dwelling units by speculative builders, although the interest rate may have been used to explain the relative attractiveness of housing as opposed to other investment opportunities.

In the usual formulation of housing market relationships the ratio of construction to changes in the total population has been determined solely by income, credit conditions, and tastes. On this basis, it has been argued that, since the ratio of housing starts to population changes remained relatively constant between the 1920's and the 1950's, the changes in credit conditions introduced by the government's insured mortgage programs have had little impact on housing markets other than to raise the price of housing.[3]

Ignoring the fact that the national ratio of dwelling units started to changes in the total population depends on the geographic composition of demand and on the type of unit demanded, one may disagree with this conclusion (and the analysis behind it) on other grounds. For example, it is clearly necessary to restrict the population variable used in these models to the population over some minimum age. But even if this change were made, there would still be no reason to expect a constant relationship between residential building and changes in the housing population with economic conditions and tastes given. The housing population at any time consists of people at different life-cycle stages. The number of separate dwelling units demanded by a given number of individuals, the type of dwelling unit demanded, and the average value of the dwelling unit demanded all vary systematically between different life-cycle stages. Moreover, these differences in housing demand by age class have remained remarkably stable over long periods of time in the United States — even as real income has risen in all age classes — and seem to be the result of relatively stable patterns of income, income expectations, family situations, and tastes over the life cycle.

Thus, it is possible for changes in age composition either to shift the ratio of housing starts to changes in the total population without accompanying changes in economic conditions or tastes or to offset the

---

[3] This argument is presented by R. J. Saulnier, Harold Halcrow, and Neil Jacoby in *Federal Lending and Loan Insurance*, National Bureau of Economic Research (Princeton: Princeton University Press, 1958), pp. 341-47.

effects of changes in economic conditions or tastes. Similarly, it is reasonable to expect that a given change in income or in credit conditions will have a different impact on residential construction depending on the age composition of the housing population at the time of the change (e.g., because asset positions vary systematically over the life cycle).

As long as the age composition of the housing population can be reasonably expected to vary over time, both the ratio of residential construction to changes in total population and the impact of changes in economic conditions on residential construction will depend on the age composition of the housing population. If the age composition of the population were not considered, fallacious conclusions about the influence of population or economic changes on residential construction could be drawn from inter-period comparisons of the ratio of housing starts to increments in the total or housing population.

It is necessary, in short, to analyze housing demand within a framework in which explicit recognition is given the constant movement of different individuals into, through, and out of the housing life cycle and to the differences in their demand for housing at different stages of this process.[4]

The Housing Life-Cycle Model

The model developed in Chapter II relates changes in housing demand to fluctuations in population growth within the framework of the housing life cycle and leads to several unexpected conclusions. For example, in the housing life-cycle model a constant periodic increase in the housing population with income and tastes given, resulting from a once-and-for-all increase in the number of births or in the level of immigration, leads to a residential building cycle instead of the expected

---

[4] Louis Winnick, in *American Housing and Its Use* (New York: Wiley, 1957), makes use of age-specific headship rates to explain the long-run trend in the average size of households and in the persons/room ratio. Bureau of Census projections of household formations are based on various assumed age-specific marriage rates and on projections of the proportion of households that will be headed by individuals or consist of unrelated persons (*Current Population Reports,* Series P-20, No. 123, for example). Department of Commerce economists have attempted to measure the backlog of housing demand after World War II and to trace the sources of household formations in the 1950's using "normal" household formations as a reference point. For this purpose, "normal" household formations are based on "normal" marriage rates, by age and sex, "normal" doubling up, and "normal" proportions of households consisting of single or unrelated individuals; for example, see S. Morris Livingston, "Family Formations and the Demand for Residential Construction," *Survey of Current Business,* Vol. 30, No. 3 (March, 1950), pp. 8-15, and L. Jay Atkinson, "Population Growth and Markets" and "Factors in the Housing Market," appearing in the April, 1953, and April, 1960, issues of the *Survey of Current Business,* respectively.

constant level of residential construction. Similarly, a constant percentage increase in the housing population leads to a long swing in the growth rate of the housing stock.

When more than one class of housing is considered, a once-and-for-all increase in births or in immigration yields a series of cyclical adjustments, with rental construction leading total and sales construction at the upper turning point and with the peak in the cycle for higher-quality (i.e., higher-priced) sales units coming several periods after the peak in total residential construction. For this reason, the peak in the average value of housing starts is reached some time after the number of housing starts turns down.

These somewhat special results (special because of the pattern of population change assumed) are indicative of the potential cyclical power of the housing life cycle. In the more general case, with births, deaths, and immigration fluctuating from period to period, the housing life-cycle model leads to the conclusion that not only will the ratio of housing starts to population increments vary widely over time, but that even with economic conditions and tastes unchanged, housing starts may move inversely to population changes. This inverse relationship was found in the United States in 1940-45 — to take one example — when mobilization reduced the effective housing population but the age composition changed so that more dwelling units were required by a smaller population. Any attempt to relate population changes to residential construction by a constant coefficient would prove misleading in this model.

Since both births and immigration have fluctuated in the past in the United States, age composition has changed and the conclusions of the housing life-cycle model are relevant to the United States housing market experience. By summing over the changes in the population in different age classes multiplied by the proportion of household heads in each age class (the headship rate) at the beginning of a period, a measure of the effect of population change alone on housing demand in different time periods was constructed (Chapter III). To trace the impact of age-weighted population changes on the tenure composition of demand, the proportion of renter- or owner-occupied units at the beginning of each period (with qualifications to be discussed later) was used. The difference (d) between the estimated change in the number of dwelling units required and the actual change measured by household formations or the change in the renter- or owner-occupied housing stock was then ascribed to the influence of changes in economic conditions or tastes. Finally, the difference between the estimated effect of population changes on housing demand and the total and tenure type of housing starts was analyzed, paying attention to the level of vacancies, the number of conversions and withdrawals, and so forth.

When the United States record was investigated in this manner (Chapters IV and V), it was found that the number of additional dwelling units required by population changes followed a decadal pattern of alternating peaks and troughs, beginning with the trough in the 1870's and continuing through the trough in the 1950's. Quinquennial data (available only from 1900-1905 on) also showed a consistent pattern of cyclical fluctuations, with the number of additional dwelling units required increasing sharply in one five-year period (1905-10, 1920-25, 1940-45), holding the high level attained for the next five-year period (1910-15, 1925-30, 1945-50), and then falling abruptly in the following period (1915-20, 1930-35, 1950-55).

These fluctuations in the population pressure for additions to the housing stock were reflected in actual household formations and in housing starts (with a much wider amplitude but a similar inter-period ordering of first differences) until the 1950's. It is significant that the similarity between the actual and estimated changes in the number of households and in housing starts is apparent only if the estimates take account of the age composition of population increments.

In other words it is not necessary to look beyond swings in required additions (the term used instead of "the number of additional dwelling units required by changes in the age-standardized housing population") to explain the long swing in household formations and residential construction from the 1870's through the 1940's. If population changes had been the sole determinant of housing demand, the same long swings as were actually experienced would have taken place in the United States in this period. Thus, if changing economic conditions or tastes did more than increase the amplitude of the cycles in residential building based on population factors, they did so through their influence on the size and age composition of population increments (e.g., via immigration), and not directly through changes in headship rates.

However, the 1950's turned out to be a special case. In this decade required additions fell by the largest amount in the 80-year period covered, but household formations and housing starts increased (the latter by a record amount). Conversions filled an important part of the increased demand for separate quarters in the Depression, and when incomes increased during the war, instead of new construction removing this backlog, wartime controls added further to it. Together with the first important change in headship rates in eight decades, this quality backlog more than offset the decline in required additions in the 1950's.

Without further changes in headship rates, now that most of the quality backlog has been removed, the relationship between housing demand and population changes found prior to the 1950's may be more useful in understanding the future than the divergent relationships found in the last decade.

The long swing in population pressure also appears in tracing out decadal and quinquennial changes in the number of rental and sales units required. Investigation of the tenure composition of demand leads to two important conclusions. First, changes in age composition alone can account for over one-third of the increase in the relative importance of owner-occupancy since the turn of the century and have been significant enough to raise sales required additions above rental required additions in some decades and five-year periods while reversing this relationship in others. Second, as suggested by the housing life-cycle model, rental required additions have served as a leading indicator, turning down in 1910-15, 1925-30, and 1945-50 as the total number of additional units required by population changes moved on to a peak.

Comparing sales and rental required additions with changes in owner- and renter-occupied housing stock shows that they moved together (with minor exceptions) until the 1950's. However, one-family and multi-family housing starts did not change with sales and rental required additions from the 1930's on. First the Depression, then World War II, and then the working off of the resulting quality backlog led to wide differences between required additions and household formations by tenure class from 1930 on and to the noted diverse relationship between required additions and housing starts by tenure class. It may be concluded that economic conditions and tastes have been relatively more important in explaining past changes in tenure composition than in explaining either the change in the occupied housing stock or the portion of the change filled by new construction.

The importance of the innovation introduced in this volume in explaining long swings in residential construction is found in the fact that changes in age composition (Chapter VI) reversed the effect of changes in the size of the housing population in several periods and determined the relative magnitude of interperiod changes in population pressure in several other periods. Perhaps the most important of the reversals occurred in 1925-30 when the contemporary change in age composition offset an increase in the size of the population increment and slightly reduced required additions — contributing to the collapse of residential construction in the late 1920's.

The observed long swings in required additions and thus in residential building could be the result of (1) periodic waves of improvement in life expectancy, (2) long swings in births — tracing out a residential building cycle beginning two to three decades after the fluctuations in births, and (3) long swings in the level of immigration to the United States.

From the Civil War to the mid-1930's, with but one exception (1920-25), fluctuations in current immigration controlled the population increments that determined required additions (Chapter VII). Mortality-rate changes served to raise the level of required additions over time (Chapter VI), but did not significantly alter the pattern of population fluctuations underlying the residential building cycle. And, until the 1940's, changes in the size and age composition of the population resulting from past swings in births both reflected the impact of prior waves of immigration on births and were dominated by current changes in immigration.

Thus, for 80 years the timing and amplitude of the long swing in required additions can be explained by the long swing in immigration. Throughout this period, only the expansion in 1920-25 would have taken place without any concurrent increase in immigration. But, even in 1920-25, the rental boom was the result of the current upswing in immigration. The ultimate explanation of the residential building cycle and of the relationship between the residential building cycle and long swings in economic growth then reduces to an analysis of the determinants of immigration to the United States.

From the Civil War to World War I, immigration apparently responded to labor market conditions in the United States, increasing as economic growth raised the demand for labor relative to the supply. The "cobweb" adjustment of immigration to an increase in the demand for labor first increased required additions rapidly; then, as past immigration closed the labor market gap and current immigration stopped increasing, required additions leveled off, leading to overbuilding, a decline in residential construction, and, finally, a depression. In this sense, the residential building cycle was endogenous to the growth process in the United States.

However, the cobweb adjustment of residential construction to the long swing in immigration — itself a response to the expansion phase of the long swing in economic growth — does not tell the whole story. Equally significant is the relationship between immigration and the change in the housing population net of immigration. Immigration tended to increase when the domestic labor force base was increasing relatively slowly and vice versa. As a result, required additions for the immigrant population varied inversely to required additions for the population change net of immigration. This suggests that, in part at least, current immigration was a function of past immigration and births and that immigration served to dampen the effect of swings in the domestic labor supply on per capita labor income and so to stabilize labor's share in national income.

Although fluctuations in immigration continued to dominate changes in the housing population from World War I to the mid-1930's, the long swing in immigration during this period was not the result of the same forces as earlier. The expansion in immigration following World War I was similar to past expansions in the sense that it occurred at the same time that the domestic demand for labor was increasing, but it differed significantly from other expansion periods in coming concurrently with a major increase in the domestic labor force. Both the trough (due to World War I) and the peak (due to restrictive legislation in 1924) were the results of the political forces shaping economic affairs and suggest that the accompanying residential building cycle was an exogenous or causative factor in the transition from postwar expansion to the Great Depression.

After the trough in 1930-35, fluctuations in current immigration were no longer significant in determining housing population increments. From the mid-1930's to the mid-1950's, required additions depended on a composite of past waves in immigration, mortality-rate changes (especially in the 1940's), and past waves in births. In the last 10 years, past waves in births (the decline from 1925-35 at the middle life-cycle stages and the increase in births from 1940 on at the early life-cycle stages) have dominated required additions and will continue to do so for the foreseeable future.

Thus, for the last 30 years population changes have been largely predetermined rather than a function of current economic conditions in the United States. World War II and the subsequent expansion tended to cover up any difficulties that might have resulted from this new situation. In the last six years we have begun to discover some of the problems and effects of a labor force base growing independently of current economic conditions.

As long as immigration could respond to an excess demand for labor, the growth in per capita labor income was not sufficiently rapid to have an important upward impact on headship rates. Similarly, a reduced level of immigration helped to maintain per capita real income as the growth rate of output slowed or the growth rate of the domestic labor force increased. The result was that while immigration dominated population changes, required additions and household formations were closely related. Immigration served both to stabilize per capita real income over time and to create the underlying waves of growth in the domestic labor force that shaped subsequent waves of immigration.

Now that immigration can no longer play this stabilizing role, it seems likely that both per capita real income and headship rates will be subject to wider swings in the future than they have been in the past. For example, it may be that the reversal of all past relationships between household formations and required additions in the 1950's is one result of the changed basis for population increments. In the 1950's, aggregate demand grew at the same time that the population at the early life-cycle stages was falling. As the resulting good job market raised real incomes for people at these stages, immigration could not respond but headship and ownership rates could. It remains to be seen how a labor force growing more rapidly than aggregate demand will affect headship rates and housing markets.

Further understanding of past residential building cycles is derived by investigating the pattern of required additions by age class, recognizing that a given level of required additions for different age classes may have a different effect on housing demand (e.g., because family responsibilities, job security, and tastes differ over the housing life cycle and account for differences in the willingness to postpone demand for separate quarters, to double up, to accept converted dwelling units, and so forth).

From 1870 to 1920, the age composition of required additions reflected the dominance of immigration (Chapter VIII). To illustrate, in 1900-1905, when immigration was increasing rapidly, a relatively large proportion of required additions was accounted for by the first three life-cycle stages (ages 15-24, 25-34, and 35-44) and rental demand increased relative to sales demand. Then, as immigration moved on to a peak in 1905-10, required additions for the second, third, and fourth (45-54) life-cycle stages were relatively most important and sales demand increased rapidly. In 1910-15, with immigration falling off slightly, required additions for the third through the fifth (55-64) life-cycle stages continued to increase, along with sales demand, at the same time that required additions for the first two life-cycle stages and rental demand fell. Finally, all life-cycle stages showed a decline in required additions in 1915-20 as the immigration cycle reached a trough.[5]

---

[5] The decrease in required additions for the 65-and-up age class in 1915-20 was the only decrease recorded in the period covered and presumably reflected the effect of the flu epidemic in 1919 on the population change in this age class. In addition to the decline in immigration, World War I contributed to the decline in required additions at the early life-cycle stages in this period.

Total and rental required additions increased rapidly in 1920-25. Then as total required additions remained at a high level in 1925-30, rental required additions fell abruptly, resulting in a large inventory of vacant rental units in multi-unit structures at the end of the 1920's. An accelerator model might explain why residential construction turned down in 1927 and led into the Depression, but consideration of the age composition of required additions is more suggestive of the source of this collapse.

In 1920-25, as a direct result of current immigration, the largest quinquennial increase from 1900 to 1955 in required additions for the 15-24 age class and the second largest increase ever for the 25-34 age class occurred. The result was the largest quinquennial increase in rental demand to date and a rental construction boom. At the same time, a huge increase in required additions for the last three life-cycle stages (which would have increased total required additions even if immigration had fallen to zero in this five-year period) led to a sales boom.

Then, in 1925-30, with required additions at the late life-cycle stages still increasing, required additions for the 15-35 age class were drastically reduced — mostly because of the drop in immigration following the Immigration Act of 1924. The resulting overbuilding of rental units tended to undermine the sales market and residential construction fell.

The key to the changes in residential building during this critical decade would seem to be the wide shift in the age composition of demand, which, while not importantly affecting the total number of additional dwellings required, greatly affected the tenure composition of demand.

Again in the 1930's (especially the first half), age composition changes were important. A decrease in immigration explains the decrease in total required additions during this decade; but, more important, the age composition shifted so that most of the decrease took place at the key third and fourth life-cycle stages, responsible for most first-time ownership and the then largest increment in headship rates over the housing life cycle. This decline (more than two times that of any other in the 35-44 age class) was predetermined, going back to the decline in immigration in 1915-20 and World War I.

Thus changes traced to the Immigration Act of 1924 started residential construction (and the economy?) down in the late twenties, but in the absence of any decrease in immigration in 1930-35 the contemporary changes in age composition would have weakened housing demand and sales required additions would have fallen, suggesting that housing markets would have been depressed in the 1930's even in the absence of a general depression. Moreover, once a decrease in economic activity was underway, the age composition of required additions in 1930-35 made residential construction highly susceptible to further reduction. The only age classes showing increases in required additions were the 25-34 and 54 and up age classes. Except for stage one (15-24), these are the life-cycle stages most likely to suffer unemployment or to postpone demand for separate quarters or accept converted units when income is falling.

In the 1940's, a residential construction boom based on population changes was cut off by World War II. One result of the war was that the effect of the decade's population changes on housing demand was concentrated in the second half of the 1940's. For example, after adjusting for the movement of people into and out of the armed forces, required additions in 1945-50 for the 25-34 life-cycle stage were greater than in any *full* decade from the 1860's to the 1950's, and sales required additions for the 25-34 and 35-44 age classes were 40 percent greater than in any prior quinquennium, which helps explain the large increase in speculative building of tract housing just after World War II. For total required additions, the increase in this five-year period was the largest from 1900-1905 to 1960-65.[6] The production of new dwelling units could not keep up with the resulting increase in housing demand and household formations exceeded housing starts, setting the stage for the residential construction boom of the 1950's.

Required additions fell by the largest amount ever during the 1950's, and required additions for the 25-34 age class fell by six times any past decline to a negative level — in other words, in 1960 fewer dwelling units would have been required to house this age group than in 1950 at 1950 headship rates. In general, the age composition of required additions was even more adverse for a building boom than in the 1930's. The same relationships in the past meant falling residential construction and general economic decline, but not in the 1950's. In this decade, household formations continued to increase, moving ever further away from required additions, and housing starts began the task of catching up, reaching record levels and exceeding household formations for the decade.

The increase in household formations came about largely as a result of increased headship rates, mostly at the first two life-cycle stages and involving so-called nonnormal families. The reasons for this change in headship rates can be found in economic expansion, low levels of unemployment (to the late 1950's), and the effect of World War II on tastes. Important to the final result was the small population growth at the early

---

[6] In fact, basing projected household formations on 1960 headship rates, the adjusted increase in required additions in 1945-50 was greater than the increase forecast for any quinquennial period through 1980-85, and the level of required additions attained in 1945-50 will not be exceeded until 1975-80.

life-cycle stages and the absence of immigration to fill the resulting labor shortage.

In the late 1950's, the sudden rapid growth in the entering population (Stage 1) contributed, along with a slowdown in economic growth, to increased unemployment. At this time, the advance in headship rates slowed and residential construction shifted in composition toward rental units. Geographic redistribution and a high level of withdrawals helped keep the number of housing starts up, but only at the expense of an increase in vacancy rates.

Thus, a new pattern of long swings in required additions is emerging; waves of immigration are no longer leading required additions and residential construction through a long swing of alternating decadal peaks and troughs. It has now been a decade and one-half since the last peak in required additions, and we are not yet back to the 1945-50 level. In the future (for the next 20 years at least), the negative changes in required additions traced to the 1925-35 decline in births followed by the huge increases traced to the wartime "baby boom" will shape the long swing in required additions.

The prospects for the next 25 years (including the present half-decade) are discussed in Chapter IX. First, it is apparent that if household formations in the 1960's are based on population changes alone (i.e., if household formations approximately equal required additions as they did prior to the 1950's), then household formations will fall relative to the 1950's, with the decline showing up primarily in the change in the owner-occupied housing stock.[7] Only continued and larger increases in headship rates and in owner-occupancy rates than in the 1950's would prevent this decline. The possibilities for continued positive increments

---

[7] A single numerical example will illustrate this point. Suppose the housing population was 100 in 1950 and 120 in 1960 and that the average headship rate was 40 percent in 1950 and 50 percent in 1960. Then "average" required additions would be estimated as $8 = (120 \times .4 - 100 \times .4)$ for the 1950's, but actual household formations would be 12 greater than required additions and would equal 20 or $(120 \times .5 - 100 \times .4)$. Now, if the population increases to 150 in 1970, but the average headship rate remains unchanged, then actual household formations (which will equal required additions) will be $15 = (150 \times .5 - 120 \times .5)$ in the 1960's. Thus, if residential construction tends to vary proportionately with household formations, the level of residental construction will fall in the 1960's despite the 50 percent increase in the population increment, unless the average headship rate continues to increase. A similar example could be constructed for population changes and ownership rates. Since changes in age composition will serve to reduce rather than increase both the average headship and the average ownership rate during the 1960's, a considerable increase in age-specific headship rates and ownership rates will be necessary to prevent a decline in household formations and in the demand for additional sales units.

in headship rates are directly related to employment opportunities at the early life-cycle stages and to improved life-expectancy at the late life-cycle stages. Short of a two-house family, the scope for increased headship rates at the middle life-cycle stages is slight.

If unemployment rates continue at their present high levels for the early life-cycle stages, then the prospects for continued improvement in headship rates would seem dim. The need is not just for economic growth sufficiently rapid to absorb a growing army of young people into the employed labor force, but, for housing markets at least, the growth in aggregate demand must be fast enough to raise the per-capita real incomes of young people as well. Otherwise, the level of household formations will fall in the 1960's relative to the 1950's.

But even if household formations do not fall, to maintain residential construction at the level of the 1950's it will be necessary to achieve a continued excess of housing starts over household formations in the 1960's. This is a possibility if withdrawals and geographic mobility remain at high levels (both are again tied to economic growth); but such an excess has never before been achieved for two consecutive decades and was only achieved in the 1920's at the expense of increased vacancies that finally led to a collapse of residential construction and a long period in which household formations exceeded housing starts.

In any event, the prospects for a significant expansion in residential construction in the 1960's — despite the large increase in the total housing population — are slim. Both the required increase in headship rates and the effect on the average value of housing starts of the age composition of demand mitigate against this happening. Thus, the expansion in aggregate demand necessary to prevent a decline in residential construction must originally occur outside the housing market; there is unlikely to be much stimulus to increased demand arising within this sector of the private economy in the 1960's.

By the 1970's, there will be such a large increase in the housing population (most of which will take place in 1970-75) that even at 1960 headship rates required additions will exceed household formations during the 1950's. So, even if headship rates do not increase (of course, they must not fall), there will be a larger increase in the population pressure for additional dwelling units in the 1970's than has ever occurred before. This unmatched increase will be coupled with an equally unmatched concentration of required additions at one life-cycle stage (the 25-34 age class). Two important questions raised by this prospect are, (1) Will employment opportunities be present to absorb the increase in people at this life-cycle stage and make their potential demand effective? and

(2) Can the housing market adapt itself to satisfactorily meet the specialized housing needs reflected in this increase without the speculative excesses of the past?

Whatever the answers, required additions will continue to expand in the 1980's. However, the rate of increase will be much slower, reflecting a trend that can be traced all the way back to the decline in births between 1925 and 1935. It will be in this manner, through fluctuations in the rate of increase in required additions rather than in the level, that the long swing in required additions will be recorded in the future.

This then is the record and the prospect. Past experience can provide a basis for understanding the future, when changes in age composition will be relatively more important than ever before and when — unlike during much of the past — we shall know of the forthcoming changes before they occur.

II. A LIFE-CYCLE MODEL OF HOUSING DEMAND

The most common population variable used in models of housing demand or of the residential building cycle is the total population of a nation. Total population may be included directly as an independent variable or used to explain household formations, which then are related to residential building. Thus, the usual approach to population growth and housing demand ignores the potential effect of the housing life cycle on new residential construction.

If the total population is divided into age classes, the ratio of heads of households to the total number in an age class first increases as older age classes are considered and then falls off. The proportion of households owning their own dwelling units and the average value of dwelling unit occupied follow a similar pattern. The proportion renting shows a different pattern. Unless the population always changes so that the age composition of the total population remains constant, these relationships mean that the total and tenure composition of housing demand and the average value of dwelling units demanded will depend on the distribution of population changes between age classes.

The Life-Cycle Pattern

Since the demand for separate quarters comes almost entirely from individuals or heads of spending units 15 years of age or older, total population is not the relevant aggregate for housing demand analysis. Rather, the housing population, defined to include all persons 15 years of age or older, should be used as a base for measuring changes in the size of the population or in calculating average headship rates for use in housing market analysis.

By dividing the housing population into five-year age intervals from 15-19 to 70-74, with an open interval from 75 years of age up, and calculating the ratio of heads of households to the total population in each interval (known as the age-specific headship rate), the characteristic

CHART 1. HEADSHIP RATES BY AGE CLASS, 1890, 1940, AND 1950

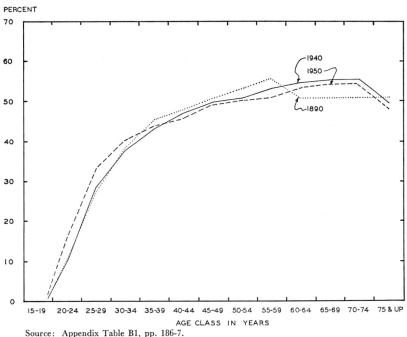

Source: Appendix Table B1, pp. 186-7.

housing life-cycle pattern is found.[8] The variations in headship rates among age classes are shown in Chart 1 for 1890, 1940, and 1950. In all three decades the housing life-cycle pattern is essentially the same: headship rates begin very low at the early life-cycle stages, increase rapidly through the age classes where most families are formed, continue to increase slowly through the middle life-cycle stages, and then turn down.

---

[8] The housing life cycle as defined in the text differs from the usual life-cycle groups discussed. In the latter, the total population is first divided into three broad age classes (18-44, 45-64, 65-and-up), and then the age classes are further subdivided by marital status and the presence or absence of children under 18 in family units. Since important changes in headship and tenure rates occur within the age classes utilized in the customary life-cycle definition, it (that definition) is not suitable for housing demand analysis. Of course, the ideal breakdown would divide the population into age classes of not more than 10 years in length, and then divide the age classes by sex, marital status, and the presence or absence of children of different ages in family units. Such data are not available for a sufficient number of decades to justify their inclusion in this study. However, since many of the life-cycle changes in marital status and family size are closely correlated with age, the changes in headship rates between the age classes used reflect the impact of these demographic variables on housing demand.

Chart 2. Housing by Tenure Class as a Percentage of
Total Nonfarm Population in Each Age Class

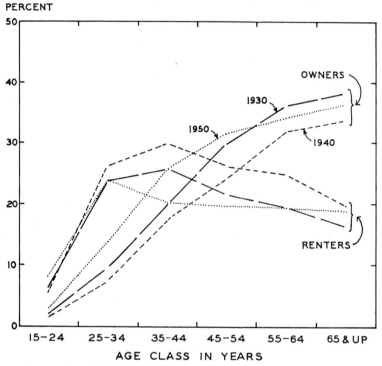

Sources: Appendix Tables B1 and B2, pp. 186-7 and 188, respectively.

Between 1890 and 1950 three changes significant for understanding developments in housing markets in the United States occurred. (1) The level of headship rates increased sharply in the 20-24 and 25-29 age classes (all of this change coming in the 1940's). (2) The peak headship rate moved from the 55-59 age class to the 70-74 age class. (3) The entire housing life-cycle pattern flattened out. These changes played an important role in this country's residential building cycle (especially the first), but even more important is the fact that the general pattern of the housing life cycle has been strikingly uniform for over half a century.

The variation in the tenure composition of demand between age classes is shown in Chart 2 for 10-year intervals in the 1930, 1940, and 1950 census years. The percentage of renters in an age class rises rapidly during the early life-cycle stages, reaches a peak in the 35-44 age class, and then falls slowly throughout the remainder of the life cycle. The percentage of owners, on the other hand, increases throughout the life cycle, relatively slowly at first, most rapidly in the 35-44 age class, and then at a decreasing rate to the end of the life cycle.

A direct implication of the tenure life cycle is that a bulge in births or in immigration that increases the population change from one period to the next at the early life-cycle stages will initially increase the demand primarily for rental units. Then, with a lag of as much as 20 years after the initial effect on rental markets is felt, the peak increase in demand for sales housing will take place. Considering the upgrading in quality of dwelling unit over the housing life cycle, especially within the ownership market, the peak impact of a population wave on some classes of sales housing may not occur until 30 or 40 years after the wave appears.

Like the housing life cycle, the tenure life cycle has changed over time while still retaining the same general pattern. The most significant development has been the increase in the percentage of owners in the early life-cycle stages (especially in the 25-34 and 35-44 age classes between the 1940 and 1950 samples) and the shift in the peak rental demand from the 35-44 age class back to the 25-34 age class in 1950. That the increase in the percentage of owners in the early life-cycle stages in 1950 did not come at the expense of renting may seem surprising, but it simply reflects the increase in headship rates at the same life-cycle stages between 1940 and 1950.

Finally, the value life cycle is shown in Chart 3 for sales and rental units for 10-year age intervals. The average value of sales and rental units occupied follows a cyclical pattern over the life cycle, increasing through the 45-54 age class and decreasing thereafter.[9]

---

[9] The percentage distribution of household heads by age-class between value classes of owner-occupied and rental-occupied dwellings follows:

Age	$0 to $2,400 Renter- occupied	Owner- occupied	$2,400 to $4,799 Renter- occupied	Owner- occupied	$4,800 to $7,199 Renter- occupied	Owner- occupied	$7,200-and-up Renter- occupied	Owner- occupied
15–24....	63%	66%	32%	25%	4%	7%	2%	2%
25–34....	47	43	41	35	10	15	2	7
35–44....	40	30	42	38	14	20	4	12
45–54....	39	26	41	39	14	23	5	12
55–64....	44	29	38	41	13	19	5	11
65-and-up	57	37	30	28	9	16	4	9

Source: See Chart 3, p. 20. The *1950 Census of Housing* (Volume II, Part I), although offering less complete information than the *1940 Census of Housing,* shows about the same distribution as this tabulation for household heads (males only) among value classes by age class.

CHART 3. THE VALUE LIFE CYCLE

VALUE CLASS IN
THOUSANDS OF DOLLARS

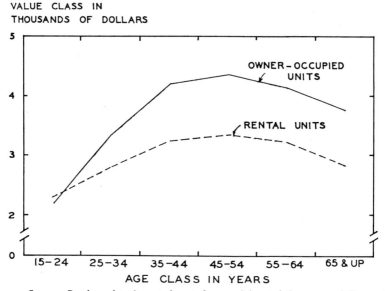

AGE CLASS IN YEARS

Source: Based on data for actual rent classes and imputed (owner-occupied) rent classes from the *Census of Population and Housing: Families, Tenure, and Rent, 1940*, United States Bureau of the Census (Washington: U.S. Government Printing Office, 1943), Table 8, pp. 41-42.

To estimate value, the rent classes were multiplied by a factor of 10. The average value in an age class (for each tenure class) was then calculated by multiplying the number of owners or renters in each value class by the mid-value for the class, summing over all value classes, and dividing by the total number of owners or renters in the age class.

A Single-Class Life-Cycle Model

In order that the potential cyclical role of a changing age composition may be highlighted, several simplifying assumptions will be made at this stage of the analysis.

(1) There is only one class of housing in the market — sales housing produced by speculative builders under conditions of perfect competition and long-run constant costs.

(2) Builders are always correct in their estimates of market demand.

(3) Dwelling units last forever.

(4) When existing dwelling units cannot be sold at current prices they are left vacant.

(5) Credit terms are fixed and the supply of credit is perfectly elastic at the fixed terms.

(6) The housing life cycle of each member of the housing population is split into M periods of equal duration and no one dies until the end of the Mth period.

(7) The headship rate follows a cyclical pattern, increasing and then decreasing from the first to the Mth period but remaining the same at all life-cycle stages from period to period.

Given these assumptions, price is a parameter of the model and supply conditions or mortgage market conditions have no influence (other than the assumed constant one) over the end result. The required stock of dwelling units (Hr) can be found by totaling the number of household heads at any time, which can be done simply by multiplying the headship rate $(h_i, i = 1, 2, \ldots, M)$ for each stage by the population in the stage $(p_i, i = 1, 2, \ldots, M)$ and summing over all stages as follows:

$$(1) \qquad Hr = \sum_{i=1}^{M} h_i p_i.$$

Construction (C) will take place if the demand for dwelling units (number of households) so measured is greater than the existing stock of dwelling units (He) at the fixed price and credit terms. If demand is less than the existing stock, then the difference will equal vacancies (V). These relationships are summed in Equation (2).

$$(2) \qquad Hr - He = C \text{ if positive and } V \text{ if negative.}$$

Putting the argument in terms of the number entering and leaving the housing population and the number at each stage of the housing life cycle, and introducing a time dimension for construction, the significance of age composition can be directly seen. Assuming for now that positive increments in the population occur only through past births and writing out (1) — after replacing p_i with p_n or the number entering the housing population in Period n — yields the following equation for the required stock at the end of Period $n - 1$.

$$(3) \qquad Hr_{n-1} = p_{n-1}h_1 + p_{n-2}h_2 + p_{n-3}h_3 + \ldots + p_{n-M}h_M.$$

In this equation people enter the housing population only at the first stage and leave (death) only at the last stage. If the duration of each stage equals 10 years and there are 6 stages, then the required stock equals the number born 15 to 24 years before times the headship rate in the first stage plus the number born 25 to 34 years before times the headship rate at the second stage, and so on through to the number born 65 to 74 years before times the headship rate at the Mth stage.

The change in the required stock during Period n will then depend on the number entering the first stage less the number leaving the first stage times the headship rate for the first stage plus the number entering the second stage less the number leaving the second stage times the headship rate for the second stage, and so on. This can be written out and related to construction and vacancies as follows:

$$(4) \quad (p_n - p_{n-1})h_1 + (p_{n-1} - p_{n-2})h_2 + \ldots + (p_{n-M+1} - p_{n-M})h_M - V$$
$$= C \text{ if positive or } dV \text{ if negative.}$$

One significant conclusion can be derived immediately from this equation. The change in the housing population in any period is defined by the single difference, $p_n - p_{n-M}$, but the change in housing demand and thus in construction depends on the sum of all the differences.

This point is relevant to clarifying relationships between construction and population increments to mark off changes in economic conditions and tastes (e.g., as Grebler, Blank, and Winnick do in their book, *Capital Formation in Residential Real Estate*).[10] The implication is that the ratio of construction to changes in the housing population may shift, with economic conditions or tastes remaining unchanged. In other words, housing population changes depend on the difference between births 15 to 25 years before and births 65 to 74 years before, but housing demand and construction depend as well on all that happened in between. Thus, construction and the housing population may well move inversely or by diverse relative amounts.

Turning to patterns of population growth and their impact on construction, suppose that a constant number (p_c) enter Stage 1 of the housing life cycle each period, starting from a zero housing stock and housing population. The result would be a residential construction cycle, with construction equal to $h_1(p_c)$ in Period 1, $h_2(p_c)$ in Period 2, and so forth, and lasting for M periods. After M periods the population entering Stage 1 would be equal to the population leaving Stage M and the housing market would be in equilibrium and residential construction would fall to zero. However, if the entering population doubled in Period M plus 1 and increased by a like amount after each M period, the cycle would be repeated. Chart 4 illustrates this cycle.

The conclusion from this somewhat special example is that despite the constant increase in the housing population, construction follows a stable cyclical pattern. The usual acceleration approach, relating the growth in the population to the level of residential construction by a constant coefficient, simply does not apply to the housing life-cycle model, except in the special cases where the population grows by a constant absolute or per-

---

[10] Leo Grebler, David Blank, and Louis Winnick, *Capital Formation in Residential Real Estate — Trends and Prospects*, National Bureau of Economic Research (Princeton: Princeton University Press, 1956).

CHART 4. POPULATION CHANGE AND RESIDENTIAL CONSTRUCTION:
A SPECIAL LIFE-CYCLE CASE[a]

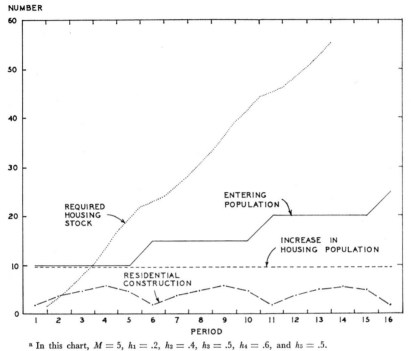

[a] In this chart, $M = 5$, $h_1 = .2$, $h_2 = .4$, $h_3 = .5$, $h_4 = .6$, and $h_5 = .5$.

centage amount, and then only after an adjustment period based on the housing life cycle lasting three-quarters of a century.[11]

Of course, a once-and-for-all increase in the entering population lasting for 60 or more years would be equally unlikely or special. However,

---

[11] If the entering population grows by an arithmetic progression, then, after M periods, construction will equal $dp \sum_{i}^{M} hi$, and the change in the housing population will also equal a constant, dpM, where dp is the common difference in the progression. Since both construction and the change in the housing population will equal constants, their ratio will be a constant. If the entering population follows a geometric progression, then, again after M periods, the ratio of construction to the change in the housing population will be a constant. In Period $M + n$, construction will equal

$$pr^n [r^M h_1 + (r^M - r^{M-1}) h_2 + \ldots + h_M].$$

In the same period, the change in the housing population will equal $pr^n (r^M - 1)$. In both equations, r is the common ratio. Since n is the only variable in either equation and pr^n cancels when construction is divided by the change in the housing population, it follows that the resulting ratio is a constant.

the pattern of population growth assumed for Chart 4 serves to illustrate very clearly the potential cyclical effect of the housing life cycle on housing demand and is a useful approximation of the population growth in a newly settled nation or region or of the impact of an increased in-migration or births (with a lag) on construction, beginning from an equilibrium position.[12]

The resulting residential building cycle demonstrates that great care should be exercised in the interpretation of past building cycles, especially if per capita housing starts or household formations are used to distinguish between the demographic and nondemographic determinants of residential building. Per capita ratios are meaningful for this purpose only if there is no housing life cycle or if the age composition of the population does not change over time — both conditions unsupported by the facts.

Whatever their heuristic value or adaptability for growth theories, all patterns of population growth discussed so far are essentially special cases. A moment's reflection on Equation (4) suggests that an infinite number of relationships between population change and residential construction are possible, some relating population increases to increasing, some to decreasing, and some to constant residential construction. With so many possibilities it is necessary to look at the actual path of population growth before drawing any conclusions about the relationship between population and residential construction in local markets or nations.

In the United States, for example, both the entering population and the housing population changes have moved up and down during the last century, bearing little resemblance to any of the special cases discussed. The fluctuations in the entering population have been sufficiently repetitive to lead to recurring cycles in residential construction (see Chapter IV), but the cycles have not been particularly similar in amplitude or duration. The housing population has not increased by a constant absolute or percentage amount from decade to decade (or from five-year period to five-year period). It is a mistake to smooth the variation in population changes to get a constant rate of growth, just because theory has assumed this sort of increase. The variation that has taken place has changed the age composition of the population and so has shifted the relationship between population changes and residential construction in the United States over the last century, and no account of the experience in United States housing markets would be complete without considering this variable.

---

[12] Equilibrium exists when the movement of people through the housing life cycle leaves the demand for housing equal to the stock from one period to the next.

Local Markets and Aggregation

All dwelling units differ from one another (in location, style, tenure, value, and so forth), so that the discussion of housing markets necessarily involves the aggregation of unlike commodities. Since dwelling units in different local markets are not close substitutes for most households and since most dwelling units are immobile, only extreme differences in price would lead households to change their location (change jobs) or lead to the physical removal of dwelling units from excess-supply to excess-demand markets. Thus, when a shift in demand leads to vacancies and falling prices in one local market and increased prices in another, profitable opportunities for new construction (with total demand in both markets unchanged) are likely in the excess-demand market. Only if shifts in demand or supply between local markets leave room for construction in all local markets — and then, only if supply conditions are similar in all local markets — is it likely that output will be unchanged when the geographic composition of supply and demand changes.

Similarly, with the exception of single-family units, dwellings are not easily shifted from one tenure class to another. With the same exception, rents tend to be inflexible downward in response to excess supply. Finally, rental and sales units in similar quality classes are often not considered close substitutes by households.[13] Together these relationships mean that when demand shifts between rental and sales markets construction will be as or more important than price changes or reclassification of the existing stock in removing excess demand. If so, then it is necessary to distinguish between rental and sales markets in explaining construction in a given local market.[14]

---

[13] The basic evidence of downward inflexibility in rents is given by Blank, Rapkin, and Winnick, *op. cit.,* Ch. 3. For information on the relative preferences of consumers for renting or owning, see the discussion in the "1955 Survey of Consumer Finances, Housing Arrangements of Consumers," *Federal Reserve Bulletin,* Vol. 41, No. 8 (August, 1955), and the Housing and Home Finance Agency, "Why People Buy the Houses They Do," *Housing Research,* Vol. 41, No. 8 (March, 1953), pp. 856-68.

[14] Even when shifts in the composition of demand leave excess demand for both rental and sales units, the more elastic response of sales production (especially in lower price classes and metropolitan areas) means that the level of production of new dwelling units is likely to be changed. The speculative builder of sales units requires less equity to get into operation, and he invests his funds for only a short period of time. For him, it is the market situation in the next half-year that is relevant. For the investor in large multi-unit rental properties, the decision involves earning a profitable return for many years to come. He must expect that the current, favorable market situation will last, and this generally will require that it has lasted some time before a decision to build is made. See Fisher and Fisher, *op. cit.,* p. 206, for a discussion of this point.

There is a certain asymmetry in the foregoing conclusion. An excess demand for sales units at the expense of rentals can be resolved by re-classification only to the extent that there are single-family units in the rental market, usually an insignificant part of the rental stock. On the other hand, an excess demand for rental units at the expense of sales units — unless it is the result of a change in tastes raising the demand for the characteristics of apartments located in multi-unit structures — can readily be filled by shifting vacant sales units to the rental market. However, in developing the multi-class housing life-cycle model, but not in analyzing the United States experience, it will be assumed that shifts in demand between rental and sales units are solely resolved by construction in the excess-demand class and by increased vacancies in the excess-supply class.

Shifts in the composition of demand between value classes (within or across tenure classes) are also likely to change the rate of output of new dwelling units. Briefly, the large gaps between alternatives open (one result of mass production), the existence of a floor on the acceptable quality of housing, and financial constraints on moving up the housing ladder make large shifts in relative prices necessary to restore equilibrium without construction when demand shifts between value classes. Thus, a shift in demand between value or quality classes may open the door to profitable construction opportunities. This will be particularly true if the excess-supply value class is below the excess-demand value class.

There are other characteristics distinguishing dwelling units, but those mentioned — location, tenure class, and value class — are both the most important and the most quantifiable.

A Multi-Class Life-Cycle Model

All the assumptions made for the single-class market, except, of course, that there is only one class of housing, will be retained in developing the first multi-class model. In addition it is assumed that vacant units in one class of housing can not be shifted to others. Thus, the analysis of the determinants of the required stock and of construction in the single-class market applies directly to a specific class of housing in the multi-class model.

Construction will occur in the jth class of rentals when the following sum is positive, and increased vacancies will result when it is negative.

$$(5) \qquad C_{rj} \text{ or } dV_{rj} = r_1^j(p_n - p_{n-1}) + r_2^j(p_{n-1} - p_{n-2}) + \ldots \\ + r_M^j(p_{n-M} - p_{n-M+1}).$$

In this equation, p_i and M are as before, r_{ji} is the ratio of the number of Class j rental units demanded in the ith life-cycle stage to the housing population at that stage, and C_{rj} and V_{rj} are construction and vacancies in the jth class of rental. The same relationships exist for the other classes of rentals, and when o_{ji} is substituted for r_{ji} and C_{oj} and V_{oj} replace C_{rj} and V_{rj}, for the various classes of sales housing.

Construction will occur in the multi-class model when the actual stock of dwelling units is less than the required stock — that is, when Equation (5) is positive — in any class of dwelling units. Since, by assumption, units in different classes are not substitutes for one another, total construction will equal the sum of the excess-demand classes and there may be positive construction for one or more classes at the same time that vacancies are increasing in other classes. Thus, residential construction may occur without any change in total market demand — just a shift in its composition — or even at the same time that there is market-wide excess supply. The required stock of all dwelling units will be the same for the same housing population, as in the single-class market (r_{ij} plus o_{ij} equals h_i), but the response of construction to a given change in the required stock will not be the same. Clearly, the ratio of rental or sales units demanded to the total stock will depend, for a given housing population, on the age composition of the population.

Considering only two classes of dwelling units, sales and rental units, a once-and-for-all increase in the entering population with an initial housing stock of zero will again lead to a residential building cycle. However, applying the tenure life cycle shown in Chart 2, the resulting long swings in rental and sales construction will be different in timing and amplitude. Rental construction will follow a time path determined by the rental headship rate at the first, second, and on to the last housing life-cycle stage, and sales construction will follow a time path determined by the sales headship rates at the same stages. Total construction will equal the sum of rental and sales construction and will vary with the headship rates at each life-cycle stage as before.

This once-and-for-all adjustment process is traced out in Chart 5. For illustrative purposes, after the first cycle is completed, it is assumed that the entering population increases for several periods and then decreases. As expected, given the tenure life cycle, rental construction moves to a peak in Period 2 and then falls off, serving as a leading indicator for sales demand and construction and also for total demand and construction. Sales construction does not reach a peak until the fourth life-cycle stage and moves with total construction throughout. When the entering popu-

Chart 5. Population Change and Residential
Construction: The Multi-Class Market
(Sales and rental units)[a]

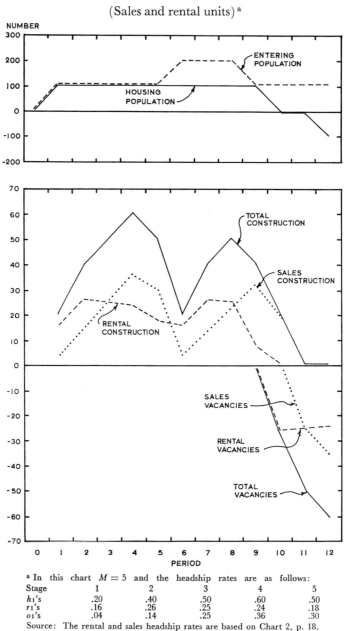

[a] In this chart $M = 5$ and the headship rates are as follows:

Stage	1	2	3	4	5
h_1's	.20	.40	.50	.60	.50
r_1's	.16	.26	.25	.24	.18
o_1's	.04	.14	.25	.36	.30

Source: The rental and sales headship rates are based on Chart 2, p. 18.

lation declines in the ninth period, we find rental construction dropping immediately, whereas sales construction continues to increase. In fact, sales construction remains positive after vacancies appear in the rental market. The extension of this analysis to additional classes of rental and sales units is obvious and would lead to a peeling off of peaks in construction for different classes of housing, beginning with the classes most suitable for the early life-cycle stages and continuing on to a final peak for units specialized to fit the needs of the last life-cycle stage.

Two important conclusions can be derived from this analysis of once-and-for-all population changes. First, one would expect to find the turning point in the construction of rental units leading the turning point in the construction of sales units and, for this reason, to find the average value of housing starts lagging behind the number of housing starts. Second, the opportunities for lags in construction behind population changes are increased in the multi-class market over the single-class market, since shifts in the demand for rentals leading to excess supply do not offset increases in the demand for sales housing based on past changes in the entering population. It is important to note that the response of the tenure composition of demand to changes in immigration would be similar to that outlined for births, since most immigrants are in the early life-cycle stages.

Fluctuations in Population Growth

In general, neither the size of the entering population nor the change in the housing population will remain constant or increase by a constant absolute or percentage amount. Once such restrictive assumptions are discarded and it is recognized that the entering population actually fluctuates from period to period, the relationship between births, population increments, and residential construction becomes very complex. Each successive entering population traces out its own cycle, and so we have different entering populations and their different cycles superimposed on one another without constraint as to the accompanying change in the housing population.

It is possible, for example, to construct a cycle in births that will lead to a zero rate of construction and increasing vacancies at the same time that the housing population is increasing — even in the single-class model. If the entering population increases sharply relative to the entering population M periods before, and if this sharp increase follows several periods of decline in the entering population, then the higher headship rates weighting the declining numbers at Stages 2, 3, and so on, may more than offset the impact of a larger number at the low headship-rate Stage 1.

The result would be a reduction in the required stock of housing at the same time that the housing population is increasing. The glow of optimism surrounding the increase in population at early life-cycle stages in the 1960's may be unjustified for exactly this reason.

Similarly, a decline in the entering population and in the housing population may continue for several periods with construction positive or even increasing. One should not be surprised (as some market analysts were in the 1950's) to find a reduction in the population in the age classes where families are usually formed associated with boom conditions in the housing market.

In the multi-class model, recent changes in the entering population (lagging changes in births by two periods) will dominate the rental market first. Thus, if births decrease sharply, after increasing for several periods, the result will soon be zero construction and increasing vacancies in rentals. However, since prices cannot quickly adjust, the excess supply of rentals will not change the impact of the earlier increases in births on the demand for sales housing at later life-cycle stages, where the peak ownership headship rate is reached. Therefore, construction may remain positive in Class 2 sales housing after vacancies have appeared in Class 1 rental and sales housing, et cetera. If no one buys Class 4 sales housing until the fourth life-cycle stage, then the entering population (and the housing population) may decline for four periods before residential construction is reduced in the fourth class of sales housing. Also, residential construction, unlike the single-class market, may exceed net household formations in the multi-class market. This relationship helps explain the excess of single-family housing starts over the change in the owner-occupied housing stock in the 1930's and the increase in the average value of housing starts in the late 1950's.

A hypothetical example of the response in a single-class and in a multi-class market to the same fluctuations in births from period to period is shown in Charts 6 and 7. Although the swings in births are wider than those experienced in the United States (the total population is allowed to fall in several periods), this example suggests several significant conclusions.

First, in both the single- and the multi-class markets, residential construction and changes in the housing population move inversely in many periods and their rates of change differ widely in several others. This suggests that when the entering population has fluctuated, a close relationship between housing starts or household formations and changes in the housing population should not be expected.

CHART 6. THE MULTI-CLASS MARKET AND
POPULATION CHANGE: THE GENERAL CASE

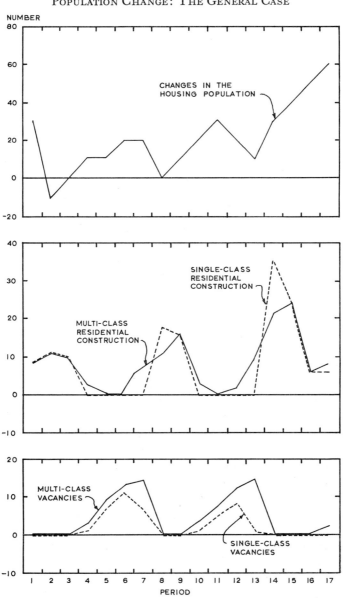

Sources: Based on 1930 tenure rates (Chart 2) and on the following headship rates: $h_1 = 10$ percent, $h_2 = 30$ percent, $h_3 = 50$ percent, $h_4 = 60$ percent, $h_5 = 60$ percent, and $h_6 = 50$ percent. Starting with Stage 1, the population was assumed to be as follows by stages in Period 1: 60, 50, 40, 30, 20, and 30. The entering population was then assumed to vary from Period 2 on as follows: (2) 20, (3) 20, (4) 40, (5) 50, (6) 70, (7) 80, (8) 20, (9) 30, (10) 60, (11) 80, (12) 90, (13) 90, (14) 50, (15) 70, (16) 110, and (17) 140.

Chart 7. Population Change and Tenure Composition
of Demand: The General Case

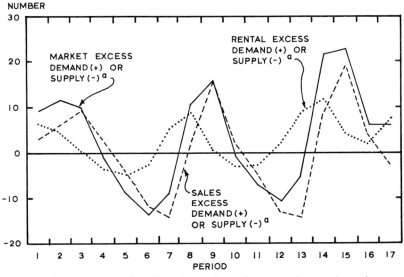

NUMBER

MARKET EXCESS
DEMAND(+) OR
SUPPLY(−)ᵃ

RENTAL EXCESS
DEMAND(+) OR
SUPPLY(−)ᵃ

SALES
EXCESS
DEMAND(+)
OR SUPPLY(−)ᵃ

PERIOD

ᵃ Rental or sales excess demand equals rental or sales construction rental or sales excess
supply equals rental or sales vacancies. Market excess supply or demand equals rental plus sales
excess supply or demand.
Source: Chart 6, p. 31.

Second, the response of a multi-class market may differ greatly from
that of a single-class market, even though the population changes are the
same. The differences can appear in the levels of construction and vacancies and in the timing of turning points. All of these differences are
explained by the fact that excess supply in one class in the multi-class
market cannot be shifted to meet excess demand in another class, but can
only be removed by increased demand in that one class.

Two examples will show how these relations lead to the observed differences. In Period 8, single-class residential construction is far above the
multi-class level. The reason for this is the concentration of a large part
of the increase in demand during the period at the fourth and fifth life-
cycle stages, which, in the multi-class market, only serves to reduce the
vacancies hanging over the sales market where demand is concentrated at
these life-cycle stages. In Period 13, on the other hand, multi-class residential construction is greater than single-class. In the single-class market
the increase in demand at the second and third life-cycle stages is offset
by the decrease in demand at the last stage. This offset does not occur in
the multi-class market, as the sales units released by the decreased de-

mand at the last life-cycle stage can not satisfy the increased demand for rentals at the early life-cycle stages.

Third, if more than one class of dwelling unit is considered, no general relationship between market demand, construction, and vacancies can be said to exist. For example, market-wide excess supply accompanies positive construction in several periods, construction and vacancies appear together in several periods, and the inverse of expected relationships between changes in these variables occur in several periods.

Finally, the leads and lags between the demands for different classes of housing in this model show clearly that there is a tendency for rental demand to lead overall market demand and for sales demand to coincide or lag at both the peak and the trough of the population cycle. Thus, the current state of the rental market acts as an indicator of things to come in the market as a whole and in the market for sales housing. However, the lead in the turning points of rental demand and construction is not the same in each population cycle and may occasionally disappear.

To this point, the conclusions derived are based on the assumption that changes in relative prices or shifts in the stock of dwelling units between quality or tenure classes cannot remove excess supply or demand. In reality, both changes in relative prices and reclassification of dwelling units take place and serve to reduce the amount of construction resulting from shifts in either the quality or tenure composition of demand.[15] However, as long as price changes or the reclassification of dwelling units can-

---

[15] Price flexibility means that excess demand leads to higher prices and excess supply to lower prices. Within the sales market, the chain of substitution between quality classes may be sufficiently close that shifts in the quality composition of demand may be resolved by only minor price changes — especially since owners must dispose of present housing to move up the quality ladder. This will be most likely when the excess-demand class is below the excess-supply class. Between the sales and rental markets the chain of substitution in similar quality classes is not close, but reclassification becomes an important possibility. An excess demand for rental units and an excess supply of sales units can be partly met by shifting dwelling units from sales to rental markets. If the tenure composition of demand later shifts back to ownership, then single-family rental units can be used to fill part of any resulting excess demand for sales units. However, the shift toward sales markets is limited at any time to a small proportion of the stock of rental units, whereas at least potentially, the entire sales stock could be shifted to rental markets. Of late, cooperative apartments, and so forth, have tended to dim the demarcation line between rental and sales markets, but for most of the period covered in this study it was clear and well defined. These considerations lead to the conclusion that a shift in the tenure composition of demand toward ownership is (or was) more likely to lead to new construction than the reverse shift. Within the rental market, since rents tend to be inflexible downward, changes in the quality composition of demand will less readily be offset without construction or conversions in the excess demand class.

not restore equilibrium without leaving scope for profitable construction, then the results derived from the model presented apply to the real world. The less downward price flexibility there is, the more the physical characteristics of dwelling units rule out their mobility between classes of housing; and the more elastic the supply of new units in a given local market, the closer the market will correspond to the multi-class model.

Thus, the applicability of these conclusions to the United States will depend on the nature of the local market considered. Such markets differ considerably in terms of the homogeneity of their dwelling units. In markets with most units included in a narrow price range and either owner- or renter-occupied (the latter is unlikely), the single-class market would most closely approximate conditions. In markets in which there are a large number of value alternatives, and in which both rental and sales units are important and multi-unit rental structures dominate the rental market, the multi-class model would be most useful. But these are just the differences found between small and large cities, between rural- and urban-oriented markets, and, to some extent, between the suburban fringe and the central city within metropolitan areas. It is safe to conclude that most of the United States housing stock and most residential construction in this century is and was located in local markets broadly similar to the market described by the multi-class model.

Before using the multi-class model to investigate the sources of residential building cycles in the United States, a word of caution about the results reached so far is in order. Conceptually, the housing life-cycle model applies to a single local market, but it will be used to draw conclusions about aggregate nonfarm residential construction in the United States. In doing this, some adjustment must be made for the effect of shifts in the geographic composition of demand on national totals.[16]

Migration

An important source of changes in housing demand comes from the migration of people from one local market to another or from one nation to another. The effect of migration on housing demand will depend on the ages of the migrants and on the pattern of migration (numbers of migrants in different periods).

---

[16] In the late 1940's and early 1950's, the condition that there be excess demand in all geographic submarkets was closely approximated in the United States. Consequently, the national market concept is more useful for these years than for earlier periods. However, the differences in the elasticity of supply between regions and, within regions, between communities of different sizes would leave output at least partly dependent on the geographic composition of demand even in the first postwar decade.

Assuming that migrants are all in the first life-cycle stage and that migration continues at a constant level over time, the result would be the same as described for a once-and-for-all increase in the level of births in the market the migrants enter and the same as a once-and-for-all decrease in births in the markets the migrants leave. That is, a construction or vacancy cycle lasting M periods and following the life-cycle pattern of headship rates and tenure rates would occur.

If migration fluctuates from period to period, the response of housing demand and construction would be similar to that of fluctuations in births. In this case, migration and construction may not be closely related in some circumstances, just as changes in the housing population resulting from past swings in births were not closely related to construction under some circumstances. For example, migration may have no effect on construction at the time of migration as the migrant population fills up vacancies in the class entered, but it may have a large impact later on as the past migrants shift their demand to classes without excess supply. Or, migration may lead to construction in the class entered even if there is market-wide excess supply.

In other words, the impact of migration on construction depends on the housing and tenure life cycles, on the numbers and age composition of the migrants, and on the excess supply and demand conditions in the different classes of dwelling units before the migration occurs. This makes generalization difficult. However, most migration between local markets in the United States has been either to urban areas in response to economic opportunities or to largely unsettled regions where the beginning housing stock was very small. Thus, migration has tended to create an excess demand for dwelling units in the markets entered, and construction has responded to migration. The same can be said for immigration to the United States in the nineteenth and early twentieth centuries.

Two important conclusions may be suggested from the preceding analysis: first, migration at the early life-cycle stages means that the maximum change in residential construction lags behind the maximum level of migration; second, as the migrants move through the housing life cycle, a constant level of migration finally is required simply to keep housing demand equal to the housing stock. In other words, once construction has adjusted the housing stock to the level required by a constant flow of migrants into and out of the housing life cycle, equilibrium would require continued migration and excess demand would require increased migration over time.

One other aspect of migration in the multi-class model deserves emphasis. The patterns of demand by class of housing for migrants can be expected to differ systematically from the pattern for nonmigrants for some time after the migrants enter a local market or reach the United States.[17] Briefly, migrants in a given age class tend to demand a larger proportion of low-cost rental units than nonmigrants do, both because the former are financially less well off and because there tends to be a larger proportion of single people among them. For the latter reason and because they have less chance of doubling up with relatives, migrants also tend to have higher headship rates. There are exceptions to both of these conclusions; for example, Negroes moving north often double up (as did immigrants to urban areas around the turn of the century), and retired persons moving south or west often become owners rather than renters. However, in general, the impact of an increase in the housing population via migration is to raise the relative demand for rental units at the time of migration and later, at each life-cycle stage, to raise the number of separate dwellings required to house a given population. If the migration does not continue or falls off, the initial adjustment of the stock of rental units will be too large, and vacancies will result as the migrant population moves through the housing life cycle or becomes established financially in the market entered.

Finally, given the immobility of dwelling units between local markets, migration between local markets means that residential construction may be positive for the nation in the absence of a nationwide excess demand for residential dwellings or in the presence of a nationwide excess supply. In this context, a national market containing a large number of noncompeting local markets is similar to a multi-class local market containing a large number of noncompeting classes of housing.

Life Expectancy and Housing Demand

Continuing the assumption of no deaths until the end of the Mth period, an increase in life expectancy, or M, would (1) raise the required stock of dwelling units by an amount dependent on the headship rates in the stages added and the population entering those stages and (2) change the tenure and value composition of the required stock. Since the proportion of sales units demanded and the average value of dwelling unit demanded are both above the life-cycle average at the last life-cycle stage, an increase in life-expectancy will increase the proportion of sales units in the housing stock and also the average value of the housing stock.

An increase in life expectancy will then raise construction or reduce

[17] For example, because a much larger proportion of migrant than of nonmigrant persons are single or, if married, have no children. See U.S. Bureau of the Census, *Current Population Reports*, Series P-20, Nos. 72, 82, and 85.

vacancies for dM periods. The impact on construction would be greater than the impact of a change in the entering population adding the same number of people to the housing population — at least for the first few periods — because of higher headship and ownership rates at late life-cycle stages than at early ones. This factor may be much more important than the lagged impact of the wartime "baby boom" in keeping residential construction at high levels during the 1960's.

The assumption that no one dies until the end of the last stage of the housing life cycle was introduced to keep the analysis simple. The question might rightfully be asked, Will dropping this assumption change any major conclusions? The answer is, No.

When it is recognized that deaths are an increasing function of age, the change in the housing population will depend on the mortality rate at each housing life-cycle stage as well as on the number in each stage at the beginning of a period and the number entering the housing population during the period. Residential construction or the change in vacancies will depend on the sum of the resulting increments in the population at each stage of the housing life cycle and on the headship rate at each stage. Compared with all earlier examples, demand will be reduced by increasing amounts through the life cycle, the peak demand will be lower, and the variation in demand over the life cycle will be greater for the same entering population.

Although a constant entering population no longer leads to a constant change in the housing population but, instead, to a constantly declining increment, it is clear from Chart 8 that a once-and-for-all increase in births will still lead to a construction cycle and to wide shifts in the ratio of housing starts to population increments. The relative timing of the turning points in rental, sales, and total construction will be unchanged. However, the total stock of sales units required when adjustment is complete will fall relative to the total stock of rental units required. The reason is that the demand for sales units (relatively speaking) and the increment in death rates both increase at the late life-cycle stages.[18]

---

[18] Reversing the foregoing analysis explains why increased life expectancy will increase the relative stock of sales units required and increase the relative importance of the late life-cycle stages. The possibility also exists for a lagged response to changed economic conditions, with headship and tenure rates affected for several periods after the initial changes. For example, an increase in income at all life-cycle stages would be expected to change the characteristics of housing demand in the 45-54 age class differently for people who will reach that stage in the future than for those presently in that age class. In other words, because increased income will affect marriage rates, family size, and the accumulation of wealth by people in the 25-34 age class more than it can the same variables for

CHART 8. POPULATION CHANGE AND RESIDENTIAL CONSTRUCTION:
DEATHS AT ALL LIFE-CYCLE STAGES[a]

NUMBER

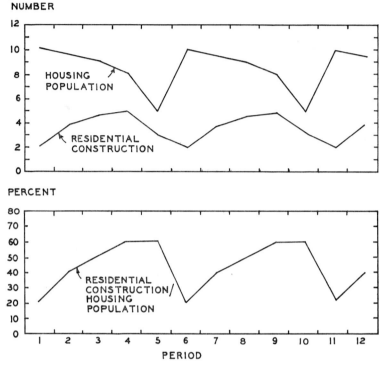

PERCENT

PERIOD

[a] In this example, $E = 10$ for five periods and then increases by 10 in period $M + 1$, 10 in $2M + 1$, and so forth. Headship rates are $h_1 = .20$, $h_2 = .40$, $h_3 = .50$, $h_4 = .60$, and $h_6 = .50$; Survivor rates (S_1) are $S_1 = 1.00$, $S_2 = .95$, $S_3 = .90$, $S_4 = .80$, $S_5 = .50$, and $S_6 = .00$. The survivor rate times the headship rates at each life-cycle stage times the housing population in the stage gives the demand for separate quarters in the stage for each period. This might be thought of as an average demand over the period.

In the general case where births fluctuate over time, the introduction of mortalities at all life-cycle stages reduces the difference between the single- and multi-class results. It also reduces the length of time it takes for the housing market to adjust to changes in the entering population. A much larger proportion of the total adjustment of the housing stock will now occur in the first few periods after the change in the entering population.

people presently in the 45-54 age class, the housing demand of the former group will differ in 20 years from that of people in the 45-54 age class at the time of the income change. Thus, in the housing life-cycle framework, changes in economic conditions and tastes may have an unexpected lagged cyclical effect on housing demand.

Other Refinements

To this point, the discussion has proceeded under the assumptions of a constant level of headship and tenure rates and a constant quality composition of demand at each life-cycle stage. This was done to emphasize the importance of the housing life cycle and to show as clearly as possible the potential cyclical effect of changes in age composition. However, non-demographic factors do affect housing demand, and they do so by changing headship and tenure rates and the quality composition of demand.

In general, economic analysis suggests that headship rates, the relative demand for ownership, and the average value of dwelling units demanded are all increasing functions of income and decreasing functions of interest rates (used as a proxy for credit conditions). Thus, changes in income, credit conditions, and tastes will affect the pattern of response of housing demand to population growth. These effects will be considered in the next two chapters.

If withdrawals of housing units (including demolitions, abandonments, conversions, and so forth) are related to past rates of residential construction in different housing classes, then part of current construction will be determined by past levels of activity. Thus, past cycles will tend to be repeated or at least to determine the present relationship between housing demand and the stock of dwelling units. The exact date of the repetition will depend on the lag between construction and withdrawals.

In essence, the introduction of replacement demand simply adds one more source of instability for residential construction. It means that the required stock must fall by more than replacement demand before construction falls to zero for a particular class of dwelling unit.

However, the filtering process by which withdrawals are determined suggests that any simple lag between the time of construction and actual replacement in a given quality class of housing is unlikely. With the passage of time, units that were produced in one price class can no longer compete with more recent additions to the housing stock in that price class, and they become substitutes for newer units in lower-price or lower-quality classes. This implies that replacement demand is necessary in a given quality class (other than the bottom class) years before the units originally produced for sale in that class wear out. Starting in the highest-price quality class, this process continues down through the market until most withdrawals occur at or near the bottom of the price-quality ladder (and generally at a price level where construction of substitutes would not be profitable). The result is that replacement is spread out over time, beginning several periods before any dwelling units are actually withdrawn from the housing stock.

When demand increases at the entering life-cycle stage, this slow filtering-replacement process tends to provide a means for meeting the excess demand from the existing stock — directly or through conversions, thus reducing construction relative to the level implied by the housing life-cycle model. However, when demand falls at the entering stage, the necessity of replacing higher quality units may keep construction above the level implied by the housing life-cycle model.

One consequence of the introduction of the filtering-replacement process is that it is necessary to consider the adjustment of the housing stock, in terms of its total and quality composition, as well as shifts in housing demand to explain the time path of residential construction and vacancies. Because of the long life of dwelling units and the spreading out of replacement via filtering, this additional consideration does not change the basic conclusions derived from the housing life-cycle model.

One final source of instability on the supply side of housing markets results from the production of dwelling units in anticipation of demand. Whether justified or not, changes in builders' estimates of demand will lead to shifts in the level of residential construction. The possibility of mistaken estimates of demand is heightened in housing markets by the fact that construction plans are usually made by a large number of builders, acting independently. With builders operating on a small scale and often without means either of investigating market demand conditions or the plans of other builders, errors may cumulate for more than one production period before they are discovered.[19] Once made, errors involving oversupply hang over the market in the form of vacancies for a long time. The tendency to make errors in demand estimates is probably an increasing function of the amplitude and duration of changes in actual demand. However, speculative building under conditions of uncertainty is more likely to accentuate construction cycles than to start them, which leaves changes in demographic factors, economic conditions, or tastes as the root cause of residential building cycles.

Even if tastes, real income, or credit terms were unchanged, there would be no reason to expect a constant amount of residential capital formation per capita of population increase in the United States. Wide shifts in this ratio can result simply from changes in age composition in the housing life-cycle framework. Thus, to argue from trends in the relationships between the housing stock or construction activity and demo-

---

[19] For a description of the construction industry, see Miles Colean and Robinson Newcomb, *Stabilizing Construction: The Record and Potential* (New York: McGraw-Hill, 1952), and Sherman Maisel, *Housebuilding in Transition* (Berkeley: University of California Press, 1953).

graphic variables to conclusions about shifts in consumer preferences or the impact of the government's mortgage insurance programs on housing markets (as was done in two recent National Bureau of Economic Research studies) is, at best, inconclusive if no adjustment is made for changes in the age composition of the population.[20]

The housing life-cycle model developed in this chapter establishes how and why swings in age composition are important in explaining residential building cycles. Wide swings in age composition, especially at the early and middle life-cycle stages, have occurred in the United States over the last century. Clearly, if we are ever to properly evaluate the place of population changes in determining past residential building cycles and long swings in economic growth, or to utilize population projections to assess the prospects for future developments in housing markets, the housing life cycle will have to be included in the analytical process.

---

[20] When Saulnier, Halcrow, and Jacoby (*op. cit.,* pp. 341-43) argue that the decline in the ratio of housing starts to population (total) increments between the 1920's and the 1940's is evidence that the FHA and VA mortgage programs had little effect on construction, they fail entirely to recognize that age composition changes could explain much of the observed decline. This decline was measured as being from 37.8 percent to 20.6 percent by Grebler, Blank, and Winnick, *op. cit.,* Table 24, p. 86. Age composition changes alone would have reduced the ratio of housing starts to population (housing, not total) increments from 32.3 percent to 28.0 percent. If the total population change were considered — inappropriate though it is — the decline due to age composition would have been almost half the total decline. The rest could be just as well ascribed to the special characteristics of the decades selected for comparison (controls, shortages, and so forth, during the 1940's) as to the ineffectiveness of FHA and VA mortgage programs. In fact, this sort of empirical "proof" is unable to meet the counter that the decline in the ratio would have been larger without the FHA and VA programs.

Similarly, Grebler, Blank, and Winnick use the decreasing trend in gross residential capital formation per capita as evidence of a decline in consumers' preferences for housing (*op. cit.,* p. 131). They also compare the 1920's with the 1940's without taking account either of the special effects of the war on gross residential capital (conversions and temporary dwellings) or of the fact that between these decades changes in age composition reduced both the number of additional units required per capita of population change and the average value of the additional units.

III. POPULATION CHANGES AND HOUSING DEMAND: ESTIMATION PROCEDURES AND INTERPRETATIONS

Taking the changes in the housing population and the headship and tenure rates for different age classes as the basic data, the number of additional dwelling units, in total and by tenure class, required by the movement of the housing population through the housing life cycle will be computed for decades and half-decades.

The estimates of the changes in the stock of rental, sales, and total dwelling units required to satisfy the additional demand resulting from changes in the age composition and size of the housing population will then be compared with the actual change in the occupied housing stock (or household formations) and with housing starts, in total and by tenure class.

In this manner, the relationship (if any) between past long swings in household formations, the tenure composition of increments to the occupied housing stock, and housing starts, and long swings in the size and age composition of the population can be determined and the relative importance of other (nondemographic) supply and demand determinants evaluated.

To save space, from here on the additional dwelling units required by population changes will simply be called "required additions," and the additional sales or rental units required by population changes will be called "sales" or "rental required additions." These terms will be modified accordingly when reference is made to the total, sales, or rental units required by changes in age composition alone or by changes in the size of the housing population with age composition held constant.

Whenever possible, total, rental, or sales required additions will be computed as follows. The population change in each age class during some time period will be multiplied by the headship rate or the appropriate tenure rate for the age class *at the beginning* of the time period and the resulting estimates of total, rental, or sales required additions by age class will then be summed.

42

The procedure outlined can be summarized by the following equations:

(6) Required Additions $(RA) = \sum_{i=1}^{M}[(p_n^i h_{n-1}^i) - (p_{n-1}^i h_{n-1}^i)] = \sum_{i=1}^{M} h_{n-1}^i \Delta p_n^i,$

(7) Rental Required Additions $(RRA) = \sum_{i=1}^{M} r_{n-1}^i \Delta p_n^i,$ and

(8) Sales Required Additions $(SRA) = \sum_{i=1}^{M} o_{n-1}^i \Delta p_n^i.$

In these equations M equals the number of life-cycle stages or age classes, p_n^i is the population in the ith age class at time n, h_n^i is the headship rate in the ith age class at time n, r_n^i is the rental headship rate in the ith age class at time n, and o_n^i is the owner headship rate in the ith age class at time n; Δp_n^i refers to the change in p^i from time $n-1$ to time n.

For some purposes, it will prove useful to divide tenure rates into two parts, the headship rate and the ratio of sales or rental units demanded to the total number of households in an age class. This makes it possible to distinguish between the effects on sales or rental demand of changes in headship rates and changes in the relative preference for a particular tenure class. If this is done, sales and rental required additions are defined by the following equations:

(9) $RRA = \sum_{i=1}^{M} r_n^{*i} h_n^i \Delta p_n^i,$ where $r_{n-1}^{*i} = r_{n-1}^i / h_{n-1}^i,$ and

(10) $SRA = \sum_{i=1}^{M} o_n^{*i} h_n^i \Delta p_n^i,$ where $o_{n-1}^{*i} = o_{n-1}^i / h_{n-1}^i.$

The difference between household formations and required additions or between the change in the renter or owner-occupied housing stock and rental or sales required additions can also be given explicit formulation. Household formations are defined by the following equation.

(11) $HHF = \sum_{i=1}^{M}[(p_n^i h_n^i) - (p_{n-1}^i h_{n-1}^i)].$

Subtracting (6) from (11) yields:

(12) $HHF - RA = \sum_{i=1}^{M} p_n^i (\Delta h_n^i) = \sum_{i=1}^{M} (p_{n-1}^i \Delta h_n^i + \Delta p_n^i \Delta h_n^i).$

Thus, household formations differ from required additions by the sum of the change in headship rate weighted by the beginning population plus the joint product of the change in headship rates times the change in the population. The first part of this sum $(p_{n-1}^i \Delta h_n^i)$ measures the additional dwelling units required by changes in headship rates alone. The second part implies that part of the difference between household formations and required additions should properly be allocated to population changes. However, for the most part in the following discussion the joint product residual will be ignored and the difference between required additions and household formations attributed to nondemographic factors.

Similar manipulations yield the following equations for the differences between the change in the owner-occupied housing stock (HO) and sales required additions and between the change in the renter-occupied housing stock (HR) and rental required additions.

$$(13) \qquad HR - RRA = \sum_{i=1}^{M} (p_{n-1}^i \Delta r_n^i + \Delta p_n^i \Delta r_n^i), \text{ and}$$

$$(14) \qquad HO - SRA = \sum_{i=1}^{M} (p_{n-1}^i \Delta o_n^i + \Delta p_n^i \Delta o_n^i).$$

The difference in each case measures the combined effect of changes in headship rates and the relative preference for sales or rental units, with the housing population fixed and varying. By dividing rental and sales headship rates into component parts, as in Equations (9) and (10), measures of the effect of headship rate changes alone ($p_{n-1}^i o_{n-1}^{*i} \Delta h_n^i$; $p_{n-1}^i r_{n-1}^{*i} \Delta h_n^i$) and of the changes in the relative preference for sales or rental units alone ($p_{n-1}^i h_{n-1}^i \Delta o_n^{*i}$; $p_{n-1}^i h_{n-1}^i \Delta r_n^{*i}$) can be derived.[21]

Turning to the computation of required additions due to changes in age composition (RA_a), an estimate was made by holding the size of the

---

[21] Derived from the equation defining the owner-occupied (or renter-occupied) housing stock. For owner-occupied housing this equation is

$$HO = \sum_{i=1}^{M} [(p_n^i h_n^i o_n^{*i}) - (p_{n-1}^i n_{n-1}^i o_{n-1}^{*i})].$$

Substituting $p_{n-1}^i \Delta + p^i$ for p_n^i, $h_{n-1}^i + \Delta h^i$ for h_n^i, and $o_{n-1}^{*i} + \Delta o^{*i}$ for o_n^{*i} in this equation and multiplying out the terms in brackets yields

$HO = p_{n-1}^i h_{n-1}^i \Delta o_n^{*i}$ (effect of changes in the relative demand for sales units only),

$+ p_{n-1}^i \Delta h_n^i o_{n-1}^{*i}$ (effect of changes in headship rates only),

$+ p_{n-1}^i \Delta h_n^i \Delta o_n^{*i}$ (joint effect of changes in headship and ownership rates),

$+ \Delta p_n^i h_{n-1}^i o_{n-1}^{*i}$ (sales required additions),

$+ \Delta p_n^i h_{n-1}^i \Delta o_n^{*i}$ (joint effect of population changes and ownership-rate changes),

$+ \Delta p_n^i h_n^i o_{n-1}^{*i}$ (joint effect of population changes and headship-rates changes), and

$+ \Delta p_n^i \Delta h_n^i \Delta o_n^{*i}$ (joint effect of all three).

population constant and measuring the change in households resulting from shifts in the proportions of the population in different age classes.[22]

$$(15) \qquad RA_a = \frac{P_{n-1}}{P_n} \left(\sum_{i=1}^{M} p_n^i h_{n-1}^i \right) - \sum_{i=1}^{M} p_{n-1}^i h_{n-1}^i.$$

Required additions due to changes in the size of the population (RA_p) were then measured by holding the proportion in each age class constant (and so holding the average headship rate constant) and finding the number of dwelling units required at the beginning and end of some time period.

$$(16) \qquad RA_p = \frac{P_n}{P_{n-1}} \left(\sum_{i=1}^{M} p_{n-1}^i h_{n-1}^i \right) - \sum_{i=1}^{M} p_{n-1}^i h_{n-1}^i = \frac{HH_{n-1}}{p_{n-1}} (\Delta P_n).$$

The effects of changes in age composition and of changes in the size of the population, with age composition constant, on sales and rental required additions were measured in a similar manner.

In summary, required additions measure the impact of changes in the size and age composition of the housing population on the required stock of dwelling units. If headship rates change, then household formations and required additions will differ by an amount determined by the change in headship rates, weighted by the population in different age classes at the beginning of the period and by the change in population by age class during the period. Similar relationships tie sales and rental required additions to the distribution of household formations between sales and rental units.

Thus, it is not a foregone conclusion that swings in total, sales, or rental required additions will be reflected in similar swings in household formations (or housing starts, for that matter), in total or by tenure class. Since the difference between the various classes of required additions and household formations or housing starts for the same classes depends to a large extent on the general level of economic activity and since business cycles and long swings in the rate of economic growth have characterized the United States economy over the last century, it would indeed be surprising if population changes told the whole story of the residential building cycle.

---

[22] Taking the proportion of the population at time n in the first age class, multiplying this ratio by the total population at time n-1, and multiplying the product by the headship rate in the first age class yields the number of dwelling units required to satisfy the housing demand by the first age class if the first age class accounts for the same proportion of the total population as at time n. Summing over all age classes and factoring out common terms then yields Equation (13).

The Determinants of Headship Rates

Economic theory suggests that headship rates will vary directly with real income and net worth and inversely with the price of separate quarters and the level of interest rates, taken as an index of both the cost and availability of credit. Headship rates will also vary with changes in consumer preferences.

Clearly, increases in real income can only raise headship rates by encouraging members of existing households to demand separate quarters. At the middle life-cycle stages, where almost half of the individuals are household heads and a large proportion of the others are married to household heads, the potential for increased headship rates is relatively small.[23] At the other extreme, the large number of unmarried individuals living in households headed by relatives or sharing quarters with other unmarried individuals provides the base for a large increase in headship rates at the early life-cycle stages when income increases. Most individuals in these age classes are not heads of households, both because of tastes and because of income, so the potential for increased headship rates is largest for the under-35 age classes. Although headship rates are high at the late (over 65) life-cycle stages, the proportion of the nonheads who are unmarried or doubled up is much larger than at the middle life-cycle stages. Thus, the potential for increased headship rates is greater at these life-cycle stages than for the middle life-cycle stages.

The response of headship rates to falling real income (and to unemployment) also depends on the characteristics of the existing households within different age classes. Households consisting of unrelated individuals are more likely to break up or to merge with other, similar, households in times of economic stress than are households formed by so-called normal (i.e., married couples or members related to the head) families. Once a normal household has been formed, separate quarters will be one of the last consumer services given up when income falls. In this context, it is interesting to note that, despite the reduction in real income and increased unemployment during the 1930's, headship rates fell only slightly between 1930 and 1935 and that two of the three age classes showing an increase in headship rates between 1930 and 1940 were in the middle life-cycle stages where the incidence of normal families is greatest. On the other hand, headship rates did decline in the 1930's at the early life-cycle stages.[24]

---

[23] Assuming that there is no significant correlation between divorce rates and real income. The small change in headship rates in the 35-to-64 age class as real incomes have increased suggests that this assumption is reasonable. See Appendix Table B1, pp. 186-7.

[24] See Appendix Table B1, pp. 186-7.

These considerations suggest the following relationships: First, that increasing real income will lead more people, and decreasing real income will lead fewer people, to demand separate quarters in all age classes. Second, that the income elasticity of demand for separate quarters is greatest at the early and late life-cycle stages and is less for changes in real income below past peak levels than for increases above levels attained in the past. Third, that the income elasticity of demand at any time will depend — for the market as a whole — on the distribution of income changes between age classes, on the ratio of nonnormal to normal households at the time of the change in income, and on the age composition of the population at the time of the change.[25]

In this context, the steady increase in the relative number of households consisting of a single person or a group of unrelated individuals since the end of World War II suggests that the income elasticity of demand today may be much greater than in the 1930's. There is, in fact, some evidence of wide shifts in headship rates in the 1954 and 1958 recessions.[26] Working in the opposite direction would be the greater stability of disposable income (resulting from the built-in stabilizers) as GNP falls and unemployment increases.

Beside their direct impact, fluctuations in real income also affect headship rates via their influence in internal mobility and on marriage and birth rates.[27] Since both increased internal mobility (by fragmenting existing households) and increased birth rates increase headship rates and are positively related to income, the indirect influence of income on these demographic variables will have the same impact on headship rates as does the direct influence. Increased marriage rates, on the other hand,

---

[25] For a discussion of the importance of nonnormal families in housing markets and of the neglect of this source of demand (L. Klein, *op. cit.,* pp. 91-92, is a perfect example) in much housing market analysis see the article by H. Blumenfeld in *Land and Public Utility Economics,* Vol. 20, No. 3 (August, 1944), pp. 264-70.

[26] Based on an annual headship-rate series derived from the annual estimates of the age distribution of households and the population given by the U.S. Bureau of the Census in *Current Population Reports,* Series P-20 and P-25. These annual estimates are subject to a relatively large sampling error and no firm conclusion can be drawn.

[27] Both marriage and birth rates are positively correlated to income and both, in turn, determine the level of headship rates. An increase in birth rates, by decreasing the desirability of doubling up and by changing the tenure composition of demand, will tend to raise headship rates. On the other hand, an increase in marriage rates may either increase or decrease headship rates, depending on whether or not the individuals involved would have independently maintained separate quarters. If the increase in marriage rates has the effect of reducing the average age of first marriages, then an increase in headship rates is the more likely outcome.

may increase or decrease headship rates, depending on whether or not the individuals marrying were previously household heads.

Finally, changes in income shift the tenure and quality composition of demand. Increased real income reduces the sacrifice necessary for home ownership and for moving up the quality ladder. Given the housing stock and number of households, such changes lead to construction or to decreased vacancies in some tenure and quality classes while increasing vacancies and, perhaps, decreasing prices in others. The structure of the housing market is such that changes of the sort described will generally lead to increased vacancies (and lower rents) in low-quality rental units. The importance of changes in the availability of rental units in attracting new households is difficult to measure, but it may be a critical factor in determining whether or not young people desert the family home and in determining the size of nonnormal households.[28] In sum, shifts in the composition of demand may increase headship rates by lowering prices at some quality levels and, more importantly, by increasing the availability of low-priced rental units.

In addition to changes in real income, changes in credit conditions, supply conditions, and tastes may also influence headship rates. Easier credit reduces the present sacrifice necessary for homeownership and shifts the supply curve of available dwelling units to the right. Although some new households may be formed to take advantage of easier credit in the sales market, evidence suggests that the major impact of easier credit will be on the tenure and quality composition of demand and on the supply of low-cost sales housing. The impact of easier credit is then similar to that of increased real income on headship rates via the quality and tenure composition of demand. The implication is that easier credit will significantly affect headship rates only when there are few, if any, vacancies in rental units prior to the change in credit conditions. Because of this, it is reasonable to assume that, except for the introduction of the government-insured mortgage programs and amortized mortgages (which

---

[28] There is undoubtedly a certain amount of inertia that must be overcome before single people or groups of unrelated individuals enter the housing market. When many alternatives are available, the mere presence of these alternatives together with the minimum expenditure of effort necessary to find and rent an apartment at such times may increase the number of nonnormal families. Thus, in good times, when easy credit moves people out of rental units into owner-occupied units, no reduction in rents may be necessary to fill up the resulting vacancies, even though little evidence existed of an excess demand for rental units before the the vacancies appeared. Once under way, the emulation effect would be expected to keep the trend going. Following this line of thought, one might argue that the government's mortgage insurance programs may be partly responsible for the rapid increase in headship rates at the early life-cycle stages in the 1950's.

influenced demand and supply after World War II), headship rates have been largely independent of credit conditions over the period covered in this study.

Supply conditions (other than responses to changes in credit conditions) influence headship rates by determining the response of the price of separate quarters to changes in demand. At one extreme, if when income increased no vacant units were available and no additions could be made, then prices would have to rise to prevent any increase in headship rates. Thus, whether price changes, output changes, or inventories of vacant units clear the market of excess supply or demand will determine the final response of headship rates to changes in income and credit conditions.

The final determinant of headship rates to be considered is the one least susceptible of analysis — changes in consumer preference. Over the period from 1880 to 1960 there seems to have been a considerable change in the nation's attitude toward the role of the family and the obligations of the family to relatives and unmarried children. These changes have tended to reduce the average size of families and so to increase the level of headship rates. However, one could argue that the splitting up of family groups is not so much the result of a change in tastes as of the general increase in real income over the last 80 years.

The Determinants of Tenure Rates

Tenure rates are determined by the same factors as headship rates. However, the income and interest elasticity of demand by tenure classes would be expected to be much greater than that for separate quarters. Relative to headship rates, swings in tenure rates in response to increasing income in the 1920's and falling income (and employment) in the 1930's were extremely large. Taking the 1930's as an example of the pre-World War II relationship, as income fell and unemployment increased large number of homeowners found it impossible to meet their mortgage obligations and lost their homes or were forced to rent their homes to others to cover the costs of ownership. Spending units that would normally (i.e., at the per capita income levels of the late twenties) have moved into the ownership market at the life-cycle stage reached in the 1930's either could not raise the downpayments or found that the usual sources of mortgage funds had dried up. As the demand for ownership fell, single-family dwelling units were shifted to the rental market, the inventory of vacant rental units was utilized, and conversions of existing units took place. In this manner, a wide shift in tenure rates occurred without any commensurate reduction in headship rates.

The introduction of government-insured mortgages, together with the functioning of the built-in stabilizers and counter-cyclical monetary policy, has largely attenuated the effect of income changes (at least downward) on tenure rates since World War II. By stimulating the use of amortization and pushing loan-value ratios and maturities up, the government-insured mortgage programs led to increased ownership. Beyond this, with per capita disposable income isolated from reductions in GNP in the relatively minor postwar recessions, the response of lenders to monetary policy tended to increase the demand for government-insured mortgages in recessions and vice versa and, as a consequence, to offset the income effect of the business cycle on tenure rates. Thus, the secular increase in real income, along with an apparent change in preferences (raising the importance of ownership) and the effect of rent controls (reducing the incentive to produce new rental units and the availability of existing rental units), contributed to the steady increase in ownership rates from 1945 to 1960. Of course, minimal down payments and long maturities have clearly reduced the difference between renting and owning for many spending units. In fact, many owners seem to believe that they are renting from lenders and that the latter should bear all the risks usually associated with ownership. Thus, tenure-rate data have become more and more difficult to interpret. The postwar increase in ownership rates may reflect an increased desire for a particular type (single-family) of dwelling unit or a particular location (suburban), rather than an increased preference for ownership per se.

Housing Starts and Household Formations

Even if required additions and household formations are the same (i.e., headship rates do not change), household formations will not necessarily be equal to housing starts. The increase in demand resulting from a positive level of household formations during a decade or half-decade can be met by converting existing dwelling units or by reducing the stock of vacant units as well as by the construction of new dwelling units.[29] Or, since some new units may be needed to replace dwellings withdrawn from the housing stock or may directly or indirectly lead to increased vacancies, housing starts may be greater than household formations and required additions. Obviously, the same possibilities exist for differences between

---

[29] In addition, household formations include people living in mobile homes, temporary dwellings, and other types of housing not included in the BLS-Department of Commerce housing starts series. In the discussion that follows, the types of dwelling units not counted in the housing starts series will be considered part of net conversions, thus retaining the basic indentity: housing starts minus household formations equals change in vacancies plus withdrawals minus net conversions.

housing starts by tenure class and the change in the renter- or owner-occupied housing stock.

The determinants of the factors (conversions, withdrawals, and the change in vacancies) separating household formations from housing starts can best be discussed in the context of the United States housing market experience. At this stage it is sufficient simply to point out a few important relationships.

First, conversions occur primarily in the rental market and, since they substitute for existing low-quality rentals, conversions are most adaptable to satisfying the demand for housing by the relatively poor and by the young and the old. Thus, conversions will tend to vary inversely with income but will be higher at any point in the business cycle, the greater the relative importance of population changes at the early and late life-cycle stages.[30] This means that the more important immigration or rural-urban migration is in total or nonfarm population changes, the larger conversions will be. Over the period covered by this study, conversions have always been positive and so have contributed to an excess of household formations over housing starts, with the excess concentrated in rental markets.

Second, withdrawals from the housing stock, apart from a random component related to natural or man-made disasters, also occur primarily in the rental market. They depend on the age composition of the housing stock and on economic conditions in local markets. But, since houses can be refurbished and do not have anything like a fixed life span, the level of withdrawals would be expected to vary primarily with economic conditions in local markets.

The influence of economic conditions depends in part on the local conditions determining the value of particular pieces of real estate for residential and other uses and in part on national conditions affecting the same relationship. For this reason, withdrawals from the housing stock would be expected to vary directly with income fluctuations. But, all in all, the available evidence suggests that the variation in withdrawals was slight relative to changes in the other factors separating household formations and housing starts until the 1950's.[31]

Withdrawals also occur from the sales to the rental market and vice versa. The downgrading of the stock of sales units accounts for a contin-

---

[30] This is particularly true during the contraction phase of the business cycle, since these same age classes also show the greatest income elasticity of demand for housing.

[31] See Grebler, Blank, and Winnick, *op. cit.*, Table A-1, p. 329, for estimates of withdrawals by decades through the 1940's. See Ch. IV, Table 2, p. 65, for the 1950's data. Withdrawals apparently increased sharply in the 1950's.

uous flow of dwellings from sales to rental markets and explains why one-family housing starts generally exceed the change in the owner-occupied housing stock. But withdrawals by reclassification also vary with supply and demand conditions in the sales market. Since single-family dwellings can be readily shifted between tenure classes, excess supply in the sales market will lead to the offer of the vacant units on the rental market. Excess demand for sales units will then return some single-family units to the sales market, reducing the stock of rental units. Thus, the level of withdrawals from the sales market will tend to vary inversely with income and credit conditions.

Finally, the level of vacancies may change either because of fluctuations in the demand for housing, in total or for a particular class, or because of changes in the stock of dwelling units. Since household formations were positive for all age classes in all decades covered and since, with three exceptions, the housing population increased in all age classes in all quinquennial periods covered, there is little evidence that fluctuations in demand were an important source of increased vacancies in the United States.[32] On the other hand, for the same reasons the continuous growth in the number of households has been the major source of reductions in vacancies.

This suggests that increased vacancies in United States housing markets have resulted largely from overbuilding or the redistribution of the housing population between local markets, which creates vacancies by shifting the location of demand without changing the location of the housing stock. If so, then increased vacancies would be expected to lag behind economic expansion or increased household formations, with the level of vacancies reaching a peak some time after the peak in income or household formations is reached.[33]

The influence of the lagged and often mistaken adjustment of builders

---

[32] Except for the 15-24 age class in 1945-50 and 1950-55 and the 25-34 age class in 1955-60, the population change was positive in all age classes in each quinquennial period from 1900-1905 to the present. Prior to the 1940's it is impossible to determine whether or not headship rates (or tenure rates) changed sufficiently to offset the effect of population growth and reduce demand in total or by tenure class absolutely. But with the exception of the 1930-35 period, both decadal headship- and tenure-rate changes and the size of the population growth by age class suggest that the demand for housing of all types increased in all age classes in each five-year period included. For the 1930-35 period, the vacancy rate in the few areas for which data are available increased sharply from 1930-32, but by 1935 it was back to the 1930 level (Ernest M. Fisher, *Urban Real Estate Markets: Characteristics and Financing* (New York: National Bureau of Economic Research, 1951) pp. 105-9. Thus, population growth rapidly cut into the vacancies created by the initial impact of the Depression.

[33] Since both the price elasticity of household formations and the relative demand for rental units are highest in precisely those age classes most susceptible to

and investors to shifts in the demand for dwelling units on the level of vacancies is both complex and interesting. Mistakes in demand estimates that might lead to increased vacancies would, in theory, be positively related to the rate of increase in housing demand. In the short run, rents, land values, and sales prices increase more than is justified — given long-run supply conditions — when demand increases. The greater the increase in demand, the greater the error. Of course, as long as demand continues to increase by the same or larger amounts, the errors made will not be readily uncovered — if one can call them errors under these circumstances. In any event, the prices and rents that spurred construction will not be attainable once the rate of increase in demand slows down, and more units will have been started than can be absorbed by the market. These mistakes result because of the atomistic productive structure and the large gaps in information that characterize the residential building industry. Because of the length of time necessary to complete large-scale rental projects and because of the longer lag between increased demand and the initiation of such projects, overbuilding is more likely to occur in rental than in sales markets.

Vacancies resulting from builders' mistakes will tend to increase sharply when the rate of growth in housing demand slows down. In other words, vacancies from this source increase before either the number of household formations or the level of economic activity actually declines. This helps to explain, as residential construction responds negatively to increased vacancies, why the residential building cycle is a leading indicator of major cyclical downturns. Once vacancies from this source have increased, given the substantial lag in completion of projects underway, they will tend to remain high for some time after economic activity falls off.

Wherever or from whatever source vacancies arise in the housing market, they are likely to end up in the rental sector, especially in large multi-unit rental structures.[34] If vacancies appear in the sales market,

---

falling income and loss of jobs during recessions, the relatively small changes in rents resulting from increased vacancies will not generally serve to remove the vacancies at such times and residential construction will remain depressed until the population grows sufficiently to fill the vacant units or until recovery spurs an increase in headship rates. On the other hand, vacancies resulting from the usual tenure and quality composition changes in expansion periods may be rapidly removed as increased "availability" raises headship rates and withdrawals are increased.

[34] The concentration of vacant units in large multi-unit rental structures in times of declining demand is shown by the experience in Denver, Colorado, and Cuyahoga County, Ohio, in the 1930's. See Fisher, *op. cit.*, Table 35, p. 106, and Table 37, p. 108.

speculative builders caught with unwanted inventories and owners of single-family dwellings will be under considerable pressure to either cut the sales price or shift their dwelling units to the rental market, where they will be under pressure to reduce rents until the units are occupied. On the other hand, the proprietors of large multi-unit structures may lose more (unless price discrimination is possible) by reducing rents than by keeping the units off the market. The result is that when vacancies appear — either throughout the housing market or in classes of housing other than multi-unit rentals — the relative price of dwelling units in multi-unit rental structures increases, the increase being a positive function of the number of units in the structure.

The stated preferences of households suggest that the price elasticity of demand for sales housing is very high. Since this preference is as much for single-family dwellings as for ownership, falling rents and prices for single-family units relative to rents in multi-unit structures would bring about a substantial substitution of the former for the latter type of housing. Thus, the burden of vacancies tends to be shifted to the multi-unit sector of the rental market.

With vacancies and withdrawals positively related to income fluctuations and conversions inversely related, the conclusion must be that, in general, housing starts will exceed household formations in decades or five-year periods containing major-cycle or long-swing expansions and be less than household formations during periods included in long-swing contractions or containing major-cycle troughs.

Feedbacks

The discussion of the differences among required additions, household formations, and housing starts begs the issue of cause and effect between population changes and income changes. For example, if required additions rise at the same time that household formations increase relative to required additions and housing starts increase relative to household formations, is it not possible that the gains in income which explain the widening difference between housing starts and required additions are the result of the population changes measured by required additions? Increased required additions will tend to raise income, and higher income will tend to raise headship rates and to raise housing starts relative to household formations, and so on.

Clearly, fluctuations in required additions might explain part of the difference between required additions and housing starts, so that the procedure of assigning this difference to nondemographic changes might underestimate the effect of population changes on the residential building cycle. But, it is also possible that the observed changes in required additions actually were determined by concurrent changes in income, so that population changes are simply a link in a chain of cause and effect rather than an exogenous determinant of demand. When national totals are used, immigration immediately comes to mind. Similarly, fluctuations in nonfarm required additions must certainly reflect the influence of income changes on farm-to-nonfarm migration.

Economic theory suggests that both of these relationships are possible, but no attempt will be made in this study to disentangle cause and effect relationships between population changes and income changes. The approach followed will be simply to break down observed changes in household formations to measure the influence of population changes from whatever source and of headship-rate changes from whatever source.

Special attention will be given to the influence of immigration on national required additions, without attempting to determine the ultimate cause of fluctuations in immigration. Since net migration and mortality changes are the only possible sources of changes in the national housing population within the decadal and quinquennial periods utilized, the raw materials are available for at least a preliminary sorting out of income and population effects on household formations.

Farm-to-nonfarm migration surely depends on long-run differences in sectoral growth rates and productivity trends as well as on national economic conditions. Separate estimates of required additions for national and nonfarm population changes will not be presented, but the relationship between national and nonfarm household formations will be discussed.

Population changes are often given an important role in accelerator or capital stock adjustment models of the business cycle, where they are treated as exogenous. Beginning with the 1930's and the elimination of immigration as a major determinant of population changes, the latter have been mainly predetermined, raising the possibility of population changes determining income fluctuations and thus determining headship- and tenure-rate changes.

Whatever the source may be, the possibility exists of an acceleration relationship between population changes and residential construction. The usual notion of the population accelerator is not used because it is based on population changes unadjusted for changes in age composition. However, required additions escape this criticism, and it may be suggested that (1) the level of residential construction is positively related to the change in required additions and (2) the difference between housing starts and required additions is positively related to the change in required additions. The implication is that a reduced positive increment in required additions will lead to a negative change in housing starts and so, *ceterus paribus,* will lead to a negative change in income and headship rates.

There are several good reasons for suggesting this acceleration relationship, especially for the decadal and quinquennial periods used in this study. First, there is the strong evidence of lagged and mistaken responses by builders and investors to changes in housing demands. A large increase in required additions from one period to the next would set off a chain of events leading to overbuilding, which, if followed by a smaller increase, would leave a heritage of unsold or unrented dwelling units hanging over the housing market. The result would be that both the difference between housing starts and required additions and the level of housing starts would vary directly with the change in required additions. It is important to note that this possibility exists for rental or sales required additions as well as for total required additions. In other words, reductions in the rate of increase in required additions for particular age classes, even though no reduction occurs for total required additions, may lead to falling one-family or multi-family housing starts.

Further, if starts do vary directly with required additions, then investment in the wide range of industries supplying construction materials and equipment will tend to vary directly with the change in required additions. An increase in the increment in required additions would then raise both residential construction and fixed capital formation in the supplying industries. But, if the increment in required additions falls, the resulting smaller increase in housing starts (ignoring overbuilding for the moment) would be wholly or partially offset by the decline in fixed capital formation in the supplying industries. Thus, the size and possibly the direction of changes in income would depend on the change in required additions, and for five- or ten-year periods the difference between housing starts and required additions and the level of housing starts would appear to be positively related to the change in required additions.

Finally, assuming that household formations move closely with required additions and noting the close relationship between household formations and the growth in demand for a wide range of consumer goods, it is possible that fixed capital formation in most sectors of the economy will be related to the change in required additions. If so, this would be one more important reason for expecting the acceleration relationship discussed to be reflected in the United States housing data.

The accelerator as used here is applied to five- or ten-year periods and therefore escapes many of the usual criticisms levied against this kind of argument. Further, the increment in required additions is positive more often than not, reducing the weight of the criticism that excess capacity will deaden or offset any acceleration effect. In fact, with all periods in which a negative change in required additions takes place, the immediately following period shows an increase in required additions far above the level reached in any prior period, and presumably far above the ability of builders or builders' suppliers to meet with existing plant and equipment. Finally, it is not argued that a precise numerical relationship exists between changes in required additions and housing starts, but only that the direction of change in housing starts can be explained by the direction of change in first differences of required additions.

IV. POPULATION CHANGE AND THE LONG SWING IN HOUSEHOLD FORMATIONS AND RESIDENTIAL CONSTRUCTION: 1850's TO 1950's

The existence of a series of residential building cycles, beginning during the Civil War and continuing to World War II, has long been established.[35] At least as a first approximation, these long swings in residential building seem to be explained by the concurrent long swing in household formations, which, in turn, can be explained either by fluctuations in headship rates or in the size and age composition of population increments.

Required additions are a measure of the influence of population factors, including age composition, on household formations. From the 1880's on, required additions traced out a series of long swings, with a peak occuring every second decade and with an ever widening amplitude of contractions, culminating in the trough of the 1950's.[36] This pattern was matched decade by decade until the 1950's by the long swing in household formations (see Chart 9 and Table 1).[37] Not only did house-

---

[35] For example, See Clarence D. Long, Jr., *Building Cycles and the Theory of Investment* (Princeton: Princeton University Press, 1940).

[36] The every-other-decade pattern of peaks and troughs from the 1880's on, together with the absence of a peak in the 1860's, might suggest that the long swing in required additions developed after the Civil War. However, the basis for a peak in the 1860's was clearly present in the age composition of the population changes during the 1850's. The war's effect on the population changes in the 20-39 age class, together with the effect of reduced immigration during the war followed by a postwar spurt carrying over into the early 1870's, prevented the expected peak from occurring.

[37] The estimates of required additions given in Table 1 are based on 1890 headship rates from the 1850's to the 1920's and on beginning-of-the-decade headship rates from the 1930's on. This means that, for example, the estimate of required additions in the 1910's differs from the level of required additions as defined in Chapter II by an amount dependent on the difference between the actual headship rate in 1910 and the 1890 headship rate used. However, since the level of required additions for the decades from the 1950's to the 1920's would differ only slightly if 1930 headship rates were used, and since the estimates of required additions correspond very closely to the actual level of household formations through the 1920's, the error introduced by the use of a constant set of headship rates is apparently insignificant.

CHART 9. HOUSEHOLD FORMATIONS AND
REQUIRED ADDITIONS, BY DECADE

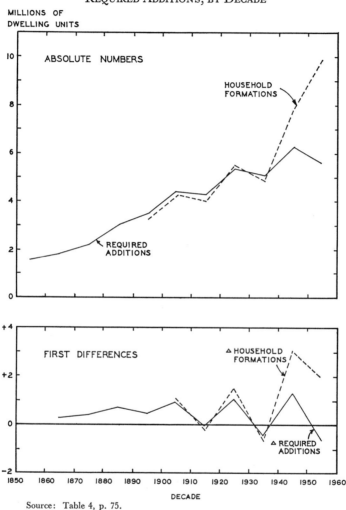

Source: Table 4, p. 75.

hold formations and required additions increase and decrease together in
five of the six decades for which a comparison is possible, but from the
1890's to the 1940's it is clear that population factors alone accounted for
most of the change in households in the United States.

Whatever the source of the long swing in required additions (and
judgment about this will be reserved until the discussion of immigration
in Chapter VI is completed), the close correspondence between required

Table 1. Household Formations and Required Additions,
by Decade
(Thousands of dwelling units)

Decade[a]	Household formations[b] (1)	Required additions (2)
1850-60	.....	1,621
1860-70	.....	1,885
1870-80	.....	2,285
1880-90	.....	3,009
1890-1900	3,273	3,485
1900-1910	4,292	4,444
1910-20	4,096	4,365
1920-30	5,553	5,419
1930-40	4,950	5,028
1940-50	7,971	6,296
1950-60	9,990	5,685

[a] Time intervals in this and subsequent tables are based on data as of July 1 of each year.
[b] As used in this and subsequent tables, household formations are the same as the change in the occupied housing stock.
Sources: Col. 1 — U.S. Bureau of the Census, *Statistical Abstract of the United States, 1963* (Washington: U.S. Government Printing Office, 1963), Table 1072, p. 759 (1960 data were adjusted to exclude Hawaii and Alaska); Col. 2 — see Appendixes A and B for a discussion of the population and headship rate data used in computing required additions.

additions and household formations — stretching over half a century — is firmly established. Neither the housing boom of the 1920's nor the Depression changed this close correspondence. That headship-rate changes were so unimportant and population changes so important in explaining household formations between the 1890's and the 1940's is a surprising result, given the wide shifts in economic conditions that occurred during this period.

However, the fact that changes in headship rates were of minor importance in housing markets from the 1880's to the 1940's does not mean that economic conditions were necessarily less important than population changes in determining the demand for separate quarters, but only that economic change had little impact on headship rates. The possibility remains that the changes in population factors that explain most of the variation in demand for dwelling units can be traced to then-current economic conditions. For example, the population changes in this period may have been controlled by contemporaneous immigration, which, in turn, may have been determined by economic conditions occurring in the United States and abroad at the same time.

In the context of the past record, the unprecedented shift in headship rates in the 1950's takes on added significance. The causes of this shift are yet to be explained. Although a complete analysis is beyond the scope of this study, some comments are in order. First, the increase in headship rates was not the result of postwar undoubling, which was largely completed by 1950. Second, unless the *level* of per capita real income was the key determinant, which might be supported, the fact that the United States experienced general economic expansion during most of the 1950's would not seem to explain the increase in headship rates. We have experienced more rapid expansion and lower levels of unemployment before without this result.

However, two factors were present in the 1950's that were not present in past periods of similar, relatively steady expansion. As per capita income rose, no offsetting surge in immigration could take place to attenuate the effect of growing real income and increased job security on people at the early life-cycle stages (the age groups that account for most of the increase in headship rates).[38] In addition, the government's insured mortgage programs helped to make possible an unparalleled boom in the production of sales housing, which had the effect of increasing the rate of turnover and so the availability of rental units. Although they are only suggestive (one would not want to ignore changes in tastes or a step-function response of household formations to changes in the level of income), these two factors perhaps help explain the completely different performance of headship rates in the 1950's from that in any past period of economic expansion.

Required Additions, Housing Starts, and Residential Construction

Population changes account for most of the observed fluctuations in national household formations, at least until the 1950's. Whether or not a similar relationship holds for national required additions and national housing starts cannot be answered directly. Through the 1950's, housing starts data are available on a nonfarm basis only; nonfarm required additions are available only from the 1920's on. Thus, a long-run comparison between population changes and housing starts must be based on the relationship between national required additions and nonfarm housing starts.

However, since nonfarm and national household formations and required additions do vary together and the rank order of their first differences is similar, the implication is that the long swings in national and nonfarm required additions and household formations were determined

---

[38] See Appendix B. Headship rates also increased significantly at the late life-cycle stages (based on the current population survey estimates).

by the same forces. Thus, so far as population changes determine household formations and household formations determine housing starts, nonfarm housing starts should vary with national household formations.[39]

In this context, it should be recalled that the increased demand for dwelling units resulting from household formations can be met by reducing the stock of vacant units, by conversions, and by new construction not counted in the available housing starts series. Similarly, housing starts may be required to replace dwelling units lost via merger, demolition, or natural disaster or may lead to increased vacancies. Thus, housing starts and household formations or required additions for even the same geographic base would not be expected to be identical. In general, one would expect to find housing starts and residential construction expenditures swinging more widely than either required additions or household formations.

Up to the 1950's, national required additions, nonfarm housing starts, and nonfarm residential construction (based on 1929 prices) followed similar decadal patterns of long swings (see Chart 10).[40] Over this period the rank order of changes in housing starts and residential capital formation was closely related to the rank order of changes in required additions, with the amplitude of the long swing in the first differences of all three series tending to increase from one cycle to the next.

As would be expected, there was a clear tendency for nonfarm housing starts and nonfarm residential construction to increase more rapidly than national required additions when the latter were increasing and to fall by more than required additions when they declined. In part, the wider amplitude of the long swings in nonfarm housing starts and nonfarm residential capital formation can be explained by fluctuations in the number of farm household formations. However, most of the difference was

---

[39] Also, as expected, farm-to-nonfarm migration followed a clear long-swing pattern, reflecting the current income and employment situation in nonfarm areas and similar in timing to the long swing in required additions. Whether this implies that population changes determined the nonagricultural economic conditions leading to swings in internal migration or were determined by these changes will be discussed in Chapter VII.

[40] The Bureau of the Census recently extended the "new" series estimates of housing starts, based on both a broader definition of starts and on improved coverage, back to 1945. The new series estimates in 1945-50 and in 1950-55 were 46 percent and 32 percent greater than the "old" series estimates, respectively. It must be assumed that a downward bias also applies to the pre-1945 old series estimates of nonfarm housing starts. However, since much of the difference is accounted for by the inclusion of nonpermit-issuing areas and of units outside incorporated areas in the new series, the special circumstances of the postwar years (rapid suburban growth in unincorporated areas, for example) would suggest that the bias was smaller prior to World War II.

Chart 10. Required Additions, Residential Capital Formation, and Housing Starts, by Decade

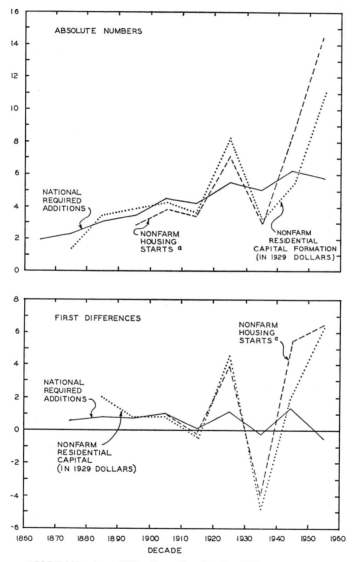

MILLIONS OF DWELLING UNITS
OR BILLIONS OF 1929 DOLLARS

ABSOLUTE NUMBERS

NATIONAL REQUIRED ADDITIONS

NONFARM HOUSING STARTS [a]

NONFARM RESIDENTIAL CAPITAL FORMATION (IN 1929 DOLLARS)

FIRST DIFFERENCES

NONFARM HOUSING STARTS [a]

NATIONAL REQUIRED ADDITIONS

NONFARM RESIDENTIAL CAPITAL (IN 1929 DOLLARS)

DECADE

[a] BLS "old" series to 1940's; Census "new" series, 1940's on.
Sources: Required additions, Table 1; housing starts, tabulation on p. 68; and residential capital formation, Table 4.

accounted for by the other factors separating housing starts and required additions, suggesting that nondemographic variables played a role in determining the amplitude if not the direction of changes in residential building.

For the first three decades covered in this study, national required additions and household formations exceeded nonfarm housing starts, largely because of continued growth in the farm population (see Table 2). Of these three decades, 1900-1910 is the most interesting. In that decade, because of the rapid expansion in urban immigration, nonfarm household formations increased much more than either national required additions or national household formations. Moreover, unlike what happened in the 1890's or from 1910-20, they exceeded nonfarm housing starts.

Since conversions are more often used to meet the housing demand of low-income groups and renters, both of which classes include a large number of immigrants, the decline in the relative importance of immigration in the 1890's and its increase from 1900-1910 might help explain why housing starts exceeded nonfarm household formations in the former decade and fell short of them during the latter when the economic atmosphere was generally more bullish.

One result of the large proportion of population growth accounted for by immigration was a smaller relative increase in residential construction than in required additions, the opposite of the relationship found in all other decades covered. The resulting backlog of relatively poorly housed spending units was slightly reduced from 1910-20, since housing starts exceeded nonfarm household formations and conversions apparently were greater than withdrawals.[41]

---

[41] The estimates of the difference between conversions plus other additions and withdrawals in Table 2 are based on the data presented by Grebler, Blank, and Winnick, *op. cit.*, Appendix A (see especially Table A-1, p. 329). The average of the two estimates given for the 1920's for withdrawals was used. Following the suggestion of Grebler, Blank, and Winnick, the number of conversions given for the 1890's to the 1910's, (based on David Wickens, *Residential Real Estate* [New York: National Bureau of Economic Research, 1941], p. 54) was multiplied by a factor of four. Chawner's (Lowell Chawner, *Residential Building*, National Resources Committee, Housing Monograph Series No. 1 [Washington: U.S. Government Printing Office 1939], p. 14) estimate for the 1920's was used rather than Wickens's. Until the 1930's no estimates of the number of dwellings — trailers, tents, boats, permanent units without housekeeping facilities, and so forth — included in the housing stock but excluded from housing starts were available. From the 1890's to the 1910's it was assumed that these units equaled 5 percent of nonfarm starts; but, because the relative importance of the kinds of dwelling units excluded from nonfarm starts would seem to be a positive function of the relative importance of the automobile as a means of transportation, this ratio was raised to 10 percent in the 1920's. The net figure (showing an excess of withdrawals over "other" additions for the first time) for the 1950's was based on the *1960 Census*

TABLE 2. RELATIONSHIP BETWEEN REQUIRED ADDITIONS AND HOUSING STARTS, BY DECADE

(Thousands of dwelling units)

Decade	Required additions (1)	Adjustment for head-ship rate changes (2)	Household formations (Col. 1 plus Col. 2) (3)	Adjustment to nonfarm[a] (4)	Nonfarm household formations (Col. 3 plus Col. 4)[b] (5)	Adjustment to housing starts[c] (6)	Nonfarm housing starts (Col. 5 plus Col. 6)[d] (7)	Other additions minus withdrawals[e] (8)
1890-1900	3,485	-212	3,273	-922	2,351	520	2,871	180
1900-1910	4,444	-152	4,292	-434	3,858	-155	3,703	213
1910-20	4,365	-169	4,096	-638	3,468	38	3,506	169
1920-30	5,419	134	5,553	147	5,700	1,359	7,059	621
1930-40	5,028	-78	4,950	-502	4,448	-1,579	2,869	1,173
1940-50	6,296	1,675	7,971	1,368	9,357	-644	8,713	1,700
1950-60	5,685	4,305	9,990	2,163	12,153	2,281	14,434	-2,674

[a] In the 1930's and 1940's Col. 4 was not adjusted for the reclassification of farm dwellings to nonfarm status [see Leo Grebler, David Blank, and Louis Winnick, *Capital Formation in Residential Real Estate — Trends and Prospects*, National Bureau of Economic Research (Princeton: Princeton University Press, 1956), pp. 330-31] because the occupancy status of the units so reclassified was not known.

[b] Nonfarm household formations for the 1950's are not comparable to earlier estimates because of a basic change in the definition of "nonfarm" in the 1960 Census. Thus, the 1950's "adjustment to nonfarm" is biased upward by this change. The 1950's nonfarm household formations have also been adjusted to exclude Hawaii and Alaska.

[c] Some of the differences between nonfarm housing starts and nonfarm household formations are the results of differences in dates. Housing starts, for example, run from July, 1890, to June, 1900, whereas household formations are counted between census dates (usually from April to April).

[d] Through the 1930's, nonfarm housing starts are based on the old series definitions. From the 1940's on, they are based on the new series. See Sources.

[e] The estimated difference between additions to the housing stock not counted in housing starts (conversions, trailers, "temporary" units) and withdrawals.

Sources: Col. 1 — Table 1; Col. 2 — household formations minus required additions (the change in headship rates weighted by the population changes — see Chapter III, p. 43); Col. 3 — Table 1; Col. 4 — nonfarm household formations minus household formations; Col. 5 — Table 1; Col. 6 — nonfarm housing starts minus nonfarm household formations; Col. 7 — 1890's to 1920's, David M. Blank, *The Volume of Residential Construction, 1889-1950*, National Bureau of Economic Research, Technical Paper No. 9 (Princeton: Princeton University Press, 1954); 1930's to 1950's, Council of Economic Advisers, *Economic Report of the President, 1964 and 1965* (Washington: U.S. Government Printing Office, 1964, 1965); 1930's Bureau of Labor Statistics old series; 1940-45, old series blown up to new series level by the 1945-50 ratio of the new to old series; 1945-50, based on new series data adjusted for construction in Hawaii and Alaska — see U.S. Department of Commerce, *Construction Review* (May, 1960), for a description of the new series; Col. 8 — see footnote 7, p. 13.

In the 1920's, the experience of the first three decades was completely reversed. Headship rates increased for the first time, the number of farm households fell, and nonfarm housing starts far exceeded national required additions (and nonfarm household formations).[42] Thus, all the relationships suggested by a priori analysis for a period of rapid economic growth are found in the 1920's.

Most of the excess of nonfarm housing starts over national required additions was accounted for by the large excess of housing starts over nonfarm household formations. Assuming that the bias in the old series leading to the upward adjustment in the nonfarm housing start series recently completed for the postwar years would be relevant to the 1920's and noting that conversions were apparently greater than withdrawals in this decade, it is obvious that a large increase in the number of vacant units must have occurred — an increase at least as large as the excess of housing starts over nonfarm household formations. Thus, population growth not only led to increased production of dwelling units but also to mistaken estimates of demand by builders and investors (especially in rental properties — see Chapter V) and consequently to a large inventory of vacancies at the end of the decade.[43]

As national required additions fell in the 1930's, housing starts virtually collapsed. As would be expected, required additions exceeded national household formations (but, surprisingly, only slightly) and national household formations exceeded nonfarm household formations as the movement off the farm was reversed by the Depression. These developments contributed to the large excess of national required additions over nonfarm housing starts, but most of the excess was accounted for by the difference between nonfarm household formations and housing starts. Even assuming that the old series estimates of housing starts understate the actual level by the same proportion as in the postwar years — which is unlikely — there would still remain a large gap between household formations and

---

of Housing (see tabulation on p. 68). Until the 1950's the estimates are at best a rough indication of the magnitude of the difference between other additions and withdrawals, but they should be reliable as to the sign of the difference.

[42] Instead of saying that headship rates increased for the first time in the 1920's, it is perhaps more correct to say that they increased more than enough to offset the decline in the 1890's. Whether the smaller negative difference between required additions and household formations in the 1900's than that in the 1890's means that headship rates increased in the 1900's is difficult to determine because of the constant set of headship rates used.

[43] Adding the excess of other additions over withdrawals to the excess of housing starts over nonfarm household formations would yield an increase in the inventory of vacant units of almost 2 million units (or about 30 percent of housing starts) in the 1920's.

housing starts to be filled by other means, and of course withdrawals during the 1930's would increase this gap. The gap could have been filled by making use of the stock of vacant units left from the 1920's, but the large increase in conversions during the 1930's suggests that they provided the majority of the dwellings required and that, as a consequence, vacancy rates remained high.[44] It is clear that the income elasticity of demand for separate quarters was far less than the income elasticity of demand for new dwelling units during the Depression.

Both national required additions and nonfarm housing starts increased during the 1940's. The increase in housing starts is biased upward by the shift from the old to the new series base; but even when the old series estimates for both decades are compared, the increase in housing starts was far greater than that called for by the concurrent increase in required additions, and housing starts exceeded national required additions for only the second time in the period covered.

The excess of nonfarm housing starts over national required additions in the 1940's is entirely explained by two factors: the first significant increase in headship rates and the large excess of nonfarm household formations over national household formations. Together, these developments raised nonfarm household formations above housing starts. Part of the increase in nonfarm household formations was offset by the census reclassification of dwelling units from farm to nonfarm status, but evidence that production of new units did not keep up with the growth in housing demand — at least in some local markets — is provided by the large estimated excess of conversions over withdrawals and the decrease in net vacancy rates from 1940 to 1950.[45] Since the gross vacancy rate increased during the 1940's, the converted units apparently provided a temporary response to the excess demand during and just after World War II and were later vacated as the production of new units expanded in the late 1940's. In any event, there is little evidence to suggest that a major dent was made during the 1940's in the quality backlog resulting from the excess of household formations over housing starts in the 1930's. In fact, except for the uncertainty involving the exact time of construction and the

[44] The census estimate of the gross vacancy rate in 1940 was 6.5 percent (U.S. Bureau of the Census, *Census of Housing, 1940,* Vol. II, Part I, p. 9), whereas Wickens's estimate (*op. cit.*) for 1930 was 5.0 percent. However, vacancy rates did fall in mid-decade, only to increase again. See Fisher, *loc. cit.*

[45] The gross vacancy rate was 6.5 percent in 1940 and 6.8 percent in 1950. The net rate (excluding seasonal units, units occupied by nonresidents, and units held for absent residents) was 3.8 percent in 1940 and 1.7 percent in 1950. For 1940 data see fn. 44. The 1950 data are based on the U.S. Bureau of the Census, *Census of Housing, 1950,* Vol. I, *General Characteristics,* Pt. 1, Table 5, p. 3.

occupancy status of the dwellings moved from farm to nonfarm status by the census, it would appear that the quality backlog was increased still further in the 1940's.

The housing market adjustments made during the Depression and during and just after World War II help to explain the almost complete break between national required additions and nonfarm housing starts that took place in the 1950's. Up to that decade, national required additions exceeded housing starts or accounted for more than 75 percent of housing starts, but in the 1950's housing starts were over two and one-half times national required additions and increased by the largest amount ever as national required additions fell. The largest portion of this huge difference was the result of increased headship rates during the 1950's. But, in addition, both the excess of nonfarm household formations over national household formations (again biased upward by a change in the definition of farm and nonfarm) and of housing starts over nonfarm household formations were greater than ever before.

The inventory of the components of change in the housing stock compiled by the Bureau of the Census in the *1960 Census of Housing* makes it possible for the first time to allocate the difference between required additions and new construction (a concept somewhat different from housing starts) to headship rate changes, the various classes of withdrawals, the change in vacancies, and other additions, but on a national basis only. Doing so makes clear the important role played in the 1950's by withdrawals which exceeded other additions for the first time and did so by a large amount, making possible most of the excess of new construction over national household formations. The following tabulation shows this allocation.

National required additions............................		5,685,000
plus adjustment to national household formations		4,305,000
equals national household formations............		9,990,000
plus dwelling units lost		
via mergers..............................	815,000	
via demolition...........................	1,933,000	
via other means..........................	1,783,000	4,351,000
equals total dwelling units required............		14,521,000
plus change in vacancies.....................		2,339,000
equals total dwelling units added..............		16,860,000
less other dwelling units added		
via net conversions.......................	807,000	
via other sources.........................	1,050,000	1,857,000
equals new construction......................		15,003,000

New construction includes all units built, not just those started during the 1950's. New construction also differs from housing starts in the inclusion of trailers, some units in hotels, and units in structures primarily intended for nonresidential use. To some extent the increase in withdrawals reflected the quality backlog built up during the 1930's and 1940's (most units demolished were of inferior quality), but it also reflected the proliferation of high-speed transportation systems (the "freeways") in most metropolitan areas. Thus, two unprecedented developments, the increase in headship rates and the excess of withdrawals over other additions, account for most of the increase in housing starts relative to national required additions in the 1950's. It remains to be seen whether these developments will continue and so continue to justify a large excess of housing starts over required additions in the future.

A more familiar aspect of a building boom was also present in the increase in vacancies during the 1950's. The national increase was closely related in size to the decrease in farm households, so it is possible that a large part of the additional vacancies were located in rural areas where they did not compete with new nonfarm units. However, the considerable increase in rental vacancy rates in the late 1950's presumably involved mostly units located in nonfarm areas. More significantly, to go on accumulating vacancies at the marginal rate (almost 19 percent of net additions to the housing stock) of the 1950's would imply a stock of vacant dwellings close to 10 percent of the total housing stock by 1970. There is reason to doubt that this proportion of vacant units can be reached before the increasing number of unsold or unrented dwellings has a depressing effect on residential construction.

It seems clear that by the end of the 1950's the quality backlog resulting from the Depression and World War II was gone. The remaining low-quality housing — especially in the urban slums — is not likely to have the same effect on housing starts. In the 1940's lower-quality or converted dwelling units were occupied by spending units that could demand better-quality housing once production controls were lifted and the housing became available. Today, these units are occupied largely by low-income minority groups without the financial capacity to demand better housing without subsidization. We may have a backlog in terms of social goals, but it hardly seems that one exists in terms of effective demand.

In some respects the similarity between the 1920's and the 1950's is striking. Both decades followed a major war, and in each the level of income was generally increasing. As a result, in both decades the tenure composition of demand shifted sharply toward sales housing (see Chapter V). In the 1950's, the combined influence of the Depression and World War II had the effect of creating a quality backlog similar to that created in the 1920's by the combined influence of heavy immigration between

1900 and 1910 and during World War I. In both instances, the postwar booms aided, and were aided by, the working off of these backlogs. Vacancy rates increased less in the 1950's than in the 1920's (1) because the large increase in headship rates in the 1950's moved a new group of households into converted and lower-quality rentals as soon as income changes moved the old occupants out and (2) because urban renewal projects, freeway systems, and so forth removed a large number of dwelling units from the housing stock. In one characteristic, however, the historical analogy completely breaks down — the expansion in residential building in the 1920's was firmly rooted in the population changes of that period as headship rates remained virtually constant, whereas the even greater expansion in the 1950's was accomplished despite the concurrent decrease in required additions.

The Quinquennial Record

Quinquennial estimates show that population changes led to three distinct long swings in required additions during the first 60 years of this century (see Table 3), with peaks occurring in 1910-15, 1920-25, and 1945-50. Housing starts and residential capital formation were closely related to these long swings through the 1930's, and, if required additions are adjusted for the effect of World War II on the housing population, this close relation continues through the 1940's. Not only did these three series move together for the most part during the first half of this century, but, despite the greater amplitude of the swings in housing starts and residential construction, the rank order of their first differences was similar over the same period.

Required additions increased by relatively large amounts in 1905-10 and 1920-25, remained at the high level attained for the next five years, and then declined sharply in 1915-20 and 1930-35. Housing starts and residential capital formation increased and decreased with required additions, but, although required additions remained on a high plateau, housing starts fell in 1910-15. In 1925-30, housing starts mirrored required additions but remained far above them, suggesting that the build-up of vacancies in the 1920's was the result of the mistaken estimates of the rate of growth in demand in the second half of the twenties. Before the war intervened, required additions, housing starts, and residential construction started to trace out the third long swing of this century in 1935-40.

During World War II, residential construction, housing starts, and required additions all fell, and all three series participated in the postwar recovery, with required additions and housing starts increasing by the largest amounts ever. The fact that residential construction had shown

Table 3. Required Additions, Housing Starts, and Residential Capital Formation, by Quinquennial Period

Quinquennial period	Required additions[a] (Thousands of units) (1)	Housing starts (Thousands of units) (2)	Residential capital formation (Billions of 1929 dollars) (3)
1885-90..........................	.....	.....	2.12
1890-95..........................	.....	1,529	2.00
1895-1900........................	.....	1,341	1.77
1900-1905........................	2,068	1,430	1.91
1905-10..........................	2,376	2,273	2.41
1910-15..........................	2,396	2,072	2.28
1915-20..........................	1,969	1,434	1.38
1920-25..........................	2,714	3,505	4.05
1925-30..........................	2,705	2,554	4.08
1930-35..........................	2,475	882	.98
1935-40..........................	2,562	1,987	2.24
1940-45..........................	1,872	1,801 (2,633)[b]	1.32
1945-50..........................	4,424	6,258[c]	3.89
1950-55..........................	2,913	7,783[c]	5.22
1955-60..........................	2,977	6,946[c]	6.17

[a] Required additions in 1940-45 and 1945-50 are based on population changes adjusted for the movement of people into and out of the armed forces (see Appendix E). Without adjustment, required additions would be 3,125 in 1940-45 and 3,171 in 1945-50.
[b] Old series estimate blown up to new series level on the basis of the 1945-50 ratio of the new to the old series.
[c] New series estimates.
Sources: Col. 1 — based on population sources and headship rate data in Appendixes A and B; Col. 2 — Table 2; Col. 3 — 1885-90 to 1945-50 from Simon Kuznets, *Capital in the American Economy: Its Formation and Financing* (New York: National Bureau of Economic Research, 1960), Table R30, p. 576; and data for the 1950's based on the estimates presented in the *Economic Report of the President, 1963* (Washington: U.S. Government Printing Office, 1963), which were converted to 1929 dollars.

a greater increase following World War I suggests the greater importance of young households (requiring dwelling units of less than average value) in 1945-50, as well as the relatively low quality of some of the early postwar housing.

In 1950-55, when required additions fell by the largest amount ever, housing starts moved up to an all-time peak and residential construction reached the second-highest level ever attained. Then in 1955-60, housing starts fell as required additions increased slightly and residential construction reached its all-time peak. In neither half of the 1950's did housing starts or residential construction appear to be greatly influenced by population changes.

In Chapter III the possibility was raised that the rate of change in required additions (and in population growth) might be more important than the level of required additions in determining housing starts. Comparing the first differences in required additions with movements in the level of housing starts shown in Table 3, it is apparent that the relative amplitude of the long swing in the increments in required additions more closely parallels the amplitude of swings in housing starts than does the long swing in the level of required additions. However, since all but one (1910-15) of the fluctuations in the first differences in required additions were the results of absolute increases or decreases in the level of required additions rather than of fluctuations in the rate of increase or decrease, little additional explanatory value attaches to the "accelerator" hypothesis.

To some extent this conclusion derives from the five- or ten-year periods for which required additions are available. Annual estimates might show a feedback from changes in the rate of increase in required additions to increases or decreases in the level of housing starts and so through income changes to increases or decreases in the level of required additions.

It was also suggested in the preceding chapter that the difference between housing starts and required additions would be positively related to the first differences in required additions. Except in 1940-45 and in the 1950's, this positive relationship was found, suggesting that in the first 40 years of this century at least, a cobweb adjustment to changes in the demand for housing was an important feature of housing markets.

In sum, even with demand correctly estimated and income unchanged, population factors alone would have led to a series of residential building cycles closely related in magnitude and timing to the residential building cycles actually experienced. There would have been the same residential construction booms in the 1880's, 1900's, 1920's, and 1940's, with housing starts and residential construction falling in the 1910's and 1930's and remaining stable or falling in the 1890's. Only the 1950's do not fit this picture. In the 1950's the largest recorded decrease in required additions was matched by the largest increase in housing starts.

Apparently national required additions and housing starts were either closely related to some third variable or bore a causal relationship to each other. If one could explain the variation in required additions, at least from 1880 to 1950, it would be possible to offer a consistent model of the residential building cycle. Certainly, the evidence presented so far is consistent with the hypothesis that long swings in population growth are the main causes of long swings in residential construction. It is not necessary that population changes control residential building — changes in economic conditions or tastes may offset their impact as they did in the 1950's — but it is apparent that population changes did have that effect for almost a century.

The obvious conclusion is that if economic changes greatly influenced the housing market prior to the 1950's, they must have done so by influencing the size and age composition of population increments. This influence might have been exercised through either farm-to-nonfarm migration or immigration. Farm-to-nonfarm migration reduced the difference between national required additions and housing starts; but, as has been noted, even if the ratio of nonfarm to national required additions had remained constant, the residential building cycle would have corresponded closely to the long swing in required additions.

On the other hand, prior to the Immigration Act of 1924, the long cycle in required additions (see Chapter VII) was determined largely by the ebb and flow of immigration to the United States, which in turn was at least partly determined by economic conditions in the United States. However, after 1924 (and to some degree in the early 1920's) changes in the housing population clearly were predetermined in the sense that any remaining influence of concurrent immigration on housing population increments was far outweighed by population factors wholly independent of income conditions. Thus, for several decades required additions have been an independent variable, determining but not determined by residential construction and gross national product.

V. POPULATION CHANGES AND THE TENURE COMPOSITION OF HOUSING DEMAND: 1870's TO 1950's

The ebb and flow of population growth has often been considered a major cause of the residential building cycle, but little or no attention has been given to the possibility that demographic variables also may influence the tenure and quality composition of housing demand. Starting from the observed variation in the tenure composition of housing demand over the life cycle, this possibility was given theoretical content in the development of the multi-class model in Chapter II. In the present chapter, the long swing in owner- and renter-occupied required additions will be investigated and compared with both the change in the owner- and renter-occupied housing stock and the production of single-family and multi-family dwelling units.

Changes in Tenure Composition of Demand

Owner-occupied required additions increased from the 1880's to the 1920's, turned down in the 1930's, and then increased to an all-time high in the 1950's (see Table 4). Excepting in 1910-20, sales required additions moved with total required additions and with the actual change in the owner-occupied housing stock. In the absence of any effect of population changes on the tenure composition of demand, sales required additions would be a constant proportion of total required additions and of rental required additions. Thus, the excess of sales required additions over rental required additions from the 1910's to the 1930's and the reverse situation from the 1880's to the 1900's and in the 1940's testify to the influence of the shifting age composition of the population.[46]

---

[46] Since part of the interdecade variation in the relationship between sales and rental required additions is the result of tenure-rate changes after the 1930's and of headship-rate changes in the 1950's, for comparative purposes it is desirable to have estimates of required additions in the 1940's and 1950's at 1940 headship and 1930 tenure rates.

	Sales required additions	Rental required additions
1940's	3,555	2,741
1950's	3,795	2,141

TABLE 4. HOUSEHOLD FORMATIONS AND REQUIRED ADDITIONS BY TENURE CLASS, BY DECADE

(Thousands of dwelling units)

Decade	Household formations (1)	Required additions (2)	Col. 1 minus Col. 2 (3)	Change in owner occupancy (4)	Sales required additions (5)	Col. 4 minus Col. 5 (6)	Change in renter occupancy (7)	Rental required additions (8)	Col. 7 minus Col. 8 (9)	Col. 5 minus Col. 8 (10)
1870-80	.....	2,285	.....	.....	1,025	.....	.....	1,260	.....	−235
1880-90	.....	3,009	.....	.....	1,394	.....	.....	1,615	.....	−221
1890-1900	3,273	3,485	−212	1,389	1,639	−250	1,884	1,846	38	−207
1900-1910	4,292	4,444	−152	1,846	2,080	−234	2,446	2,364	82	−284
1910-20	4,096	4,365	−269	1,813	2,211	−398	2,283	2,144	139	67
1920-30	5,553	5,419	134	3,166	2,843	323	2,387	2,577	−190	266
1930-40	4,950	5,028	−78	916	2,716	−1,800	4,034	2,312	1,722	404
1940-50	7,971	6,296	1,675	8,364	3,058	5,306	−393	3,238	−3,631	−180
1950-60	9,990	5,685	4,305	9,146	3,640	5,506	841	2,045	1,204	1,595

Sources: Cols. 1, 4, and 7 — Bureau of the Census, *Statistical Abstract of the United States, 1963* (Washington: U.S. Government Printing Office, 1963), Table 1,072, p. 759; Col. 2 — Table 1; Cols. 5 and 8 — derived by multiplying required additions by age class by tenure rates by age class — 1930 tenure rates were used through the 1930's, 1940 tenure rates were used for the 1940's, and 1949 tenure rates were used for the 1950's (sources of tenure-rate data are given in Appendix B).

Sales required additions exceeded the actual change in the owner-occupied housing stock in the first decades covered. The excess is partly explained by the use of 1930 tenure rates to estimate required additions by tenure class for the decades prior to the 1930's; the 1930 tenure rates reflect the shift toward home ownership in the 1920's and therefore would tend to overestimate the demand for owner-occupancy prior to the 1920's. However, the excess of estimated over actual additions to the owner-occupied housing stock in the 1890's and 1910's (but not the 1900's), the reversal of the sign of the error in the 1920's, and the large overestimate in the 1930's are as would have been expected, given the economic conditions in these decades.

From 1910-20, age-standardized population changes "predicted" an increase in the change in the owner-occupied housing stock at the same time that total required additions were falling. The increase did not materialize, both because of the slowdown in economic growth from 1910 to 1914 and because of the wartime controls in the latter part of that decade. The implication is that a reduction in owner-occupancy rates more than offset the increased growth of the population in the age classes where owner-occupancy is relatively most important. However, the decline in the incremental demand for sales housing was relatively much smaller than the decline in total household formations.

In the 1920's, owner-occupied required additions increased by the largest amount in the period covered by this study. The increase was accompanied by a substantial rise in owner-occupancy rates, resulting in a boom in sales markets. Since this boom was soundly based on predetermined population growth, it could be argued that the economic expansion of the 1920's was at least partly the result of the prior increases in immigration and births (from 1900-1910, for example) that led to the contemporary population changes at the middle and late life-cycle stages.

The decline in owner-occupied required additions in the 1930's broke a string of four straight decadal increases, and, following as it did the peak increase of the 1920's, this decline must have been an important factor in explaining the collapse of sales production in the early 1930's. More important for understanding this key period in our economic history, the reduction in owner-occupied required additions in the 1930's would have taken place in the absence of any depression (see Chapter VII), and it is therefore properly classified as one of the causes of the Depression.

Clearly, the largest reduction in rental required additions in the period covered would still have occurred in the 1950's even if tenure rates had not changed to favor ownership during the 1940's.

If adjustment is made for the upward bias introduced by the use of 1930 headship rates, the estimated and actual changes in the owner-occupied housing stock were closely related through 1930. The Depression then turned an estimated decline into a major collapse in the demand for owner-occupancy. From 1930 on, population factors were clearly of subsidiary importance in explaining the change in owner-occupancy. A combination of changed tastes, rising real income, revolutionized mortgage terms, and rent controls served to raise the actual change in the owner-occupied housing stock to two and one-half times the estimated change in the 1940's. The continuance of all of these factors except the last pushed the increase in owner-occupancy to almost three times the level justified by population factors alone in the 1950's. Considering that the estimates of sales required additions for the 1950's are based on tenure rates in 1949 and thus have been adjusted for the increase in owner-occupancy rates during the 1940's, the extent of the sales boom in the 1950's seems even more remarkable. Future prospects will be discussed in detail in the concluding chapter, but here it might be remarked that within the last few years the increase in owner-occupancy rates has been dampened and the importance of population factors (especially of age composition) has been correspondingly increased.

The experience with rental required additions is just the reverse of that with sales required additions. Rental required additions fell slightly short of the actual change in the early decades covered and then exceeded the actual change in the 1920's. That relatively large increase was immediately followed by a substantial decrease in the 1930's, once again suggesting the importance of predetermined population changes as a cause of the Depression. Of course, the actual (positive) change in renter occupancy during the 1930's was the largest in the period covered.

As part of the large increase in household formations explained by population changes in the 1940's, rental required additions reached their peak level in that decade, exceeding sales required additions for the first time since 1900-1910. However, a rental boom not only did not materialize, but contemporary changes in tenure rates reduced the number of renter-occupied dwelling units below the level reached in 1940. Rent controls, new arrangements (the F.H.A. and V.A. programs) for financing the construction of tract housing and ownership, changing birth rates, and increasing real incomes all contributed to the decline in renter-occupancy rates during the 1940's. With this change included, the level of required additions for renters fell in the 1950's to the lowest level since the 1890's.[47]

---

[47] From the 1920's on (earlier data are not available), much the same pattern of decadal changes in required additions by tenure class occurred in the nonfarm

A Further Look at the Last Three Decades

The 1930-60 period deserves special attention. In all three of its decades, population factors do not come close to estimating the change in
the occupied housing stock by tenure class, but in the 1930's and 1940's
at least, they do explain most of the change in the number of households.

In the 1930's household formations were only 0.08 million less than
the number expected on the basis of population factors; the change in
the owner-occupied housing stock was 1.80 million less than expected,
and the number seeking rental units increased by 1.72 million more than
expected. It is clear that tenure-rate changes were far more important
than headship-rate changes or population changes in determining the
tenure composition of demand in the 1930's. It is also clear that the
tenure composition of demand responded much more to the impact of
the Depression than did the number of units demanded by each one
thousand of the housing population. Even if required additions had estimated household formations perfectly (the error was less than 1.5 percent), required additions by tenure class would still have differed by over
50 percent from the actual change in the occupied units by tenure class.

In the 1940's, household formations were 1.68 million more than expected on the basis of estimates of required additions. This is a considerable difference (about 28 percent) but small compared with the error
resulting from the impact of nonpopulation factors on the tenure composition of demand. The gain in the number of households seeking sales
housing (5.31 million more than expected) would have given the largest
increase in demand for owner-occupancy on record, even in the absence
of any change in the housing population or in headship rates during the
1940's. The related decline in renter-occupancy rates, which more than
offset the concurrent change in headship rates and the greater growth in
the housing population, brought about the largest drop in the number of
rental household formations in 80 years. In fact, the change in renter-
occupancy was negative and 3.63 million units less than rental required
additions.

The level of sales required additions was still far short of the actual
change in owner-occupancy in the 1950's, but most of the difference was
explained by the concurrent change in headship rates rather than the
change in tenure rates. As a result, the change in renter-occupancy was
positive once again.

The conclusion one reaches is that population factors were far less

---

sector. The swings were wider because of a shift in the level of farm-to-nonfarm
migration (especially in the 1940's).

important in determining the tenure composition of demand than they were in determining the number of household formations. By analogy, economic conditions and tastes were relatively more important. In other words, the income elasticity of demand for owner-occupancy was much greater than the income elasticity of demand for separate quarters. With demand swinging toward sales units in expansions and back to rental units in contractions, this helps to explain (given the possibility of converting existing units to meet increased rental demand) the wider amplitude of fluctuations in housing starts than of those in household formations.

Quinquennial Estimates

Data giving the actual tenure composition of the occupied housing stock are not available for five-year periods, but estimates for quinquennial periods of the required additions to the owner- and renter-occupied housing stock reveal at least two very interesting relationships between population changes, especially changes in age composition, and the total and tenure composition of household formations.

First, both rental and sales required additions trace out a series of long swings, similar in duration but different in the timing of peaks and troughs (see Table 5). The difference in timing is the same at the peaks, with the peak in rental required additions leading the peak in sales required additions in each long swing. The pattern was less consistent at the trough; rental required additions led only in 1930-35.[48]

Since both sales required additions and total required additions reached peaks in the same half-decade, apparently rental required additions served as a leading indicator of the upper turning point in population pressure for additions to the housing stock in all three long cycles for which quinquennial data are available. Thus, the experienced pattern of leads and

---

[48] If tenure rates are held constant (at the 1930 level) and headship rates are not allowed to change after 1940 (the 1930-40 change was insignificant), the following quinquennial estimates of sales and rental required additions from 1935-60 result.

	Sales required additions	Rental required additions
1935–40	1,425	1,137
1940–45	1,715	1,410
1945–50	1,840	1,331
1950–55	1,926	1,124
1955–60	1,869	1,107

These constant tenure-rate estimates remove the lead of rental required additions at the trough in 1930-35 and show that, in the absence of tenure- and headship-rate changes, changes in age composition would have continued the lead of rental required additions over sales and total required additions at the upper turning point in the long swing in total required additions through the 1950's.

TABLE 5. TENURE COMPOSITION OF REQUIRED ADDITIONS,
BY QUINQUENNIAL PERIOD
(Thousands of dwelling units)

Quinquennial period	Owner-occupied required additions	Renter-occupied required additions	Total required additions
	(1)	(2)	(3)
1900-1905[a]	958	1,110	2,068
1905-10	1,122	1,254	2,376
1910-15	1,195	1,201	2,396
1915-20	1,016	953	1,969
1920-25	1,359	1,355	2,714
1925-30	1,485	1,221	2,706
1930-35	1,375	1,100	2,475
1935-40	1,233	1,329	2,562
1940-45[b]	1,481	1,644	3,125
1945-50[b]	1,579	1,592	3,171
1950-55	1,860	1,052	2,912
1955-60	2,011	966	2,977

[a] From 1900-1905 to 1930-35, 1930 tenure rates were used in estimating required additions by tenure class. In 1935-40, 1940-45, and 1945-50, 1940 tenure rates were used. In 1950-55, 1950 tenure rates were used, and in 1955-60, 1955 tenure rates were used.
[b] If adjusted for the effects of mobilization during and demobilization after World War II, then sales required additions would be 1,243 in 1940-45 and 1,815 in 1945-50, and rental required additions would be 629 in 1940-45 and 2,609 in 1945-50.
Sources: Cols. 1 and 2 — see Appendix B for a discussion of the basic tenure-rate data used in making estimates of required additions by tenure class; Col. 3 — Table 1, p. 60.

lags at cycle peaks between renter- and owner-occupied required additions is precisely the one suggested by the model outlined in Chapter II, a conclusion of the first importance both for understanding past building cycles and for future planning. At the lower turning point of the long swing in total required additions, rental required additions coincide with total required additions in all three cycles.

Second, the collapse of residential construction and the increase in rental vacancies that presaged the Depression must have been at least partly the result of the variation in rental required additions in the 1920's. The largest increase in rental required additions took place in 1920-25, pushing vacancies to low levels, leading to speculation in existing rental properties, and encouraging the construction of new dwelling units for the rental market — a time-consuming, emulative process that masks the true state of the market until several of the new structures are completed in a given locality. With this boom in progress, the second-largest decrease in rental required additions occurred in 1925-30, leaving many unfinished projects high and dry and undercutting the earlier speculative optimism.

The resulting increase in rental vacancies served to place a damper on the sales market as well, and even through owner-occupied required additions continued to increase in 1925-30, construction of sales units fell (see p. 88).

Housing Starts and the Change in Occupied Units by Tenure Class

Responding to changed economic conditions and tastes, the tenure composition of demand shifted far more widely from the 1930's to the 1960's than did required additions by tenure class. To find out (1) whether or not these wide swings in tenure composition were reflected in the type of dwelling unit started and (2) if the production of dwelling units conformed by structural type to the changes in the tenure composition of demand before the 1930's when population factors accounted for most of these changes, two steps were taken. Single-family starts were compared with the changes in the owner-occupied housing stock and sales required additions, and multi-family starts were compared with the changes in the renter-occupied housing stock and rental required additions (see Table 6).

This procedure introduces a definite bias in that, whereas most sales demand is for one-family structures, a significant portion of all renter-occupied units also consists of one-family units. Although the ratios of owner- and renter-occupied single- and multi-family units to owner-occupancy and renter-occupancy may be relatively stable, the marginal ratios (e.g., the change in owner-occupied one-family units to the change in owner-occupancy) would be expected to vary with changes in economic conditions and tastes. For example, about 60 percent of all renter-occupied units are multi-family units, but in the 1950's the increase in multi-family renter-occupied units was just over 200 percent of the total change in renter-occupancy.[49] For this reason, rather than attempting to allocate the change in owner- or renter-occupancy or the number of sales and rental required additions between single- and multi-family starts, it seemed less misleading to make the indicated comparison, keeping in mind the built-in bias.[50]

---

[49] Multi-family renter-occupancy increased by 1,337,000, whereas total renter-occupancy increased by only 636,000, with the difference accounted for by an absolute decline in one-family renter-occupancy. See Table 7.

[50] In 1950, 88.0 percent of owner-occupants were housed in one-family structures, 10.9 percent in multi-family structures, and 1.1 percent in trailers. In 1960, these percentages by structure type were respectively, 89.2 percent, 9.4 percent, and 1.4 percent. In 1950, 40.5 percent of renter-occupants were housed in one-family structures, 58.1 percent in multi-family structures, and 1.4 percent in trailers. By 1960, these ratios had changed to 39.7 percent, 59.8 percent, and 0.5 percent (see U.S. Bureau of the Census, Census of Housing, 1960, op. cit., Table 1, p. 28). Although applying these average ratios to allocate sales or rental

TABLE 6. ONE-FAMILY AND MULTI-FAMILY HOUSING STARTS AND REQUIRED ADDITIONS BY TENURE CLASS, BY DECADE

(Thousands of dwelling units)

Decade	Sales required additions (1)	Adjustment for national change in owner-occupancy (2)	Adjustment to nonfarm base (3)	Adjustment to one-family starts (4)	Nonfarm one-family starts (Total of Cols. 1-4) (5)	Rental required additions (6)	Adjustment for national change in renter-occupancy (7)	Adjustment to nonfarm base (8)	Adjustment to multi-family starts (9)	Nonfarm multi-family starts (Total of Cols. 6-9) (10)
1900-1910	2,080	−234	−182	708	2,372	2,364	82	−252	−863	1,331
1910-20	2,211	−398	−68	535	2,270	2,144	139	−550	−497	1,236
1920-30	2,843	323	366	736	4,268	2,577	−190	−219	623	2,791
1930-40	2,716	−1,800	−224	1,511	2,203	2,312	1,722	−278	−3,090	666
1940-50	3,058	5,306	25	−3,485	4,904	3,238	−3,631	1,362	207	1,176
1940-50[a]	3,058	5,306	25	−1,360	7,029	3,238	−3,631	1,362	715	1,684
1950-60[a]	3,640	5,506	1,040	1,852	12,038	2,045	−1,204	1,115	440	2,396

[a] Based on new series housing starts adjusted to exclude Hawaii and Alaska.

Sources: Col. 1 — Table 4. Col. 2 — the national change in owner-occupancy minus sales required additions and rental required additions respectively — see Table 4. Col. 3 — the nonfarm change in owner-occupancy and renter-occupancy minus the national changes — nonfarm data are from the same source as national data and have been adjusted to exclude Hawaii and Alaska in the 1950's. Col. 4 — nonfarm one-family starts and nonfarm multi-family starts minus the nonfarm change in owner-occupancy and the nonfarm change in renter-occupancy respectively. Col. 5 — for the 1900's through the 1920's, one-family and multi-family starts are from David M. Blank, *The Volume of Residential Construction, 1889-1950*, National Bureau of Economic Research, Technical Paper No. 9 (Princeton: Princeton University Press, 1954), p. 68; for the 1930's and the 1940's the old series starts are from Council of Economic Advisers, *Economic Report of the President, 1964* (Washington: U.S. Government Printing Office, 1964), Table C-38, p. 253; for the 1940's and the 1950's the new series starts (see tabulation on p. 68) between structure classes on the basis of the old series ratio of one-family to total starts in 1940-45, 1945-50, 1950-55, and 1955-60, respectively. This procedure is probably biased toward understating one-family starts.

Sales required additions moved with one-family starts in all except the 1910-20 decade. They were fewer than one-family starts (as expected) in all decades except the 1930's, but the extent of the divergence in the 1940's and 1950's clearly cannot be explained by the absorption of one-family units into rental markets. Rental required additions moved with multi-family starts until the 1950's and, again as was expected, were greater than multi-family starts in four of the six decades covered. Only in the 1920's and 1950's did multi-family starts exceed rental required additions.

In the first two decades covered, most of the difference between housing starts and required additions by tenure class arose from the excess of one-family starts over the change in nonfarm owner-occupancy and the opposite relationship between multi-family starts and the change in nonfarm renter-occupancy. In fact, the excess of one-family starts would have been just about sufficient to meet the rental deficiency. However, considering withdrawals (from both tenure and structure classes) and the fact that some part of ownership demand is for multi-family units, the conclusion must be that a large part of the deficit in the rental sector was filled by conversions, which exceeded withdrawals in both decades.

In the 1920's, the excess of one-family starts over sales required additions increased significantly. The difference was increased for the first time by a gain in ownership (and headship rates) and by a net decline in the number of farm households. But, as before, most of the difference resulted from the continued excess of one-family starts over the change in nonfarm owner-occupancy.

The most important development in the twenties, however, was the reversal of the expected relationship between rental required additions and multi-family starts. This took place despite the facts that (1) the change in tenure rates more than offset the increase in headship rates and reduced the national change in renter-occupancy below rental required

---

required additions between one-family and multi-family starts would be misleading, they do provide a basis for determining the direction of the probable difference between housing starts and household formations or required additions by tenure class. In approximate terms, then, if sales required additions were four times rental required additions, then, *ceterus paribus*, one-family starts would equal sales required additions and multi-family starts would equal rental required additions. If sales required additions were less than four times rental required additions (the usual relationship), then one-family starts would be greater than sales required additions and multi-family starts would be less than rental required additions. The relationship if sales required additions were greater than four times rental required additions then follows directly. Substituting the change in owner-occupancy and the change in renter-occupancy for sales and rental required additions yields the same conclusions, always assuming that the marginal and average ratios are relatively similar.

additions and (2) part of the increase in rental demand (unlike the change in ownership demand) occurred in farm areas. The excess supply of new multi-family units was somewhat greater than the excess implied in Table 6, since part of the increase in rental demand was probably met by single-family units and since conversions (almost entirely additions to the rental stock) exceeded withdrawals.

The excess of single-family starts over the change in nonfarm owner-occupancy in the 1920's was in line with past experience, but the excess supply of multi-family units was both unwanted and unprecedented. Thus, the twenties ended with a large inventory of vacant rental units in multi-family structures. In effect, the production of rental units continued at the rate suggested by the 1920-25 increase in rental demand for some time after rental required additions had begun to fall.

Tenure rates shifted widely during the 1930's. However, the production of dwelling units by tenure class did not follow the changed tenure composition of demand. The increase in nonfarm renter-occupancy was over four times as great as the increase in nonfarm owner-occupancy, yet one-family starts were about three and two-thirds times as large as multi-family starts. Since the excess of one-family starts over the change in nonfarm owner-occupancy was far less than the deficit of multi-family starts relative to the change in nonfarm renter-occupancy, the transfer of one-family units to rental markets could not fill the rental gap unless some of the units were converted to multi-family structures. The high level of conversions (see Table 3, p. 71) suggests that this is what happened during the 1930's and it also suggests that the Depression shifted the quality composition as well as the tenure composition of demand. Households that under more favorable circumstances would have become homeowners became renters and occupied a disproportionate number of lower-quality converted units. However, at the same time, the production of new sales units remained relatively high (and far above the change in owner-occupancy) — direct evidence of the low elasticity of substitution between different quality classes of sales housing.

In the 1940's, the tenure-rate changes of 1930-40 were sharply reversed. In fact, the shift toward owner-occupancy was so strong that, with sales required additions also increasing, the production of one-family units could not keep pace with the growth in ownership demand, and for the first time one-family starts were less than the increase in nonfarm owner-occupancy (although far above sales required additions).

Multi-family starts, on the other hand, exceeded the change in the nonfarm renter-occupied housing stock for only the second time in the period covered. Part of the excess went to replace vacated war housing and converted dwellings, as housing standards were raised in the late 1940's, and this led to increased vacancies. Another part of the excess went to satisfy the increase in ownership demand. Because of the huge shift in tenure rates, rental required additions were greater than multi-family starts in the 1940's, and the entire increase in nonfarm renter-occupancy was the result of farm-to-nonfarm migration (and census reclassification).

To meet the deficit in the sales market, single-family units were shifted from renter- to owner-occupancy. This helps to explain the high level of conversions that was reached in the 1940's even though multi-family starts exceeded the change in the nonfarm renter-occupied housing stock. The converted units were required to replace the single-family units transferred from rental to sales markets, and in some local markets they were necessary because the exceptional geographic redistribution of the population left both one-family and multi-family starts below household formations.

With some sales units being lost to conversions and with withdrawals positive (and, possibly, as was true in the 1950's, heavily concentrated in one-family structures), the deficit shown in Table 6 understates the resulting quality backlog. For two decades prior to the 1950's, conversions and other makeshift (trailers, mergers) and relatively low-quality dwelling units provided a significant part of the adjustment to shifts in the total and tenure composition of demand. Thus, the basis for the building boom of the 1950's is clear.

The large excess of one-family housing starts over the change in owner-occupancy in the 1950's was sufficient to provide all the dwelling units required by the growth in rental demand. At the same time, multi-family housing starts were positive and greater than both rental required additions and the change in nonfarm renter-occupancy. The net effects were an increase in withdrawals relative to other additions and an increase in vacancies, with increased withdrawals especially important. As a prelude to the discussion of future prospects in Chapter IX, it will be useful to look briefly at the approximate allocation of the difference between sales and rental required additions and one-family and multi-family starts during the 1950's (see Table 7). This can be shown only on a national basis and thus obscures the role of farm-to-nonfarm migration (which, ignoring changes in census definitions, accounted for most of the increase in nonfarm renter-occupancy as renter-occupancy rates continued to decline).

Most of the difference between national one-family new construction and sales required additions was the result of the increase in headship

TABLE 7. RELATIONSHIP BETWEEN ONE-FAMILY AND MULTI-FAMILY
NEW CONSTRUCTION AND SALES AND RENTAL REQUIRED ADDITIONS
IN THE 1950's

(Thousands of dwelling units)

One-family structures		Multi-family structures	
New construction[a]............ 12,155		New construction............	2,445
plus other additions		plus other additions	
other...... 717		other...... 334	
mergers.... 557.........	1,274	conversions . 1,582	
equals gross additions.........	13,429	mergers.... 219.......	2,135
		equals gross additions.........	4,580
minus withdrawals			
demolition.... 1,048		minus withdrawals	
other......... 1,200		demolition.. 533	
conversions.... 485		other...... 195	
unallocated... 1,604....	4,166	conversions . 119	
equals net additions..........	9,263	mergers.... 625	
		unallocated. 273.......	1,745
minus other one-family uses		equals net additions...........	2,835
change in renter-			
occupancy...... −729		minus other multi-family uses	
change in vacancies. 1,380	651	change in owner-	
equals change in one-family		occupancy....... 535	
owner-occupancy.........	8,612	change in vacancies.. 963	1,498
		equals change in multi-family	
plus other owner-occupancy		renter-occupancy..........	1,337
change in multi-			
family.......... 535		plus other renter-occupancy	
change in trailer.... 204	739	change in one-	
equals total change in owner-		family........ −729	
occupancy..............	9,352	change in trailer... 28	−701
		equals total change in renter-	
minus adjustment to sales required		occupancy...............	636
additions.............	5,712		
		minus adjustment to rental required	
equals sales required additions..	3,640	additions............... −1,409	
		equals rental required additions	2,045

[a] One-family new construction was allocated 79 percent to owner-occupancy, 11 percent to renter-occupancy, and 10 percent to vacancies; 1,210,000 of one-family additional vacancies were in newly built units. Multi-family new construction was allocated 10 percent to owner-occupancy, 76 percent to renter-occupancy, and 14 percent to vacancies; 332,000 of multi-family additional vacancies were in new units.

Source: U.S. Bureau of the Census, *U.S. Census of Housing: 1960* (Washington: U.S. Government Printing Office, 1962) — Table 1, p. 28; Table 2, p. 36; and Table 3, p. 46.

and ownership rates in the 1950's. Next in importance was the high level of one-family withdrawals, which far exceeded one-family other additions.[51] Also important (accounting for 15 percent of net one-family

[51] Withdrawals for both structure types contain an unallocated portion reflecting the fact that the number of units reported in 1950 less the number of units reported as the same in 1959 is greater in both structure types than the sum of the units reported changed by conversions or mergers or lost.

additions) was the increase in one-family vacancies and the absolute decline in one-family renter-occupancy, which served to increase the proportion of one-family units available for owner-occupancy. The change in owner-occupancy was greater than net one-family additions, but this was the result of multi-family units and trailers satisfying about 8 percent of the increase in ownership demand.

In the multi-class market, other additions were almost as large as new construction and apparently greater than withdrawals. Thus, multi-family net additions were greater than new construction and over four times as great as the change in renter-occupancy. The difference was split in declining order of importance between increased multi-family vacancies (34 percent of multi-family net additions and almost 40 percent of multi-family new construction), a shift of rental demand from one-family to multi-family units, and the ownership component of multi-family demand (19 percent of net additions).[52]

The increase in rental vacancies (greater than the increase in renter-occupancy) is somewhat disturbing. However, it may have been the result of shifts in the location of the population and so may not have had a depressing effect on multi-family construction, since only one-third of the increase in multi-family vacancies was in newly constructed units. On the other hand, it is significant that over nine-tenths of the increase in single-family vacancies was in newly constructed units.

For one-family construction, a continued high level would seem to depend primarily on a continued high level of withdrawals plus a continued excess of the increase in owner-occupancy over sales required additions.[53] Otherwise, even if sales required additions were to double or triple (i.e., if the increase in the population base for ownership were to double or triple), one-family starts could still fall in the 1960's.

In summary, because the income elasticity of housing demand by tenure class is very high and because shifts in the tenure composition of demand can be met by shifting single-family units back and forth from

[52] The net changes by type of structure mask a large redistribution of dwellings from renter- to owner-occupancy and the reverse; for example, 2.64 million units that were owner-occupied in 1950 were renter-occupied in 1959, and 2.32 million units that were renter-occupied in 1950 were owner-occupied in 1959.

[53] Of particular importance in the 1950's was the combination of increasing labor demand and small or negative changes in the labor supply at the early life-cycle stages, which encouraged early marriage, early families, and early home-ownership by sharply increasing the per capita real income of young people. Also, government-insured mortgage programs and rent controls had a once-and-for-all effect on ownership rates which extended into the early 1950's. Unless the changes in ownership rates continue there may be trouble ahead. Population changes during the 1960's will slow down the growth rate of sales demand at a constant owner-ship rate (see Ch. IX).

rental to sales markets or by converting or merging existing units, the relationship between sales and rental required additions and sales and rental
housing starts is subject to wide variation. Through boom, bust, and
war, from the 1920's to the 1940's, the sources and causes of differences
between required additions by tenure class and the production of single-
and multi-family units differed sufficiently to preclude generalization.
However, it is clear that the housing boom of the 1950's was greatly influenced by the response of residential construction to the Depression and
World War II. It is also clear that the relationship between the tenure
compositions of residential construction and of housing demand in the
1950's is more closely akin to their relationship in the 1920's than to that
in any other decade of this century.

A Note on the Quinquennial Relationship Between Housing Starts and Required Additions by Tenure Class

One-family starts followed the general pattern of the quinquennial
long swing in sales required additions (see Chart 11) through the 1940's.
From 1900-1905 to 1915-20 and from 1915-20 to 1930-35, one-family
starts increased by more than sales required additions, when the latter
were expanding most rapidly, and then fell as the population base for one-
family starts continued to increase at a much slower rate. However, in
1910-15 and in 1925-30, one-family starts remained above sales required
additions at these stages of the long swing; and then, when sales required
additions fell, one-family starts fell even more and were exceeded by the
additional sales units required by population changes. This order of
events suggests that in each of the five-year periods the response of the
residential building industry to the initial increase led to overproduction,
which then reduced the level of one-family starts in the subsequent five-
year period.

After falling far below sales required additions in the early 1930's (as
the relative demand for ownership fell), one-family starts recovered much
of the ground lost and then followed the changes in sales required additions resulting from mobilization and demobilization during the 1940's.
However, although one-family starts far exceeded sales required additions
in 1945-50, they did not exceed the increase in ownership demand resulting from the change in tenure rates in the same period.[54] Thus, in 1950-

---

[54] Quinquennial estimates of household formations by tenure class are not
available, but they can be approximated by multiplying the number of household
heads by age class in 1945, 1950, 1955, and 1960 by the estimates (see Appendix
B) of tenure rates by age class in 1940, 1949, 1954, and 1959, respectively, and
then computing and summing the changes in owner- and renter-occupancy by age

CHART 11. HOUSING STARTS AND REQUIRED ADDITIONS,
BY TENURE CLASS

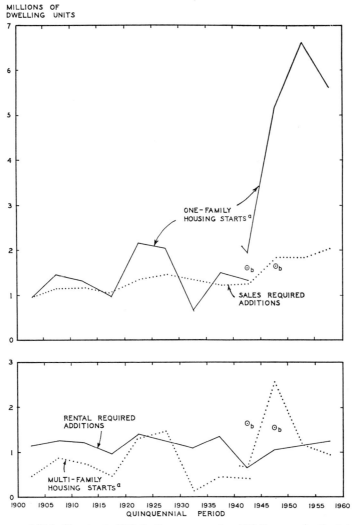

MILLIONS OF
DWELLING UNITS

ONE-FAMILY
HOUSING STARTS [a]

⊙b   ⊙b

SALES REQUIRED
ADDITIONS

RENTAL REQUIRED
ADDITIONS

⊙b   ⊙b

MULTI-FAMILY
HOUSING STARTS [a]

QUINQUENNIAL   PERIOD

[a] BLS old series to 1940-45; Census new series, 1945-50 on; and estimated
for 1940-45.
[b] Unadjusted for mobilization and demobilization.
Sources: Sales and rental required additions, Table 5; one-family and multi-
family starts, Table 3 and tabulation on p. 68.

55, as headship rates rose and tenure rates continued to shift to favor ownership, one-family starts increased even further as sales required additions moved sideways. Finally, in 1955-60, one-family starts fell slightly (as the backlog was erased) at the same time that sales required additions increased; but by this time one-family starts were so much greater than sales required additions that little or no relationship between these changes would have been expected.

Over the same 60-year period, rental required additions and multi-family starts were much more closely related, moving in opposite directions only in 1925-30 (an important exception) and in 1955-60. The relationship would be even closer if adjustment were made for the one-family component of rental demand. Since tenure rates did not change much, a large number of conversions must have been necessary to fill the gap between rental required additions and multi-family starts in 1900-1905 and in 1915-20; an excess of one-family units was not available for this purpose. Despite appearances, the same cannot be said for the 1930's, when the changes in owner-occupancy and in renter-occupancy were respectively far below and far above sales and rental required additions.

What happened in rental markets in the 1920's seems especially interesting. In response to the large increase in rental required additions, multi-family starts boomed in the first half of the 1920's — so much so that if adjustment is made for the excess of conversions over withdrawals and the part of rental demand satisfied by one-family units, then it appears that there was an excess supply of new units in both tenure classes in 1920-25. Tenure rates did change to reduce the surplus in the sales market, but this could be done only at the expense of a greater excess in the rental sector. The lagged, speculative adjustment to the rapid increase in rental required additions could not be easily halted when tenure rates changed to favor ownership and when rental required additions fell in 1925-30. As a result, multi-family starts kept on increasing and, finally, multi-family vacancies built up rapidly.

Much the same relationship existed in the 1950's. In 1950-55, one-family starts were far above sales required additions and multi-family starts were about equal to rental required additions. Then in 1955-60, starts were greater than required additions in both tenure classes. Moreover, as they did in the twenties, tenure rates changed to aggravate the

---

class over five-year periods. The results are as follows: the estimated change in owner-occupancy in 1945-50 was 7,036,000, in 1950-55 it was 5,158,000, and in 1955-60 it was 4,241,000; the estimated change in renter-occupancy in 1945-50 was —1,168,000, in 1950-55 it was —194,000, and in 1955-60 it was 785,000. This procedure assumes that the entire change in tenure rates in the 1940's occurred in 1945-50.

excess supply of new units in the rental sector in 1950-55.[55] But, unlike what happened in 1925-30, the gap between multi-family starts and the actual change in renter-occupancy was reduced in 1955-60, as the increase in headship rates more than offset the smaller ownership-rate changes and withdrawals far exceeded other additions. Thus, the present excess of multi-family starts over rental required additions does not necessarily imply that the same sequence of events as that which occurred in the 1920's is developing, but it does suggest care in evaluating the prospects for new multi-unit structures.

[55] In fact, nationally, the change in renter-occupancy was negative in 1950-55, although farm-to-nonfarm migration probably increased nonfarm renter-occupancy.

VI. AGE COMPOSITION, CHANGES IN LIFE EXPECTANCY, AND HOUSING DEMAND: 1870's TO 1950's

Housing starts, household formations, and to a lesser extent the tenure composition of housing starts and housing demand have until very recently followed a long swing resembling the long swing in required additions in total and by tenure class. The close correspondence between the residential building cycle and the cycle in housing demand traced out by population factors prior to the 1950's raises several questions about the ultimate causes of long swings in residential construction — questions which must be answered before the present and prospective status of the residential building cycle in the United States can be analyzed.

Examples of such questions are: What factors account for the long swings in total and in renter- and owner-occupied required additions? Is the long swing in required additions based on a consistent pattern of population changes or does each episode in the long swing differ from prior and subsequent expansions and contractions in required additions? Have the population changes determining the fluctuations in required additions in a given period been independent of the economic conditions of the period, and therefore an exogenous determinant of those conditions, or have they been determined by concurrent economic conditions in the United States? This last question must be answered before is will be possible to determine whether the residential building cycle has been primarily a cause or an effect of the experienced long swings in economic growth in the United States.

In the present chapter, the influence of changes in age composition and life expectancy on required additions (and thus on housing starts and household formations) will be analyzed. In the following chapter, the role of immigration in determining past population cycles will be discussed.

Age Composition and Housing Demand

The absolute and relative impact of changes in age composition on required additions varied greatly from period to period between the

1860's and the 1950's, accounting for as few as 4,000 units and less than 0.5 percent of required additions in the 1870's (see Table 8) and for as many as 1,992,000 units and 32 percent of required additions in the 1940's. The peak in importance of changes in age composition by five-year periods was reached in 1945-50 (1,102,000 units and 35 percent of

TABLE 8. CHANGES IN SIZE AND AGE COMPOSITION OF THE
POPULATION AND REQUIRED ADDITIONS, BY SELECTED PERIOD
(Thousands of dwelling units)

Period	Household formations (1)	Required additions (2)	Required additions due to population changes only (3)	Required additions due to changes in age composition (4)	Column 4/ Column 2 (5)
By decade					
1850-60...........	.....	1,621	1,516	72	5%
1860-70...........	.....	1,885	1,566	249	13
1870-80...........	.....	2,285	2,269	4	..ᵃ
1880-90...........	.....	3,009	2,887	86	3
1890-1900.........	3,273	3,485	3,076	333	10
1900-1910.........	4,292	4,444	4,176	202	5
1910-20...........	4,096	4,365	3,249	957	22
1920-30...........	5,553	5,419	4,961	390	7
1930-40...........	4,950	5,028	4,121	815	16
1940-50...........	7,971	6,296	4,070	1,992	32
1950-60...........	9,990	5,685	5,083	497	9
By quinquennial period					
1900-1905.........	.....	2,068	1,966	90	4%
1905-10...........	.....	2,376	2,235	120	5
1910-15...........	.....	2,396	1,904	457	19
1915-20...........	.....	1,969	1,385	541	28
1920-25...........	.....	2,714	2,455	215	8
1925-30...........	.....	2,705	2,499	175	7
1930-35...........	.....	2,475	1,985	456	18
1935-40...........	.....	2,562	2,146	387	15
1940-45...........	.....	3,125	2,316	756	24
1945-50...........	.....	3,171	2,025	1,102	35
1950-55...........	.....	2,912	2,033	830	29
1955-60...........	.....	2,977	3,299	−324	−11

ᵃ Less than 0.5 percent.
Sources: Col. 1 — Table 1, p. 60; Col. 2 — Table 1, p. 60, and Table 3, p. 71; Cols. 3 and 4 based on the population sources given in Appendix A and the headship rate data shown in Appendix B following the procedure described in Chapter III, p. 43.

required additions) and the minimum occurred in 1900-1905, when age composition accounted for only 4 percent of required additions.[56]

With the exception of the 1955-60 period, changes in age composition added to the level of required additions in each decadal and quinquennial period. In several periods, the inclusion of age composition significantly reduced the absolute difference between required additions based on changes in the size of the population alone and the actual change in the number of households, and thus the proportion of household formations explained by population factors was greatly increased. Obviously, leaving out the housing life cycle and age composition would lead to a considerable error in the interpretation of the relative importance of demographic and nondemographic factors in determining fluctuations in housing demand.

The positive contribution of changes in age composition to required additions from the 1860's to the 1950's reflects the continued increase in the average age of the housing population over the last century. However, this fact is less significant than the inter-period fluctuations in the contribution of changes in age composition. In the years from 1900 to 1920, a large decrease in the housing population increment was substantially offset (see Chart 12) by a contemporary rise (from 5 percent to 22 percent of required additions) in the relative importance of age composition. The increases in required additions between 1905-10 and 1910-15 were solely the results of concurrent increases in the influence of age composition.

In the 1920's, the relative importance of the age composition fell as the housing population increased greatly compared with the gain of the prior decade. More important, considering subsequent events, is the fact that within the 1920's the drop in required additions in 1925-30 following the large rise in 1920-25 occurred because a decline in the importance of age composition more than offset a slight gain in the housing population increment.

The importance of age composition increased again in the 1930's and reached its peak significance and accounted for the entire increase in required additions in the 1940's. Thus, even though the expansion in the

---

[56] The wide fluctuations in the relative importance of age composition shown in Table 8, together with the stability of headship rates through 1940, suggest that most fluctuations in average headship rates (households, ÷ by the housing or total population) from the 1850's to the 1940's can be explained by changes in age composition rather than in economic conditions and tastes. In fact, if variations in average headship rates are treated as resulting solely from taste changes or income fluctuations, an error of as much as 80 percent of the correct (i.e., age-standardized) weight of population factors might be made.

Chart 12. Decadal Estimates of the Size and Age
Composition of Population Increments and
Required Additions[a]

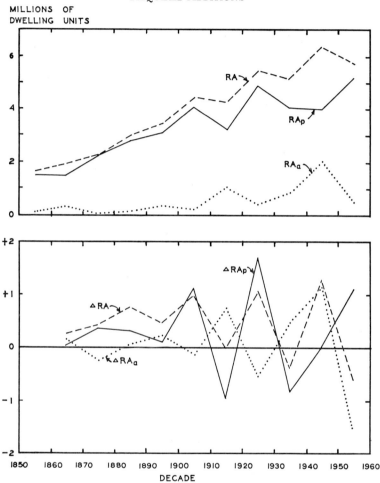

[a] RA = required additions; RA_p = required additions due to population changes
only; and RA_a = required additions due to changes in age composition only.
Source: Table 8, p. 93.

housing population was smaller in the 1940's than in the 1930's, over one
million more dwelling units were required because of the change in the
age composition of the population.

Ignoring the movement of the housing population into and out of the
armed services, the changes in required additions in both 1940-45 and
1945-50 were controlled by the contemporary changes in age composi-

tion. The 1945-50 period illustrates what took place and stands as a transitional phase in the role of age composition. The declines in immigration after 1924 and in births in the 1930's combined to reduce the size of the housing population increment in this half-decade. At the same time, the gain in the number of people at the late life-cycle stages, a direct result of the rise in immigration around the turn of the century, was increasing the demand based on changes in age composition.

Finally, in the 1950's, the largest drop in 80 years in the influence of age composition more than offset the effect of the increase in the housing population increment on required additions and led to the largest decline in required additions during the last century. That decline can be divided into two distinct patterns.

In 1950-55, the unstandardized population increment remained at about the same level as in the prior quinquennium. Thus, the drop in required additions in this period resulted entirely from the contemporary change in age composition. However, the relative importance of age composition in explaining required additions remained very high. Then in 1955-60, for the first time, the change in age composition taken alone would have reduced required additions. The large rise in the housing population in those years was heavily weighted by people in the entering life-cycle stages, reflecting the first impact of the wartime baby boom, whereas the increment in the housing population at the middle life-cycle stages was falling as a result of the declines in immigration after 1924 and in births during the 1930's. Together, these changes meant that a smaller number of dwelling units was required to meet the demand arising from a given population increment in 1955-60 than ever before.

For both decades and quinquennial periods, the influence of changes in age composition on required additions followed a cyclical pattern. By decades, the peaks were reached in the 1860's, 1890's, 1910's, and 1940's; the troughs occurred in the 1870's to 1880's, 1900's, and 1920's. Thus, the long swing in the influence of age composition bore a consistent, inverse relationship to the long swing in required additions, household formations, and housing starts from the Civil War down to World War II. The rate of economic growth was closely related to residential construction over these decades, which means that our economy grew most rapidly when the population at the early life-cycle stages was growing most rapidly and vice versa. With this pattern repeated over three cycles in the long swing covering a span of 80 years, it seems that the source of the residential building cycle up to World War II may be found in the cyclically varying importance of population growth at the early life-cycle stages in the United States. Even in the 1950's, although residential construction diverged from required additions, the past relationship between the influence of age composition on required additions and residential construction was evidenced once again.[57]

In other words, in the past the largest increase in required additions over the population cycle corresponded to the largest increase in the population at the early life-cycle stages over this same cycle. As required additions reached a peak and turned down, the proportion of total required additions at the later life-cycle stages rose. Thus, the largest increment in required additions over the long swing in required additions tends to have been associated with the lowest relative importance of changes in age composition and vice versa.

Briefly anticipating the discussion of the following two chapters, the inverse relationship between required additions and required additions based on changes in age composition alone resulted from the concurrent and lagged impacts of changes in the foreign-born population at different life-cycle stages. The immediate impact of immigration was concentrated at the early life-cycle stages; the lagged impact occurred as immigrants moved on through the later life-cycle stages and as their children entered the housing life cycle. Through the 1930's, required additions (and likewise household formations and housing starts) varied directly with immigration, thus explaining the observed inverse relationship between the influence of age composition on required additions and total required additions. After the 1930's, the long swing in required additions due to changes in age composition must be explained by the movement of past immigrants and their children through the housing life cycle, with past waves in immigration leading 15 to 20 years later to similar waves in the entering housing population. However, from 1950 on, the first- and second-generation waves in population increments derived from past waves in immigration have been and will be strongly influenced by the sharp decline in birth rates from 1925 to 1935 and by the even sharper rise in birth rates in the 1940's. The effect of war mobilization on the

---

[57] For the nonfarm area the relationship between required additions and changes in age composition was similar to that discussed for national totals. However, the change in the age composition of the nonfarm population was less important in explaining the interdecade changes in required additions than was the change in the age composition of the national population. The reason for this difference was the impact of farm-to-nonfarm migration on nonfarm required additions. In the 1940's, for example, when the national housing population increased by about the same amount as in the 1930's, the nonfarm population increased by much more than in the 1930's. Consequently, required additions based on the unadjusted housing population increase were far more important for nonfarm areas than nationally, and, since most migrants were in the early life-cycle stages, the number of additional units required for each 100 people added to the nonfarm housing population was less than for the national housing population.

housing population provides an interesting special case illustrating con-
vincingly the potential impact of shifts in age composition on the housing
demand. Between 1940 and 1945, the movement of individuals into the
armed services would have reduced the demand for separate quarters by
over 2,000,000 dwelling units if the age composition of the population had
remained unchanged. However, this number of dwelling units and 500,000
more were needed to meet the increase in demand resulting from the
contemporary change in age composition. Mobilization largely affected
those at the early life-cycle stages and did not have much impact on the
large expansion in the number of people in the life-cycle stages from 35-44
on. For each additional 100 people added at the late life-cycle stages,
as many as 600 might leave the housing population at Stage 1 (15-24)
without reducing the demand for separate quarters, so the increase in the
housing population at the late life-cycle stages during World War II more
than offset the large reduction in the total housing population, raising the
demand for separate quarters.

This entire situation was reversed when the troops returned in 1945-
50. However, the resulting reduction in the influence of age composition
did not even come close to offsetting the increase in the housing population. Thus, after adjustment for the movement of individuals into and
out of the armed forces, required additions increased by more in 1945-50
than in any prior five- or ten-year period.

Finally, the inclusion of age composition improves the "fit" of popu-
lation-based estimates of household formations to actual household formations and housing starts. However, whether or not the inclusion of age
composition raises or lowers the average deviation between population-
based estimates and household formations and housing starts is not so
important as the fact that this step improves our understanding of the precise role of demographic changes in housing markets. Whether or not it
also "estimates" household formations and housing starts more accurately
in any period will depend on the relative importance of population and
nonpopulation factors during the period. Whatever the case, the inclusion
of age composition gives a better basis for estimating the impact of nonpopulation factors on housing markets. Students of the residential building cycle would arrive at widely differing interpretations of the relative
importance of population changes, tastes, and economic conditions, depending on whether or not they had taken account of changes in age composition in their model.

Age Composition and the Tenure Composition of Housing Demand

The influence of changes in age composition on the tenure composition of demand is directly shown by the fact that rental required additions

exceeded sales required additions in the 1870's, 1880's, 1890's, 1900's, and 1940's, but fell short of owner-occupied required additions in the 1910's, 1920's, and 1930's. (See Table 9.) With a constant set of headship and tenure rates used to estimate sales and rental required additions from the 1870's to the 1930's, any changes in the relative importance of sales and rental required additions in this period must be explained entirely by changes in age composition.[58]

Changes in age composition were absolutely and relatively more important in explaining sales than in explaining either rental or total required additions. From 1910-20 on, such changes accounted for 15 percent or more of sales required additions, reaching a peak in both relative and absolute importance in the 1940's (39 percent and over one million units). Thus, behind the sales boom in the postwar years was a truly significant increase in the proportion of the total population in the age classes where owner-occupancy is most often found.

Shifts in age composition reversed the influence of changes in the size of the housing population on the incremental demand for sales units in all decades save two and in all but three quinquennial periods. As a result, total owner-occupied required additions moved inversely to the change in the housing population in 1910-20 and in 1940-50 and in 1910-15, 1940-45, and 1945-50. In many other periods, shifts in age composition either accounted for most of the change in sales required additions or offset a large proportion of the influence on owner-occupancy of changes in the size of the housing population.

Briefly, changes in age composition help explain why there was a rise in the number of additions to the owner-occupied housing stock in the 1910-20 period, when housing starts and total required additions were

---

[58] At a constant 1930 set of tenure rates and with headship rates unchanged from 1940 on, the ratio of renter- to owner-occupied required additions by decades would be as follows:

Decade	Percent
1870's	122.9
1880's	115.8
1890's	112.6
1900's	114.1
1910's	96.9
1920's	90.6
1930's	85.1
1940's	77.1
1950's	56.4

The excess of rental over sales required additions in the 1940's disappears if tenure rates are held constant, but the ratio of rental to sales required additions does increase in this decade, if the 65-and-up age class is excluded from both the 1930's and the 1940's.

TABLE 9. CHANGES IN THE SIZE AND AGE COMPOSITION OF THE POPULATION AND REQUIRED ADDITIONS BY TENURE CLASS, BY SELECTED PERIOD

(Thousands of dwelling units)

Period	Sales required additions				Rental required additions				Col. 1 minus Col. 5
	In total	Due to changes in the size of the housing population	Due to changes in age composition	Col. 1/Col. 3	In total	Due to changes in the size of the housing population	Due to changes in age composition	Col. 5/Col. 7	
	(1)	(2)	(3)	(4)	(5)	(6)	(7)	(8)	(9)
Number, by decade									
1870–80	1,025	1,042	−17	−2%	1,260	1,227	21	2%	−235
1880–90	1,394	1,306	64	5	1,615	1,581	22	1	−187
1890–1900	1,639	1,399	195	12	1,846	1,677	138	7	−207
1900–1910	2,080	1,913	127	6	2,375	2,263	75	3	−295
1910–20	2,211	1,495	615	28	2,144	1,754	342	16	67
1920–30	2,843	2,325	437	19	2,577	2,636	−47	−2	266
1930–40	2,716	1,969	665	24	2,312	2,152	150	6	404
1940–50	3,058	1,723	1,195	39	3,238	2,347	797	25	−180
1950–60	3,640	2,747	774	21	2,045	2,335	−278	−14	1,595
Change from preceding decade									
1880–90	369	264	81	…	355	354	1	…	…
1890–1900	245	93	131	…	231	96	116	…	…
1900–1910	444	514	−68	…	518	586	63	…	…
1910–20	131	−418	488	…	−210	−509	267	…	…
1920–30	632	830	−178	…	422	882	−389	…	…
1930–40	−127	−356	228	…	−264	−484	197	…	…
1940–50	342	−246	530	…	926	195	647	…	…
1950–60	582	1,024	−421	…	−1,193	−12	−1,075	…	…

TABLE 9. (CONTINUED)

Period	Sales required additions				Rental required additions				Col. 1 minus Col. 5
	In total	Due to changes in the size of the housing population	Due to changes in age composition	Col. 1/Col. 3	In total	Due to changes in the size of the housing population	Due to changes in age composition	Col. 5/Col. 7	
	(1)	(2)	(3)	(4)	(5)	(6)	(7)	(8)	(9)
Number, by quinquennial period									
1900-1905	958	901	50	5%	1,110	1,065	40	4%	−152
1905-10	1,122	1,025	84	7	1,254	1,210	36	3	−132
1910-15	1,195	875	295	25	1,201	1,028	162	13	−16
1915-20	1,016	643	347	34	953	742	194	20	63
1920-25	1,359	1,162	180	13	1,355	1,293	35	3	4
1925-30	1,485	1,172	274	18	1,221	1,327	−99	−8	264
1930-35	1,375	949	399	29	1,100	1,036	50	5	275
1935-40	1,233	899	312	25	1,329	1,247	75	6	−96
1940-45	1,481	891	550	37	1,644	1,425	206	13	−163
1945-50	1,579	784	738	47	1,592	1,050	488	31	−13
1950-55	1,860	1,076	721	43	1,052	834	108	10	808
1955-60	2,011	1,952	41	2	966	1,347	−366	−38	1,045
Change from preceding quinquennial period									
1905-10	164	124	34	...	144	145	−4	...	...
1910-15	73	−149	211	...	−53	−182	126	...	...
1915-20	−179	−233	52	...	−248	−286	32	...	...
1920-25	343	519	−167	...	402	551	−159	...	...
1925-30	125	10	94	...	−134	34	−138	...	...
1930-35	−110	−223	125	...	−121	−291	149	...	...
1935-40	−142	−50	−87	...	229	211	25	...	...
1940-45	248	−8	248	...	315	182	131	...	...
1945-50	98	−107	188	...	−52	−375	282	...	...
1950-55	281	292	−17	...	−540	−116	−380	...	...
1955-60	151	876	−680	...	−86	413	−474	...	...

Sources: Cols. 1 and 5 — Table 4, p. 75; Cols. 2, 3, 6, and 7 — derived from the population and headship and tenure rate data discussed in Appendix A and B following the procedure outlined in Chapter III, p. 43.

TABLE 10. GROWTH IN THE RELATIVE IMPORTANCE
OF OWNER-OCCUPANCY, BY DECADE

Decade	Change in owner-occupied housing stock/ household formations	Sales required additions/ total required additions[a]
	(1)	(2)
1870-80	..	45%
1880-90	..	46
1890-1900	37%	47
1900-1910	44	47
1910-20	44	51
1920-30	56	52
1930-40	24	54
1940-50	105	56
1950-60	91	64

[a] At 1890, 1930, and 1940 headship rates and 1930 tenure rates.
Sources: Col. 1 — Table 4, p. 75; Col. 2 — Table 5, p. 80.

falling. They also explain why the increase in sales required additions was smaller in the 1950's than in the 1920's despite a larger increase in the housing population in the 1950's.

The trend in this century toward a larger and larger share of owner-occupied housing stock relative to total additions is well known, but it is not often recognized that a substantial portion of the increase (see Table 10) can be explained by changes in age composition. From 1900-1910 to the 1950's, the net change in the number of households owning their homes climbed from 44 percent to 91 percent of total household formations. Over the same period, changes in age composition raised the ratio of sales to total required additions from 47 percent to 64 percent, accounting for almost one-third of the increase in the relative importance of owner occupancy. Because of emulation effects and economies of scale realized from tract-building for a mass market, it is possible that the shift in age composition in this century — particularly the change in the 1950's — may have been responsible for considerably more than 30 percent of the increase.

Changes in age composition were relatively less important in determining rental required additions, reaching a maximum of slightly less than 25 percent of rental required additions in the 1940's and determining the direction of change in rental required additions only in 1925-30 and 1955-60.

The significance of the change in age composition in the former period is particularly striking. The drop in rental demand in 1925-30 that undercut the rental boom of the 1920's was solely the result of the contemporary change in age composition — a completely neglected factor in most discussions of the events leading up to the Great Depression.

Also, it was the change in the influence of age composition between the 1940's and the 1950's that accounted for most of the large drop in rental required additions between those two decades. Thus, the low level of production of multi-family units in the 1950's was a response to the changing age composition of the housing population in the 1950's as well as to the increased relative preference for sales housing.

Mortality Rates and Required Additions

In Table 11, the numbers of additional units required by changes in mortality rates by age classes are compared with the total changes in required additions in the age classes for selected periods. The results are weighted by the beginning age composition in each case and do not take account of variations in death rates within the 10-year age classes used in calculating the estimates. Since the estimates are based on mortality rates at the beginning and the end of the periods shown, they would overestimate the actual number of additional units required by changes in death rates unless they were adjusted in some manner. In Table 10, an adjustment toward the actual change due to variations in mortality rates was made by dividing the base estimate in each case by two. With this adjustment, only in the 1940's does the variation in mortality rates account for more than 5 percent of total required additions.

Turning to the importance of mortality rate changes in different age classes, this factor accounted for less than 10 percent of the required additions in each age class in all but four instances. In the 1930's, a drop in the mortality rate explained 13 percent of the required additions in the 35-44 age class, and in the 1940's, slightly under 16 percent of the total required additions in the 65-and-up age class. The other two exceptions involved the 15-24 age class in each of the last two decades covered in the study and were unimportant in terms of the number of units required. In fact, only the change in the 1940's in the 65-and-up age class was significant in this sense.

Changes in mortality rates were never a controlling factor in determining the changes between decades in required additions. The changes would have been similar if mortality rates had remained the same from

TABLE 11. CHANGES IN MORTALITY RATES AND REQUIRED ADDITIONS,
BY DECADE
(Thousands of dwelling units)

Decade	Age classes						Total
	15-24	25-34	35-44	45-54	55-64	65-and-up	
	Number						
1900-20[a, b]							
Req. Add.	123	858	1,185	1,062	703	473	4,405
Req. Add.^{M}	4	18	35	42	37	31	165
RA^M/RA	3%	2%	3%	4%	5%	7%	4%
1920-30							
Req. Add.	225	560	1,345	1,363	1,004	922	5,419
Req. Add^M	8	55	63	24	−2	32	178
RA^M/RA	4%	10%	6%	2%	...	3%	3%
1930-40							
Req. Add.	85	775	512	1,235	1,186	1,235	5,028
Req. Add.^{M}	7	52	65	68	51	46	289
RA^M/RA	8%	7%	13%	6%	5%	4%	6%
1940-50							
Req. Add.	−29	795	1,386	943	1,473	1,728	6,296
Req. Add.^{M}	4	40	67	81	97	270	553
RA^M/RA	14%	5%	5%	9%	7%	16%	9%
1950-59[c]							
Req. Add.	−80	−314	1,074	1,680	1,131	1,764	5,255
Req. Add.^{M}	3	13	25	42	53	58	192
RA^M/RA	4%	4%	2%	3%	4%	3%	4%
Change from preceding decade							
1920-30							
Req. Add.	102	−298	160	301	301	449	1,014
Req. Add.^{M}	4	37	28	−18	−39	1	13
1930-40							
Req. Add.	−140	215	−833	−128	182	313	−391
Req. Add.^{M}	−1	−3	2	44	53	14	111
1940-50							
Req. Add.	−114	20	874	−292	287	493	1,268
Req. Add.^{M}	−3	−12	2	13	46	225	264
1950-59[c]							
Req. Add.	−53	−1,109	−312	737	−342	36	−1,040
Req. Add.^{M}	−1	−26	−42	−39	−44	−212	−361

[a] In this table, Req. Add.^{M} = RA^M refers to the required additions in each decade resulting from changes in mortality rates over the decade. The estimates shown in the table are the base estimates divided by two as suggested in the text.
[b] The data for 1900-20 are shown on a decade basis.
[c] The 1950-59 data were converted to a decade basis.
Sources: See Appendix D for a discussion of the methods and procedures used in estimating the impact of changes in mortality rates on required additions.

period to period.[59] However, changes in required additions due to shifts in mortality rates did account for over 20 percent of the total change in required additions in the 1940's and for about 35 percent in the 1950's. In the 1930's, the drop in required additions would have been almost one-third larger in the absence of the continuing increase in required additions due to mortality-rate changes.

Within age classes, the influence of shifting mortality rates on the changes in required additions was most important in the 45-54 and 55-64 age classes in the 1930's and in the 65-and-up age class in the 1940's and 1950's. If required additions resulting from shifts in mortality rates had not fallen in the 1950's, the increase in required additions in the 65-and-up age class would have been many times larger. Only in this decade does a change in mortality rate alter the interpretation of the impact of population factors within an age class. Without the decline in required additions resulting from mortality rate changes in the 1940's and the 1950's, required additions for the 65-and-up age class would have been about the same in the 1940's and 1950's. For all other periods and for all age classes, changes in mortality rates influenced neither the direction nor the relative magnitude of inter-period changes in required additions.

In summary, one can say that with the exception of their effects on the 65-and-up age class in the 1940's and 1950's, mortality-rate changes were unimportant compared with other population factors in influencing required additions between 1900 and 1960.

Mortality Rate Changes and the Tenure Type of Required Additions

Very briefly, in the 1920's the age classes affected by mortality-rate changes were such that rental demand was increased relative to owner-occupancy, but in total the effect was minor. In the other periods for which data are available (1900-1920, 1930's, 1940's, 1950's), the effect of mortality-rate changes was to increase owner-occupied required additions relative to renter-occupied required additions. Only in the 1940's was this significant, accounting for about one-third of the gain in owner-occupied required additions in that decade.

---

[59] In other words, if required additions resulting from changes in mortality rates were zero or constant from 1900 on, the direction and relative interperiod magnitude of required additions would be the same as they would be with required additions resulting from changes in mortality rates varying between periods.

VII. IMMIGRATION AND HOUSING DEMAND: 1850's TO 1950's

The striking uniformity in the pattern of changes in the relative importance of age composition over the long swing in required additions from one episode to the next suggests that past cycles in required additions were related to one another and may be explained by the same set of determinants. In this chapter, the possibility that fluctuations in immigration established the basis for the past long swing in required additions will be explored.

If this long swing were dependent on population changes net of immigration, then it would clearly be a function of predetermined variables and, within the structure of feedbacks relating residential construction to the remainder of the economy, a determinant of the long swing in economic growth. Immigration, on the other hand, has been at least partly dependent on job opportunities, and therefore on current economic conditions, in the United States. If immigration has been the major source of the fluctuations in required additions, then the presumption is that the long swing in residential building was determined by the long swing in economic growth.

Immigration and Required Additions

Immigration had its peak impact on required additions in 1900-1910, both relatively and absolutely (see Table 12). Prior to 1900, required additions due to immigration, hereafter referred to as RAi, increased from the 1860's to the 1880's and then fell in the 1890's. After 1900-1910 the number of additional units required to meet the needs of concurrent immigrants fell, until from the 1930's on immigration was no longer a significant factor in determining required additions. Thus, decadal data trace out two long cycles in RAi, from the 1860's to the 1890's and from the 1890's to the 1930's, on a trough-to-trough basis. Only the second of these was reflected in required additions.

However, this conclusion understates the importance of immigration. Quinquennial data reveal additional cycles in RAi and show that they

TABLE 12. IMMIGRATION AND REQUIRED ADDITIONS,
BY DECADE
(Thousands of dwelling units)

Decade	Required additions (1)	Required additions due to immigration (2)	Base required additions (Col. 1 minus Col. 2) (3)	Col. 2/Col. 1 (4)
		Number		
1850-60.	1,621	617	1,004	37%
1860-70.	1,885	580	1,305	30
1870-80.	2,285	626	1,659	27
1880-90.	3,009	1,124	1,785	37
1890-1900.	3,485	868	2,617	24
1900-1910.	4,444	2,146	2,298	48
1910-20.	4,365	1,379	2,986	32
1920-30.	5,419	958	4,461	18
1930-40.	5,028	129	4,899	3
1940-50.	6,296	272	6,024	4
1950-60.	5,685	629	5,056	11
		Change from preceding decade		
1860-70.	264	−34	298	. .
1870-80.	400	46	354	. .
1880-90.	724	498	126	. .
1890-1900.	476	−256	832	. .
1900-1910.	959	1,278	−319	. .
1910-20.	−79	−767	688	. .
1920-30.	1,054	−421	1,474	. .
1930-40.	−391	−829	438	. .
1940-50.	1,268	143	1,125	. .
1950-60.	−611	258	−968	. .

Sources: Col. 1 — Table 1, p. 60; Col. 2 — Appendix C.

were matched by similar fluctuations in required additions (see Table 13). Inspection of the direction of changes in required additions, in required additions net of immigration (hereafter RAb), and in RAi shows that the direction of change in required additions, and likewise the direction of the influence of population factors on residential construction, was determined by concurrent immigration in several decades and quinquennial periods.

By quinquennial periods, RAi reached peaks in 1870-75, 1880-85, 1905-10, and 1920-25 and troughs in 1860-65, 1875-80, 1885-90, 1915-20, and 1930-35 — a total of four cycles, with an average trough-to-trough duration of two and one-half quinquennial periods. Excluding the war

TABLE 13. IMMIGRATION AND REQUIRED ADDITIONS,
BY QUINQUENNIAL PERIOD
(Thousands of dwelling units)

Quinquennial period	Required additions	Required additions due to immigration	Base required additions	Col. 2/Col. 1
	(1)	(2)	(3)	(4)
1900-1905............	2,068	936	1,132	45%
1905-10..............	2,376	1,209	1,167	51
1910-15..............	2,396	1,077	1,319	45
1915-20..............	1,969	302	1,667	15
1920-25..............	2,714	613	2,101	23
1925-30..............	2,705	345	2,360	13
1930-35..............	2,475	51	2,424	2
1935-40..............	2,562	78	2,484	3
1940-45[a]............	1,323	44	1,365	3
1945-50[a]............	4,973	228	4,761	5
1950-55..............	2,912	288	2,624	10
1955-60..............	2,977	364	2,613	12

[a] The estimates of required additions and base required additions for 1940-45 and 1945-50 are adjusted for the effects of war mobilization and demobilization. The unadjusted estimates would be 3,125 and 3,171 for required additions and 3,081 and 2,943 for base required additions in 1940-45 and 1945-50, respectively.
Sources: Col. 1, Table 3, p. 71; Col. 2, Appendix C.

years, RAi have continued to expand from 1930-35 to the present, and the long swing in this component of the demand for additional dwelling units has disappeared.

Comparing RAi with the predetermined component of required additions, or RAb, it is apparent that they had a tendency to vary inversely; e.g., by decades RAb reached a peak in the 1890's, contracted in 1900-1910, and then expanded until the 1940's — just the reverse of the long swing in RAi over the same decades. Thus, changes in RAi account for the increase in required additions in 1900-1910 and for the decreases in required additions in 1910-20 and 1930-40. By quinquennial periods, RAb expanded from 1900-1905 to 1940-45. In other words, all reductions in required additions (e.g., in 1915-20, 1925-30, and 1930-35) must be explained by changes in RAi over the first half of the twentieth century. Considering the magnitude of the quinquennial changes in RAi relative to the decadal changes in required additions, it seems likely that required additions followed the path traced out by RAi in 1865-70, 1880-85, 1890-95, 1895-1900, and 1900-1905.

Of particular interest is the fact that the declines in required additions in 1925-30 and in 1930-35 were the results of contemporary declines in immigration. In both periods, required additions would have increased if immigration had remained at the level of the preceding quinquennial period. Thus, the largest peacetime decrease in required additions between 1900 and 1950 would have been avoided in 1930-35. In evaluating the causes of the Great Depression, perhaps too little attention has been given to the political conditions leading to the Immigration Acts of 1921 and 1924.

The influence of immigration on the long swing in the rate of change in required additions is shown by the first differences in Tables 12 and 13. In these tables, the interperiod change in RAb measures the change in required additions that would have occurred if immigration had remained unchanged from one period to the next.

From the 1870's to the 1910's, fluctuations in the first differences in required additions were the results of similar fluctuations in the interdecade increments in immigration, which more than offset the consistently inverse movements of the first differences in RAb.

Thus the accelerated increase in required additions in the 1880's compared with the increase in the 1870's would not have occurred if the rate of increase in immigration had not quickened in the 1880's.[60] And, the slower rate of increase in housing demand in the 1890's, which undoubtedly contributed to overbuilding and the relatively large increase in vacancies in the 1890's, would not have taken place in the absence of the concurrent decline in immigration. Similarly, if immigration had remained at the level of the prior decade, rather than reaching a peak in 1900-1910, required additions would have fallen after the turn of the century, and for opposite reasons there would have been a major increase in required additions in the 1910's. Finally, without a decline in immigration, the population pressure for additions to the housing stock would have increased rather than decreased in the 1930's.

By quinquennial periods, the direction of the long swing in first differences in required additions was determined by RAi in 1910-15 and 1915-20, and its amplitude was controlled by the interperiod change in immigration from 1900-1905 to the mid-thirties.

---

[60] For example, immigration in 1880-85 was the largest the United States had experienced up to that time and more than twice the level of the preceding five-year period. Because of both the small initial effect of immigration on housing demand and the lagged adjustment of residential building to increased housing demand, the continued increase in residential capital formation after immigration turned down (but remained above any past level) in 1885-90 is not surprising. Nor is it surprising that overbuilding resulted from this construction boom, which would explain why the very slight increase in RAi in 1890-95 was associated with a decrease in residential capital formation.

The evidence so far presented leads to the conclusion that from the Civil War to the 1890's the rate of change in required additions — and from the 1890's to the 1930's, the direction of change — was controlled by the long swing in immigration. The sole important exception occurred just after World War I, when the cumulated impact of past immigration outweighed the effect of the contemporary change in immigration.

No increase in immigration between 1915-20 and 1920-25 would have been necessary to bring about the largest increment in required additions since the turn of the century. In fact, had immigration fallen to zero in 1920-25, the level of required additions still would have increased. For the decade as a whole, the same story can be told. Thus, the residential construction boom of the 1920's was apparently the result of population changes that were largely independent of economic conditions during the 1920's. However, as will be shown in the following chapter, the impact of immigration in 1920-25 on the age composition of required additions was important in determining the extent of the response of residential construction to population changes in the 1920's.

Immigration and Residential Construction

Not only was the long swing in required additions greatly influenced by immigration, but from the 1870's to the 1910's and again in the 1930's there was a close connection between the long swing in immigration and the long swing in household formations and housing starts or residential capital formation (see Chart 13). Residential capital formation did increase in the 1890's as RAi fell, but the increase was much smaller than in the prior decade. However, the increase in housing starts in the 1920's took place despite the decline in current immigration, reinforcing the conclusion that both the building boom and its population base in the 1920's were the result of predetermined population changes. From the 1940's on, the change in immigration was so small relative to housing starts that one can only say that both seem to be related to the same determinant.

The argument that fluctuations in immigration were the sources of those in residential building can be stated most strongly in terms of quinquennial data. From the 1870's to the 1930's, residential building and RAi varied together (see Chart 14) in all but three half-decades, and the lagged adjustment of residential construction to changes in housing demand could explain all three exceptions.

In summary, from the Civil War to World War II the long swing in immigration was the dominant source of the long swing in required additions and so of the residential building cycle in the United States. Thus,

CHART 13. DECADAL ESTIMATES OF IMMIGRATION AND
RESIDENTIAL CONSTRUCTION

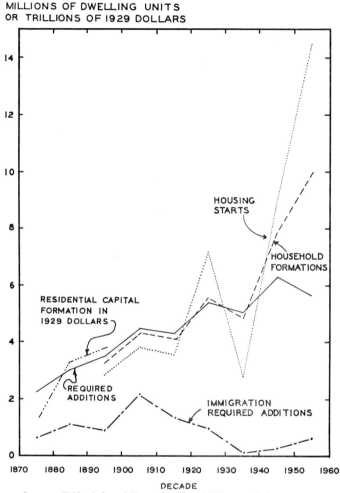

MILLIONS OF DWELLING UNITS
OR TRILLIONS OF 1929 DOLLARS

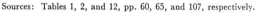

Sources: Tables 1, 2, and 12, pp. 60, 65, and 107, respectively.

so far as immigration fluctuated in response to the long swing in economic growth in the United States, the residential building cycle was endogenous to the growth process, resulting from swings in growth rates and contributing to the amplitude and duration of such swings.

If this is a fair characterization of past residential building fluctuations in the United States, then it is clear that we are moving into an entirely new era. Population changes affecting the number of dwelling units re-

CHART 14. QUINQUENNIAL ESTIMATES OF IMMIGRATION AND RESIDENTIAL CONSTRUCTION

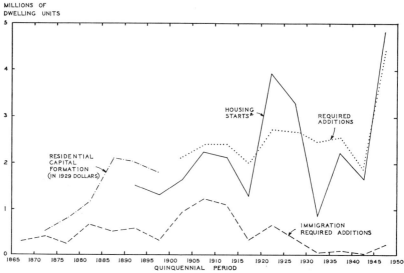

^a To account for the expected lag, starts in this chart run from January, 1871, to December, 1875.

Sources: For housing starts data, Table 2, p. 65; for immigration required additions, Table 13, p. 108.

quired can no longer respond importantly to current economic conditions. Instead, from the 1940's on, the growth in the housing population has been (and will be) almost entirely predetermined.[61] In the 1940's and 1950's, first the war and then the postwar adjustment masked the effect of this new situation. How the economy — and the housing market — will respond to population growth that is not itself a response to economic growth is one of the key questions of the 1960's, and the future will be still further outside the range of past experience.

The Long Swing in Immigration

It might be argued that the fluctuations in immigration that apparently were important in explaining the residential building cycle in the United States down to World War I took place in response to the swings in economic growth rates (and so in labor demand) resulting from the

---

[61] From the late 1930's to the first half of the 1950's, the lagged impact of past waves of immigration (directly and through births) determined the changes in the size and age composition of the housing population. Since 1955, the decrease in birth rates between 1925 and 1935 and the increase during and after World War II have been the dominant factors explaining variations in required additions.

long swing in business capital formation. The pattern of response, assuming an independent long swing in business capital formation, would be from expansion in business investment to increased demand for labor and on to increased immigration and thence to a residential construction boom and further expanding income, keeping growth rates high as the initiating force behind the long-swing expansion tailed off.[62]

Overadjustment both by builders and by immigrants responding to job opportunities or the fact that high but nonincreasing growth rates can explain high but nonincreasing levels of immigration would then lead, in the first instance, to a direct cutback in residential construction and, in the second, to a stable level of investment and consequently falling growth rates and finally falling immigration and residential construction. The end result would be the same in either event: a depression seemingly beginning in the housing sector of the economy and spreading elsewhere.[63] Recovery — starting outside the housing market with the exploitation of some new technology or geographic region — would then lead to a repetition of the long swing in immigration and residential building, culminating in another depression.

It could equally well be argued, however, that immigration responded to swings in the supply of labor, given what otherwise would have been a relatively steady growth in final demand. It was pointed out that RAi and RAb tended to move inversely to one another. From the Civil War on, immigration tended to increase or to be high in periods when the base population (especially at the early and middle life-cycle stages) was falling or low and vice versa.

In effect, increasing demand for labor created labor shortages and plentiful job opportunities in those periods when the base population increment was small, leading to a spurt in immigration and a building boom. Then, more rapid growth in the base population (traceable to some previous spurt in immigration) cut into immigration and reduced the total population increment, bringing an end to the residential building boom and leading the economy into depression. In fact, one could argue that the Civil War set off a chain of events similar to those described that

---

[62] This is the set of relationships suggested by Moses Abramovitz in his article, "The Nature and Significance of Kuznets Cycles," *Economic Development and Cultural Change,* Vol. 9, No. 3 (April, 1961), pp. 225-48. Further support for the demand-pull explanation of long swings in immigration is given by Richard Easterlin in his paper, "Long Swings in U.S. Demographic and Economic Growth: Some Findings on the Historical Pattern," delivered at the June, 1964, meeting of the *Population Association of America,* at San Francisco.

[63] Building activity turned down before the general level of economic activity did in three of the four (1870's, 1890's, and 1930's) major depressions between the Civil War and World War II in the United States.

explained the residential building cycle for half a century and are still influencing the level of required additions.

Assuming a constant birth rate, the slow growth in the base population just before and during the Civil War, which at the time could not be compensated by immigration, meant that another period of slow growth in base population would occur in the 1880's (the increase in the population from zero to 20 between 1855 and 1865 determining the increase in the base population between 25 and 45 in the decade of the 1880's). Similarly, the rapid growth in immigration following the end of the Civil War led to a spurt in the base population increment in the 1890's. Finally, the increase in the base population in the late seventies, associated with the decline in immigration in that period, established the source of the slowdown in the base population increment in 1900-1910 that helps to explain the rush of immigrants to the United States just after the turn of the century.

Whether immigration fluctuated in response primarily to predetermined population changes or to the long swing in business capital formation or to some combination of the two, from 1915 on to World War II the population changes explaining required additions were determined exogenously to current economic conditions in the United States.

First, World War I prevented immigration, which the labor-supply hypothesis suggests would have fallen anyway. Then, past immigration and births led to an increase in the base population which far overshadowed the concurrent postwar increase in immigration. Finally, restrictive legislation brought about the reduction in immigration that explains the decline in required additions in 1925-30 and 1930-35. From the latter period on, changes in the base population have resulted from past fluctuations in immigration and births.

This raises the question of the continuance of the residential building cycle. If it resulted from the long swing in immigration and that long swing no longer can occur, won't the future see a more even growth in the housing stock? Of course, the experience in the 1920's would suggest otherwise, if long swings continue in the base population. However, the present building boom cannot be explained by population factors and so presumably bears no relationship to past residential building cycles. Looking beyond the more obvious manifestations of population–housing-demand relationships, it appears that fluctuations in headship rates have stepped in to replace fluctuations in immigration. A labor shortage cannot lead to a significant increase in immigration so it must be the source of significant increases in per capita income at the early life-cycle stages. These, in turn, mean increased headship rates. Taking this possibility —

which fairly well describes events from the end of World War II until the late 1950's — one step further, it implies that if the base population is growing more rapidly than job opportunities, then headship rates will be adversely affected and the demand for additional dwelling units will be depressed. Since the rate of growth of job opportunities is within the realm of economic policy, the foregoing situation need never occur; but the possibility of a reduction in housing starts as headship rates respond to increasing relative unemployment should not be taken lightly in the circumstances of the present decade.

Immigration and Required Additions by Tenure Class

Immigration was relatively unimportant in sales markets (see Table 14), never accounting for more than 35 percent of sales required additions and determining the direction of the change in sales required additions only in 1900-1910, in the 1930's (an important exception), and in 1915-20. However, immigration did shape the cycle in sales required additions between 1890 and 1920. The small decrease from 1890-1900 to 1900-1910 due to predetermined population factors was turned into a peak increase, and the big increase in sales required additions due to predetermined population factors from 1900-1910 to 1910-20 was sharply reduced by the current change in immigration. After the early 1930's, immigration was an insignificant factor in the sales market and can be ignored.

It is relevant to the interpretation of the transition from war to boom to final collapse between 1915 and 1935, that even had immigration fallen to zero in the 1920's, the largest increase in sales required additions between 1870 and 1960 would still have taken place in the 1920's. Nor was the contemporary decline in immigration the sole source of the sharp drop in sales required additions in 1930-35, since this period saw the first decline in predetermined required additions to the sales stock in the twentieth century.

Thus, so far as the expansion in sales markets supported the residential construction boom of the 1920's, this boom was "in the cards." The sales housing part of this boom was not the result of concurrent changes in nonpopulation factors (but possibly it was the cause). Similarly, the die was cast for sales markets in the early stages of the Depression by prior changes in immigration, especially in the 1910-20 period. The contemporary decline in immigration simply made the situation worse.[64]

---

[64] However, the influence of immigration on the age composition of housing demand in the 1920's and in 1930-35 may have been important in explaining the transition from boom to bust. See Ch. VIII, pp. 126-9, for a discussion of this point.

TABLE 14. IMMIGRATION AND THE TENURE COMPOSITION OF REQUIRED
ADDITIONS, BY SELECTED PERIOD
(Thousands of dwelling units)

Period	Required additions (1)	Required additions due to immigration (2)	Base required additions (3)	Change from the preceding period in		
				Col. 1	Col. 2	Col. 3
Owner-occupied						
Decade						
1870-80........	1,025	209	816	...	...	...
1880-90........	1,394	368	1,026	369	159	210
1890-1900.....	1,639	270	1,369	245	−98	343
1900-1910.....	2,080	721	1,359	441	451	−10
1910-20........	2,211	477	1,734	131	−244	375
1920-30........	2,843	341	2,502	632	−136	768
1930-40........	2,716	52	2,664	−127	−289	162
Quinquennial period						
1900-1905.....	958	317	641	...	...	...
1905-10........	1,122	404	718	164	87	77
1910-15........	1,195	367	828	73	−37	110
1915-20........	1,016	110	906	−179	−257	78
1920-25........	1,359	220	1,139	343	110	233
1925-30........	1,485	121	1,364	125	−99	224
1930-35........	1,375	20	1,355	−110	−101	−9
1935-40........	1,233	32	1,201	−142	12	−154
Renter-occupied						
Decade						
1870-80........	1,260	417	843	...	...	...
1880-90........	1,615	756	859	355	339	−13
1890-1900.....	1,846	596	1,250	231	−160	391
1900-1910.....	2,374	1,424	950	528	828	−300
1910-20........	2,144	902	1,242	−230	−522	292
1920-30........	2,577	617	1,960	433	−285	718
1930-40........	2,312	77	2,235	−264	−540	276
Quinquennial period						
1900-1905.....	1,110	619	491	...	...	...
1905-10........	1,254	805	449	144	186	−42
1910-15........	1,201	710	491	−53	−95	42
1915-20........	953	192	761	−248	−518	270
1920-25........	1,355	393	962	402	201	201
1925-30........	1,221	224	997	−134	−169	35
1930-35........	1,100	31	1,069	−121	−193	72
1935-40........	1,329	46	1,283	229	15	214

Sources: Col. 1 — Tables 4 and 5, pp. 75 and 80; Col. 2 — Appendix C; Col. 3 — derived
by subtracting Col. 2 from Col. 1.

As might be expected, immigration was far more important in rental markets, accounting for 40 to 60 percent of rental required additions in three of the five decades from the 1880's to the 1930's and for over 60 percent in the first three half-decades of this century. The direction of the change in rental required additions was determined by immigration in 1880-90, 1900-1910, 1910-20, and 1930-40 and in every half-decade except one (1920-25) through the first half of the 1930's, after which its influence rapidly declined.

The importance of immigration in rental markets derives from the concentration of immigrants in the age classes in which rental units are relatively most important. In fact, the estimates presented probably understate the impact of immigration on rental markets, since one would expect that the immigrants in a given age class would rent more often than the average for the age class.

Unlike total and sales required additions, rental required additions would have been lower in the decade of the 1920's than in the prior decade, had immigration fallen to zero. The peak interperiod increase in predetermined rental required additions came just previous to and during World War I. The effect of this increase was held off by the war and added in 1920-25 to another substantial increase in required additions net of the current change in immigration. Together with the increase in immigration in this period, the predetermined increase in rental required additions raised the additional rental units required by age-standardized population changes by more than in any other five-year period from 1900 to 1960. Even if immigration had not declined in 1925-30, the sharp drop in the rate of increase in predetermined required additions to the renter-occupied stock would probably have brought an end to the rental boom, especially after the speculative excesses engendered by the unparalleled increase in the 1920-25 period. With the decline in immigration that did take place, the decline in rental required additions in the second half of the 1920's was the largest for any five-year period prior to 1945-50. It continued through 1930-35 and in that period was entirely accounted for by the contemporary reduction in immigration.

VIII. THE PATTERN OF REQUIRED ADDITIONS
BY AGE CLASS: 1870's TO 1950's

Little has been said thus far about the pattern of required additions by age class adds significantly to our understanding of the residential age composition of demand in different historical periods. In all past periods, but particularly in tracing the chain of events leading from World War I to the Great Depression, consideration of required additions by age class adds significantly to our understanding of the residential building cycle. Perhaps even more important, only by investigating the effect of past changes in the age composition of required additions is it possible to establish a reference point for the analysis of the truly exceptional shifts in age composition that are presently taking place and that will continue to take place in the next 15 years.

Residential Construction and Required Additions by Age Class

A given level of required additions will have a varying impact on residential construction and the demand for complementary goods and services depending on the following relations: (1) the proportion of the required additions satisfied by conversions; (2) the proportion offset by the postponement of household formations, the premature dissolution of existing households, or the doubling-up of existing households; (3) the extent to which vacancies arising at one or more life-cycle stages offset positive required additions elsewhere in the market; and (4) the impact of the required additions on income and therefore on the extent of the feedback to housing demand through (a) related expenditures and (b) the average value and financing of required additions.

Since all of these determinants may be expected to vary among age classes, the impact of a given level of required additions on residential construction may be expected to vary with the age composition of required additions.

The greater the relative importance of rental demand, the lower is the average income and net wealth; and the larger the proportion of non-

118

normal households in an age class, the greater is the likelihood that conversions will be suitable in meeting the demand for additional dwelling units in the age class. On all counts then, required additions are most likely to lead to conversions instead of to housing starts at the first and last life-cycle stages and are least likely to do so at the middle life-cycle stages.

For the same reasons, when income is falling, households at the first, second, and last life-cycle stages are the ones most willing to accept converted dwelling units. They are also the most likely to be forced to accept conversions, since households at these life-cycle stages are the ones most susceptible to loss of income in depressions. On the other hand, when real income is moving beyond past peak levels, required additions for the early and late life-cycle stages are most likely to underestimate the actual demand for new housing starts. The income elasticity of household formations is greatest at these stages and, because conversions are more important in normal times at these stages, the shift away from converted units as income increases is also greatest at these stages.[65]

When headship rates remain relatively stable and the supply of new units is relatively elastic, required additions will not be offset by postponement, premature dissolution, or doubling-up. However, in other periods the impact of a given level of required additions on housing markets will depend on the relative propensity of the individuals involved to postpone household formations, or of existing households to dissolve or double up. In turn, these propensities will depend on the age composition of required additions.

Again, the largest potential for differences between required additions and housing starts exists at the early and late life-cycle stages. Postponement will be most important at the first life-cycle stage (with the second life-cycle stage next in line). Doubling-up or dissolution will be most important at the second and last life-cycle stages, before and after the major pressure to maintain separate quarters.

Single-family dwellings may substitute for multi-family units when the former become vacant, but the reverse seldom occurs. Similarly, households in a given income class will move up the housing ladder when better-quality housing becomes available at lower prices or rents but will seldom move to lower-quality dwellings under similar circumstances. This

---

[65] On the other hand, in periods of extreme housing shortage the willingness to substitute converted units or temporary quarters for others should be greatest at the first, second, and last life-cycle stages. This conclusion is based on the differences between the types and sizes of households at these stages and at the other life-cycle stages.

simply means that a positive level of required additions at the first and
second life-cycle stages is more likely to be offset by a negative level at the
middle life-cycle stages than the reverse. With required additions positive
at all life-cycle stages with one or two exceptions, this has not been an important consideration in the past. However, at present headship rates,
negative required additions will occur at the middle life-cycle stages in
the next two decades. Any resulting vacancies would clearly be close
subsitutes for new construction to meet the increased demand at the early
life-cycle stages in the same period.[66]

The larger the number of new households and the larger the number
of first-time owners associated with a given level of required additions,
the greater would be the expected feedback effect. For example, if all required additions are for Stage 1, then the number of additional new
households and required additions would be identical. But, if all required additions are for Stage 6, then required additions would exceed
the number of new households by the amount of required additions.[67]
In the first instance, the demand for goods and services associated with
the formation of new households (furniture, appliances, laundries, and so
on) would increase, tending to stimulate activity elsewhere in the economy. In the second instance, the demand for these goods would remain
unchanged, having a neutral or even a negative effect in an economy
geared to growth.

In the same way, first-time ownership may vary widely relative to
required additions. An increase in first-time ownership from one period
to the next is likely to have an even greater impact on the rest of the
economy than an increase in new household formations. An extreme example of this difference in impact can be seen by comparing the probable
costs of furnishings, transportation, and so forth, for a one-room effi-
ciency flat near the downtown area with the same items for a three-
bedroom house located on the suburban fringe. It might be added that
the second step up the ownership ladder (for all but a few) will involve
much smaller complementary expenditures than the first — hence the
importance of first-time ownership.

---

[66] See Ch. IX for estimates of required additions by age class in the next
20 years.

[67] With all required additions at Stage 1, the number entering and leaving at
each subsequent stage must be the same and therefore household formations will
be the same at these stages. But, since all households entering Stage 1 are new
households, the number of new households will increase over the preceding period.
With all required additions at Stage 6, following the same reasoning, household
formations at all earlier stages must remain unchanged from the preceding period,
and, since there are almost no new households at Stage 6, the number of new
households formed will be almost the same as in the preceding period.

CHART 15. NUMBER OF NEW HOUSEHOLDS PER 1,000 INCREASE
IN THE POPULATION IN SPECIFIED AGE CLASSES[a]

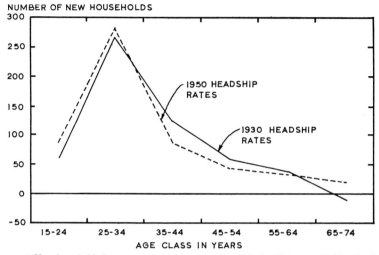

NUMBER OF NEW HOUSEHOLDS

[a] New households in an age class = for example, 1000 (headship rate 35-44 — headship rate 25-34). This assumes all households formed in the 25-34 age class remain in existence when the head reaches the 35-44 age class.
Source: Appendix B.

Since most new households are formed at Stage 2, with Stage 3 and Stage 1 next in importance, and most first-time ownership occurs at Stages 3 and 2 (in that order), the significance of required additions for these age classes should be apparent (see Charts 15 and 16). An increase or decrease in the number of required additions, for Stages 2 or 3 especially, would seem to have significance ranging far beyond the direct impact on residential construction. Because of the combination of effects and because of the greater weight attached to first-time ownership and to normal rather than nonnormal household formations, the third stage is likely to be most important in this respect.

The influence of age composition does not stop with complementary expenditures. The larger the average value of a given level of required additions, the larger the feedback one would expect. As was shown in Chapter II, the peak average value would be reached when all required additions are for Stage 4, with Stages 3 and 5 not far behind. Thus, the more concentrated required additions are at the center of the life cycle, the greater the contribution of residential construction to total investment expenditures will tend to be.

The final impact of an increase in the average value of a given number of required additions should depend on how the increase was financed.

Chart 16. Number of New Homeowners per 1,000 Increase
in the Population in Specified Age Classes[a]

NUMBER OF FIRST-TIME OWNERS

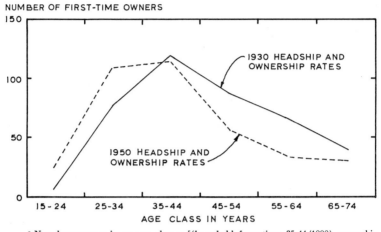

[a] New homeowners in an age class = [(household formations 35-44/1000) ownership rate 35-44 — (household formations 25-34/1000) ownership rate 25-34].
Source: Appendix B.

At one extreme the increase might be financed by an increase in current savings and at the other, by new debt. As financial arrangements move from the first to the second extreme, one would expect the impact on the economy of a given increase or decrease in the average value of required additions to be larger. In this sense, required additions at the second and third life-cycle stages will have a more inflationary impact than required additions at the other stages.[68]

In sum, most of the considerations raised point to Stage 3 as the key age class. A large increase in required additions at this stage would be expected to have a widely felt complimentary effect on the rest of the economy, along with leading directly to the construction of an equivalent number of new units at a higher-than-average per unit value. If there are no offsetting reductions at other stages (to be offsetting, the total

---

[68] See Federal Reserve Board, *Consumer Installment Credit* (Washington: U.S. Government Printing Office, 1947), P. 1, Vol. 2, Table D-1, pp. 232ff., for data on the relationship between age and debt-financing.

The age composition of required additions tends to determine the response of housing starts to monetary policy. The age classes most dependent on credit are the second and third. In periods when required additions are particularly large for these age classes, credit policy may have an important impact on the tenure composition of demand and consequently on housing starts. On the other hand, when required additions are concentrated at late life-cycle stages, credit policy is less likely to have much impact. Tight credit cannot deter moves up the housing ladder as easily as it can bring a halt to tract building for the first-time owner.

reduction in required additions at other stages would have to be larger than the increase at Stage 3), the result may be a large feedback effect, raising headship rates and reducing the importance of conversions. Similarly, a large decline in required additions for Stage 3 is likely to be disastrous in the absence of a larger increase at other stages or deliberate action by the government to stimulate changes in headship or tenure rates.

After Stage 3, the second life-cycle stage seems most important. Both the direct and the indirect impacts of required additions at Stage 2 are relatively large. The trend toward earlier household formations and the related trend toward earlier marriages and younger parents have increased the relative importance of first-time ownership at Stage 2 in recent years. Consequently, this stage has been gaining in importance at the expense of Stage 3, a fact that may be of critical importance in housing markets in the next decade when required additions for Stage 3 will be negative and required additions for Stage 2 will be increasing.

Finally, one may conclude that the larger the proportions of required additions are at Stages 1 and 6, the smaller the number of housing starts for a given level of required additions will be and the greater the variation in the ratio of required additions to housing starts as income changes or shortages arise.

The Age Composition of Required Additions in Different Periods
The Melting Pot: 1870 to 1920

In this period, changes in required additions by age class were dominated by the concurrent and lagged impact of immigration. For example, the juxtaposition of past and contemporary fluctuations in immigration (see Table 15) clearly established the basis for a major building boom after the turn of the twentieth century. Immigration reached a peak in 1900-1910 and raised required additions for the 25-34 age class to the highest level reached thus far in this century. At the same time, the increase in immigration which had occurred in the 1880's served to increase required additions for the 45-54 age class by the largest amount prior to the 1950's. With concurrent immigration more than offsetting the impact of the decline in the 1890's on required additions for the 35-44 age class, both the number and age distribution of required additions were conducive to a residential building boom during the 1900-1910 period.

In a similar fashion, each upsurge and subsequent downswing in immigration between 1870 and 1920 left its mark on the age composition of housing demand. In the decades when immigration rose (1880-90, 1900-1910), required additions for the early life-cycle stages (under

Table 15. Required Additions by Age Class During
the Melting-pot Era, by Selected Period
(Thousands of dwelling units)

Period	Age class						Total	$RA_a/$ RA^a
	15-24	25-34	35-44	45-54	55-64	65- and-up		
	(1)	(2)	(3)	(4)	(5)	(6)	(7)	(8)
Number, by decade								
1870-80........	139	595	565	509	477		2,285	+0%
1880-90........	127	780	737	592	410	363	3,009	3
1890-1900.....	133	755	1,027	728	490	352	3,485	10
1900-1910.....	196	1,013	1,147	1,055	579	455	4,444	5
1910-20........	51	704	1,223	1,069	826	492	4,365	22
Change from preceding decade								
1880-90........	−12	185	172	83	296		724	..
1890-1900.....	6	−25	290	136	80	−11	476	..
1900-1910.....	63	258	120	327	89	103	959	..
1910-20........	−145	−309	76	14	247	37	−79	..
Number, by quinquennial period								
1900-1905.....	96	475	552	473	260	212	2,068	4%
1905-10........	100	538	594	582	319	243	2,376	5
1910-15........	33	430	640	607	416	270	2,396	19
1915-20........	18	274	583	462	410	222	1,969	28
Change from preceding quinquennial period								
1905-10........	4	63	42	109	59	31	308	..
1910-15........	−67	−108	46	25	97	27	20	..
1915-20........	−15	−156	−47	−145	−6	−48	−427	..

[a] RA = required additions; RA_a = required additions due to changes in age composition.
Sources: Cols. 1 to 6 — Appendixes A and B; Cols. 7 and 8 — Table 8, p. 93.

35) constituted a relatively large proportion of the total increase in
demand. When immigration fell in the following decades, the movement
of the preceding decade's increase in immigration through the housing
life-cycle kept required additions increasing from age 35 on, whereas the
concurrent decline in immigration tended to reduce required additions at
the first two life-cycle stages. The result was that the importance of
changes in age composition as a source of required additions increased in
the decades when immigration fell and decreased in the decades when

immigration increased. Since required additions also rose and fell with immigration from the 1890's to the 1910's, it is not surprising to find that the relative importance of age composition moved inversely with both required additions and housing starts.

Table 15 shows that in the first five years of the century, required additions were highly concentrated in the first three housing life-cycle stages. In the second quinquennial period, when immigration reached a peak, required additions continued to increase at the early stages of the life cycle, but the major gain occurred in the 45-54 age class on which the impacts of the 1880's increase in immigration and the concurrent one were combined. Then, in 1910-15, as immigration fell, the influence of the increase in the preceding 10 years was sufficient to expand total required additions slightly (but by much less than in 1905-10). In this instance, the expansion came almost entirely in the last three life-cycle stages and the resulting increase in required additions was due entirely to the concurrent change in the age composition of demand. The higher headship rates at the middle and late life-cycle stages more than offset a decline in the housing population increment (concentrated at the early life-cycle stages) in this period. In other words, the age composition of the immigrant population was such that, for a time after immigration turned down, the influence on required additions of increased immigration in the recent past offset that of the concurrent decrease. Finally, in the last five-year period (1915-20), the immigration cycle was completed. Required additions continued to fall at the early life-cycle stages, and the decline in immigration in the 1910-15 period caught up with the 35-44 and 45-54 age classes, bringing down required additions for these classes as well. This entire cycle would tend to be repeated again, beginning 15 to 20 years after the initial increment in immigration, as the children of the 1900-1905 immigrants entered the housing population.

From 1900 to 1920, the age composition of required additions was probably the most favorable for residential construction in the 1905-10 period. Whereas the number of required additions edged upward in 1910-15, the shift in the age composition of required additions at this stage of the immigration cycle tended to reduce the ratio of housing starts to required additions. For example, the sharp drop in required additions for the 25-34 age class in 1910-15 very likely had a greater adverse impact on residential building than the numerically offsetting increment in the 55-64 age class. On a priori grounds, it would be expected that the reduced importance of first-time owners or occupants of required additions, together with the slower rate of growth in total demand, would have reduced residential construction at this stage of the

TABLE 16. REQUIRED ADDITIONS BY AGE CLASS DURING THE
POST–WORLD WAR I BOOM, BY SELECTED PERIOD
(Thousands of dwelling units)

Period	Age class						Total	$RA_a/$ RA[a]
	15-24	25-34	35-44	45-54	55-64	65- and-up		
	(1)	(2)	(3)	(4)	(5)	(6)	(7)	(8)
Number, by decade								
1910-20........	51	704	1,223	1,069	826	492	4,365	22%
1920-30........	225	560	1,345	1,363	1,004	922	5,419	7
Change from preceding decade								
1920-30........	174	−144	122	294	178	430	1,054	..
Number, by quinquennial period								
1915-20........	18	274	583	462	410	222	1,969	28%
1920-25........	136	497	568	533	534	446	2,714	8
1925-30........	89	63	777	830	470	476	2,705	7
Change from preceding quinquennial period								
1920-25........	118	223	−15	71	124	224	747	..
1925-30........	−47	−434	209	297	−64	30	−9	..

[a] RA = required additions; RA_a = required additions due to changes in age composition.
Sources: Cols. 1 to 6 — Appendixes A and B; Cols. 7 and 8 — Table 8, p. 93.

immigration cycle, even if required additions had increased slightly. It is
a matter of record that housing starts did fall in the United States in
1910-15.

The 1920's: The Post–World War I Boom

As a result of increased births following the peak immigration of 1900-
1910, required additions for the entering population reached an all-time
high in the 1920's. But at the same time, and despite the increase in
immigration in the first half of the 1920's, required additions for the
important 25-34 age class fell to the lowest level between the 1880's and
the 1950's (see Table 16). Therefore, unlike that of 1900-1910, the
housing boom of the 1920's took place despite a decline in required additions for the age class responsible for the second largest life-cycle increase
in home ownership, for most of the formation of normal households, and
for the peak life-cycle demand for rental units.

There was a slight increase in required additions for the 35-44 age class in the 1920's, mostly because the large increase in immigration in the early part of the decade more than offset the impact of the decline in immigration in 1910-20 on this age class. However, the major strength in the housing market came from increased required additions for the last three life-cycle stages, the largest increase in required additions for these age classes in the period covered by this study. This increase can be directly traced to the increases in immigration in 1880-90 and 1900-1910 and, to some extent, to the flu epidemic following World War I.

Thus, the age composition of demand in the 1920's was similar to that in 1900-1910, with the glaring exception of the 24-34 age class. Since the decline in this age class resulted in only a slight net gain in required additions for the first two life-cycle stages, the age composition of required additions in the 1920's is particularly difficult to reconcile with the concurrent rental boom. In fact, even with the largest increase in total required additions from 1880 to 1940 occurring during the 1920's, one might have expected that the decline in demand in the 25-34 age class would have prevented a rapid increase in residential construction.

However, looking at the decade as a whole covers up the most interesting part of the story. Within the 1920's, the age composition of required additions shifted in a way that helps to explain both the boom and the subsequent rapid decline in residential construction. In 1920-25, the largest gain in the 15-24 age class and the second-largest in the 25-34 age class for any five-year period in this century took place. The latter increase, which was especially important in establishing the basis for the residential construction boom in the first half of the 1920's, was entirely the result of the concurrent rise in immigration. In fact, without any increase in immigration in 1920-25, required additions for the key 25-44 age classes would have fallen.

At the same time, past increases in immigration were sharply expanding required additions at the last three life-cycle stages. This expansion was so large that required additions would have risen in 1920-25 without any increase in concurrent immigration.

Thus, one might argue that the residential building boom of the 1920's was based on predetermined population factors and would have taken place in the absence of any expansion in immigration. The increase that did occur simply added to the population pressure arising from earlier waves of immigration. However, the strength of the residential building boom in the first half of the 1920's depended in part on the age composition of required additions, which in turn depended on immigration.

Without the large increase in immigration in 1920-25, there would have been no increase in required additions for the 25-44 age class. With this change, the age composition of demand in 1920-25 would have resembled that in 1910-15, when required additions rose but housing starts fell.

In the second half of the 1920's, this picture was completely reversed. In fact, the decline in required additions for the 25-34 age class was even more outstanding than the increase in the preceding five years. At the same time that required additions fell in the first two life-cycle stages (and in the fifth), the largest five-year increase in required additions for the 45-54 age class and the second-largest for the 35-44 age class took place.

The large decline at the first two stages resulted from the decline in immigration in the second half of the twenties, the decline in the absolute increase in births which had occurred in the 1890's, and, at the second stage, the effects of World War I. The large increase in required additions for the middle life-cycle stages resulted from the increases in immigration that had occurred in 1920-25 and 1900-1910. Thus, the pattern of required additions by age class was still largely determined by past and concurrent changes in immigration during the 1925-30 quinquennium.

Total required additions declined only slightly in 1925-30, but behind this was a very large shift in age composition. As a result, the demand for dwelling units one or two steps up the sales ladder greatly increased, the number of new units required for first-time owners fell, and the demand for additions to the stock of rental units dropped sharply.

This was not a set of market relationships likely to generate much optimism among speculative builders or promoters of large-scale rental projects, particularly if they were carrying to completion projects based on the extrapolation of the rate of increase in demand at the first or last two life-cycle stages in the 1920-25 period. That housing starts fell sharply in the late 1920's after having reached a peak in 1925 is probably explained by the combined impact of the contemporary shift in the age composition of demand and the sharp decline in the growth of required additions compared with that in the first half of the 1920's. That housing starts remained in excess of 1925-30 required additions can best be explained by the concentration of required additions at the middle life-cycle stages and by the continuing strength of population pressure. The speculative buildup in the first half of the 1920's, together with the shift in age composition in 1920-25 and the lagged adjustment of rental and low-priced tract-building to this shift, provided a large inventory of vacant units on the eve of the Depression.

TABLE 17. REQUIRED ADDITIONS BY AGE CLASS DURING THE GREAT
DEPRESSION, BY SELECTED PERIOD
(Thousands of dwelling units)

Period	Age class						Total	$RA_a/$
	15-24	25-34	35-44	45-54	55-64	65-and-up		RA^a
	(1)	(2)	(3)	(4)	(5)	(6)	(7)	(8)
Number, by decade								
1920-30........	225	560	1,345	1,363	1,004	922	5,419	7%
1930-40........	85	775	512	1,235	1,186	1,235	5,028	16
Change from preceding decade								
1930-40........	−140	215	−833	−128	182	313	−391	..
Number, by quinquennial period								
1925-30........	89	63	777	830	470	476	2,705	7%
1930-35........	48	407	198	560	676	586	2,475	18
1935-40........	36	370	302	681	513	660	2,562	15
Change from preceding quinquennial period								
1930-35........	−41	344	−579	−270	206	110	−230	..
1935-40........	−12	−37	104	121	−163	74	87	..

[a] RA = required additions; RA_a = required additions due to changes in age composition.
Sources: Cols. 1 to 6 — Appendixes A and B; Cols. 7 and 8 — Table 8, p. 93.

The Depression Decade: 1930-40

In the first five years of the 1930's, the largest decline in required additions since the 1880's (see Table 17) occurred. Moreover, it took place at the middle life-cycle stages. A more disastrous circumstance for residential construction cannot be imagined. Required additions for the 35-44 age class fell by more than twice the decline in any other five-year period from 1870 to 1950 and by more than the total increase from 1900 on. Required additions for the 45-54 age class also fell. Both of these reductions were the undesired heritage of the past, traceable to the effect of World War I on the population increment in the 15-35 age class, to the decrease in immigration between 1910 and 1920, and to the increase in these age classes in the preceding half-decade due to the upswings that took place in immigration in 1920-25 and in 1905-10.

Even with the sharp decline in total required additions, the demand for housing did not fall in all age classes. Required additions for the

25-34, 55-64, and 65-and-up age classes increased. However, the increase in required additions for the important 25-34 age class was far smaller than the decrease for the even more important 35-44 age class. The increase at the late life-cycle stages can be traced back period by period to the expansion in immigration after the turn of the century, and the increase in the 25-34 age class resulted from the increases in immigration in the 1920-25 and 1910-15 periods.

If it had been possible to restore immigration between 1925-30 and 1930-35, there would have been no decline in required additions in the later period. However, the sharp drop in demand in the 35-44 age class far exceeded the decline in immigration, so that restoring immigration would neither have prevented the wide shift in age composition nor have kept demand from falling at the center of the housing life cycle.

Since the decline in required additions for the 35-44 and 45-54 age classes far exceeded the impact of the decline in concurrent immigration on required additions for these age classes, it might be argued that the decline in residential construction in the early 1930's was the result of predetermined population factors and would have occurred without depression elsewhere in the economy.[69] Support for this argument is offered by the fact that the relatively large increase in the 25-34 age class in this period probably went primarily to fill up vacant rental units created by overbuilding in the late 1920's and therefore provided little stimulus to residential construction in 1930-35.

In the absence of a depression brought about by factors outside the housing market, the concurrent changes in residential construction would have tended to pull the economy toward one in 1930-35. With a depression already underway, the fact that most of the increase in required additions called for by past population changes came in the age classes most susceptible to unemployment or falling income in depression periods (25-34, 55-and-up) further reduced the effective demand associated with population changes in this period. Finally, it might be noted that these same age classes are the ones most likely to have demand for separate quarters satisfied by converted rather than new dwelling units.

This brief discussion of the housing market situation in the early 1930's does little more than suggest some possible relationships of interest. However, it seems clear that breaking down the total change in required additions into changes within age classes offers more insight into the causes of changes in residential construction between 1920 and 1935 than it would be possible to gain by looking at population totals only.

---

[69] And, of course, the decline in immigration in 1930-35 was largely the result of prior legislation rather than of current economic conditions in the United States.

During the last half of the 1930's, required additions increased slightly, but the gain was far from large enough to bring required additions near the level reached before the collapse in 1930-35. Most of the increase occurred in the 35-44 and 45-54 age classes. The increase in the 35-44 age class can be explained by the 1920-25 expansion in immigration. The gain in the 45-54 age class seems to be related to this same spurt in immigration and to the contemporary reduction in mortality rates in this age class.[70]

The changes in required additions for the 1930's as a whole were clearly dominated by the change in the first half of the decade. Almost the entire decline in required additions in this decade was accounted for by one age class (the 35-44 age class), and this decline went directly back to the decline in the entering population in the 1910-20 period. It is somewhat frightening to realize that the large decline in required additions for this age class in the 1930's is about to be doubled (at 1960 headship rates) in the 1960's.

War and Its Aftermath: 1940 to 1950

After the 1930's, the impact of population changes on housing markets became less important than the impact of other factors. Still, it is interesting to trace the age composition of required additions through World War II and the immediate postwar years, if only to make clearer the extent of the break between population change and the housing market in this period. This is shown in Table 18.

Had it not been for the outbreak of World War II, another residential construction boom would have been in the making in the 1940's. The level of required additions for the 35-44 age class recovered from the 1930's to an all-time peak. The doubling of required additions for this age class, which went back to the increase in the entering population in the 1920's, would have provided a powerful stimulus to residential construction in the absence of war-time controls. The rest of the increase in required additions in the 1940's came in the 55-and-up age classes and was accounted for by two factors: the decline in mortality rates at these life-cycle stages during the decade and the lagged impact of the increase in immigration in 1900-1910.

The first half of the 1940's set the pattern for the decade's changes. In most respects, the first and second halves of the 1940's were similar to past peak and post-peak five-year periods. In 1940-45, required additions were relatively concentrated in the early life-cycle stages. In 1945-50, the

---

[70] See Appendix C.

TABLE 18. REQUIRED ADDITIONS BY AGE CLASS DURING
AND IMMEDIATELY AFTER WORLD WAR II,
BY SELECTED PERIOD
(Thousands of dwelling units)

Period	Age class						Total	$RA_a/$ RA^a
	15-24	25-34	35-44	45-54	55-64	65- and-up		
	(1)	(2)	(3)	(4)	(5)	(6)	(7)	(8)
Number, by decade								
1930-40........	85	775	512	1,235	1,186	1,235	5,028	16%
1940-50........	−29	795	1,386	943	1,473	1,728	6,296	32
Change from preceding decade								
1940-50........	−114	20	874	−292	287	493	1,268	..
Number, by quinquennial period								
1935-40........	36	370	302	681	513	660	2,562	15%
1940-45........	45	442	609	552	696	781	3,125	24
1945-50........	−76	353	777	391	777	947	3,171	35
Change from preceding quinquennial period								
1940-45........	9	72	307	−129	183	121	563	..
1945-50........	−119	−89	168	−161	81	166	46	..
Quinquennial period adjusted for war backlog								
1940-45........	−429	−289	561	552	696	781	1,872	..
1945-50........	400	1,084	825	391	777	947	4,424	..
Change from preceding quinquennial period								
1940-45........	−465	−659	259	−129	183	121	−690	..
1945-50........	829	1,373	264	−161	81	166	2,552	..

[a] RA = required additions; RA_a = required additions due to changes in age composition.
Sources: Cols. 1 to 6 — Appendixes A and B; Cols. 7 and 8 — Table 8, p. 93.

center of demand shifted toward the older age classes; the 35-44 class reached a peak, but required additions fell for the 25-34 age class. All in all (with the major exception of an absolute decline in demand in the 15-24 age class in 1940-45), this is a picture very similar to that presented in quinquennial periods 1900-1905 and 1905-10 and in periods 1920-25 and 1925-30. The difference is that the pattern in the 1940's resulted from the lagged impact of immigration rather than from the current change in immigration.

The foregoing discussion of required additions in the two halves of the 1940's abstracted from the impact of war mobilization on the size and age composition of the housing population. If account is taken of the movement of the housing population into and out of the armed services in the 1940's, a very large shift in the age composition of required additions between the first and second halves of the 1940's is uncovered. The large reduction in required additions for the under-45 age classes in 1940-45 was more than offset by the increase in the second half of the decade. The adjusted estimates of required additions shown for 1945-50 in Table 18 may have a slight upward bias, but it would not be sufficient to explain either the rise in required additions for the 15-24 age class to two or three times the level reached in any full decade or the rise for the 25-34 age class to a level one-third greater than that reached in any full decade. Further, required additions for the 35-44 age class reached an all-time peak in the 1945-50 quinquennium. It should be clear that extreme pressure on the residential building industry must have resulted from the growth in demand for separate quarters in the critical 25-44 age class. It must also be remembered that these estimates do not take account of the additional growth in demand coming from the increase in headship rates during the 1945-50 period.

The Unprecedented Boom of the 1950's

The decade of the 1950's was a most unusual one for housing markets. At the same time that total required additions fell by the largest amount of any decade covered in this study and the age composition was as unfavorable as possible from the viewpoint of stimulating construction, household formations and housing starts far exceeded past peak levels. Required additions by age class for this period are shown in Table 19.

The decline in required additions — to a negative level — was six times larger than that in any other decade for the key 25-34 age class. Although far smaller than the drop in the 1930's, the decline in required additions for the 35-44 age class was the second largest on record. Whatever strength was contributed to housing demand by population changes in the ten-year period came from the 45-54 and 65-and-up age classes. In some ways then, the age composition of required additions in the 1950's resembled that of the 1930's, but, with required additions for both the 24-34 and 35-44 age classes declining, the situation was less favorable in the 1950's.

In the absence of any increase in the headship rate at Stage 2, the negative level of required additions for this stage would have meant that households leaving Stage 2 and wanting to sell existing units and move

TABLE 19. REQUIRED ADDITIONS BY AGE CLASS IN THE 1950's,
BY SELECTED PERIOD
(Thousands of dwelling units)

Period	Age class						Total	$RA_a/$ RA^a
	15-24	25-34	35-44	45-54	55-64	65-and-up		
	(1)	(2)	(3)	(4)	(5)	(6)	(7)	(8)
Number, by decade								
1940-50......	−29	795	1,386	943	1,473	1,728	6,296	32%
1950-60......	−66	−328	1,165	1,548	1,154	2,212	5,685	9
Change from preceding decade								
1950-60......	−37	−1,123	−221	605	−319	484	−611	..
Number, by quinquennial period								
1945-50......	−74	353	777	391	777	947	3,171	35%
1950-55......	−205	105	593	647	592	1,180	2,912	29
1955-60......	168	−459	627	934	582	1,125	2,977	−11
Change from preceding quinquennial period								
1950-55......	−131	−248	−184	256	−185	233	−259	..
1955-60......	473	−564	34	287	−10	−55	65	..

[a] RA = required additions; RA_a = required additions due to changes in age composition.
Sources: Cols. 1 to 6 — Appendixes A and B; Cols. 7 and 8 — Table 8, p. 93.

up the housing ladder would have had difficulty doing so without capital loss. Even with the more than offsetting increase in the headship rate that did occur, it is reasonable to suppose that the decline in required additions at beginning headship rates had a depressing effect on the market for low-priced sales housing. However, because a relatively large proportion of those leaving Stage 2 vacate rental units, this depressing effect on sales markets was probably far less in the 1950's than it will be in the 1960's, when required additions will be negative for the 35-44 age class. In any event, nothing in this picture would have pointed to a construction boom in the 1950's, and this makes the boom that did occur all the more remarkable.

A development deserving special attention was the huge increase in required additions for the entering population in 1955-60, marking the first impact of the "baby boom" on housing markets. In fact, in 1955-60 almost all of the increase in population pressure relative to the first half of the 1950's took place at the first and the last life-cycle stages. Undoubtedly, the growing production of special housing tracts and accommodations for retired people was in response to these population changes. Similarly, the upswing in the construction of multi-family rental structures gained impetus from the expected effect of the war-time baby boom on the tenure structure of housing demand.

The changes in required additions in the 1950's can be traced by age class to earlier changes in the entering population or in immigration. The increase in required additions for the 65-and-up age class went back to the wave of immigration in 1900-1910. The gain for the 45-54 age class reflected the expansion in immigration in the early 1920's and the increase in births in 1900-1910. The declines in required additions for the 35-44 and 55-64 age classes can be explained by the declines in immigration in the 1930's and 1910's, respectively. Finally, the decline at the first two life-cycle stages was a direct result of the decline in births from 1925 to 1935, which was partly the result of the decline in immigration after 1925. Thus, almost three decades after the door was closed, the size and age composition of required additions was still importantly influenced by past swings in immigration.

However, as a result of the growing importance of past swings in births and birth rates, a new pattern of required additions in total and by age class began to emerge in the second half of the 1950's. By 1955-60, the peak in required additions was three half-decades past and required additions were still below the peak level. The relatively uniform pattern of alternating peaks and troughs by decades that held from 1900 on through the 1950's is in the process of being replaced by a new pattern as the effects of past swings in immigration every other decade wear off. This new pattern, based on swings in births of somewhat longer duration and subject to somewhat less sharp changes on the down side than the swings in immigration, will dominate the housing market in the 1960's and 1970's.

Sales and Rental Required Additions by Age Class

The tenure composition of required additions by age class from the 1870's to the 1950's is indicated in Table 20. However, the discussion in this section will be restricted to the three key periods of major interest — the first and second postwar booms and the Great Depression — and will be based on quinquennial data.

The Post–World War I Boom

In 1920-25, rental required additions increased for all age classes except the 35-44 age class (see Table 21). However, the major increase

TABLE 20. TENURE COMPOSITION OF REQUIRED ADDITIONS
BY AGE CLASS, BY DECADE
(Thousands of dwelling units)

| Decade | Age class | | | | | | Total |
| | 15-24 | 25-34 | 35-44 | 45-54 | 55-64 | 65-and-up | |
	(1)	(2)	(3)	(4)	(5)	(6)	(7)
Owner-occupied							
1870-80............	14	145	250	285	142	189	1,025
1880-90............	12	193	326	331	268	264	1,394
1890-1900..........	13	188	454	407	320	257	1,639
1900-1910..........	19	256	506	590	378	331	2,080
1910-20............	5	174	541	597	540	359	2,211
1920-30............	21	138	594	762	655	672	2,843
1930-40............	8	186	213	681	732	896	2,716
1940-50............	−3	179	511	456	829	1,095	3,058
1950-60............	−17	−119	642	949	727	1,458	3,640
Renter-occupied							
1870-80............	136	439	315	224	76	70	1,260
1880-90............	115	587	411	261	142	99	1,615
1890-1900..........	120	567	573	321	170	95	1,846
1900-1910..........	177	758	640	465	201	124	2,364
1910-20............	46	530	682	472	286	133	2,144
1920-30............	204	421	751	601	349	250	2,577
1930-40............	77	589	299	554	454	339	2,312
1940-50............	−26	616	875	487	653	633	3,238
1950-60............	−49	−209	523	599	427	754	2,045

Sources: Cols. 1 to 6 — Appendixes A and B; Col. 7, Table 4, p. 75. The tenure rates used by decade are also from Table 4.

came at the first two life-cycle stages, reaching a pre–1955-60 peak at the first stage. Sales required additions also rose for all age classes except the 35-44 age class, but in this sector of the market most of the increase occurred at the last three life-cycle stages. However, as in the other periods (1905-10, 1940-45) when total required additions increased most rapidly, sales required additions were relatively large at the second life-cycle stage in this half-decade. Thus, the proportion of first-time owners to sales required additions was high in 1920-25. As a result, the market for sales housing put up by speculative builders probably flourished.

Because of the age composition of the population increment in 1920-25, required additions tended to increase more rapidly than their value and the average value tended to fall. A principal feature of the 1920-25 period was that a relatively substantial part of residential building involved large-scale rental projects on which it was not easy to shut off production once it had begun. With the change in required additions at this stage of the population cycle having the major positive feedback effect on housing demand, it is likely that the resulting boom left many of these projects "running on air."

TABLE 21. Tenure Composition of Required Additions
from the Turn of the Century to the End of the
Post–World War I Boom, by Age Class,
by Quinquennial Period
(Thousands of dwelling units)

Quinquennial period	Age class						
	15-24	25-34	35-44	45-54	55-64	65-and-up	Total
Number, owner-occupied							
1900-1905..........	9	117	244	264	170	154	958
1905-10............	10	139	262	326	208	177	1,122
1910-15............	3	106	282	339	272	194	1,195
1915-20............	2	68	258	258	268	162	1,016
1920-25............	13	124	251	298	348	325	1,359
1925-30............	8	15	343	464	307	347	1,485
Change from preceding period							
1905-10............	1	22	18	62	38	23	164
1910-15............	−7	−33	20	13	64	17	73
1915-20............	−1	−38	−24	−81	−4	−32	−179
1920-25............	11	56	−7	40	80	163	343
1925-30............	−5	−109	92	166	−41	22	125
Number, renter-occupied							
1900-1905..........	87	358	308	209	90	58	1,110
1905-10............	90	399	332	256	111	66	1,254
1910-15............	30	324	358	268	144	73	1,201
1915-20............	16	206	325	204	142	60	953
1920-25............	123	373	317	235	186	121	1,355
1925-30............	81	58	424	366	163	129	1,221
Change from preceding period							
1905-10............	3	41	29	47	21	8	144
1910-15............	−60	75	15	12	33	7	−53
1915-20............	−14	−118	−37	−64	−2	−13	−248
1920-25............	107	167	−7	31	44	61	402
1925-30............	−42	−315	107	131	−23	8	−134

Sources: Table 15, p. 124; Table 16, p. 126; and Appendix Table B2, p. 188.

Within five years of the initial spurt in rental demand, rental required additions for the first life-cycle stage fell and for the second life-cycle stage they practically disappeared, dropping to one-fourth of the lowest level reached prior to 1925-30. With the reduction in rental demand coming primarily in the age classes that had stimulated the prior period's increase, overbuilding of dwelling units specialized to the needs of this sector was likely to result. The contemporary increase in rental required additions at Stages 3 and 4 probably involved a type of rental unit different from those produced in the 1920-25 period, since those units had been tailored to the tastes of households at the first two life-cycle stages. Moreover, with real income continuing to grow, a considerable part of the possible increase in rental required additions at Stages 3 and 4 was shifted to ownership markets.

As the age composition of demand changed to reduce rental required additions in 1925-30, total and sales required additions moved on to their respective peaks (the latter with much more gusto than the former). There was a large expansion in the number of households seeking sales units in all the age classes from 35-44 up, providing the basis for an increase in the production of better-quality housing. On the other hand, the sharp decline in owner-occupied required additions at Stage 2, involving most first-time owners, must have disappointed more than a few tract builders.

The Great Depression

In the first five years of the Depression, as the rental decline continued, the trend of the sales market was reversed. The decline in sales required additions for the key 35-44 age class was the largest ever experienced (see Table 22), bringing such additions down to one-third the lowest past level. Sales required additions for the 45-54 age class also fell sharply. The concurrent increase for the 25-34 age class far from offset these declines, and total sales required additions fell. This was probably of less importance, however, than the wide shift in age composition in depressing the market for sales housing in 1930-35. Moreover, the previously unmatched decline in sales required additions for the 35-44 age class seems to have resulted from the 1925-30 reduction in immigration and not from any current change in economic conditions — a fact that reinforces the conclusion that if no depression had started elsewhere in the economy in 1930-35, one very likely would have started in residential construction in this half-decade.

As was noted earlier, the sharp decline in sales required additions was matched by a continuing decline in rental demand, this time primarily at

Table 22. Tenure Composition of Required Additions
During the Great Depression by Age Class,
by Quinquennial Period
(Thousands of dwelling units)

Quinquennial period	Age class						Total
	15-24	25-34	35-44	45-54	55-64	65-and-up	
Number, owner-occupied							
1925-30............	8	15	343	464	307	347	1,485
1930-35............	5	101	88	313	441	427	1,375
1935-40............	4	83	111	330	286	419	1,233
Change from preceding period							
1925-30............	−5	−109	92	166	−41	22	125
1930-35............	−3	86	−245	−151	134	80	−110
1935-40............	−1	−18	23	17	−155	−8	−142
Number, renter-occupied							
1925-30............	81	48	424	366	163	129	1,221
1930-35............	43	306	110	247	235	159	1,100
1935-40............	32	287	191	351	227	241	1,329
Change from preceding period							
1925-30............	−42	−325	107	131	−23	8	−134
1930-35............	−38	258	−314	−119	72	30	−121
1935-40............	−11	−19	81	104	−8	82	229

Sources: Table 17, p. 129, and Appendix Table B2, p. 188.

the third and fourth life-cycle stages, which had experienced a sharp increase in the preceding five-year period. Rental required additions did recover at the second life-cycle stage, but not to the level reached in 1920-25, and it is very possible that most of the increase went to fill the vacancies left over from the past. If so, then the effective decline in rental required additions in 1930-35 was probably the largest ever in the United States.

Those age classes in which rental and sales required additions did increase in 1930-35 were very susceptible to loss of employment and income in the Depression, so the very large decrease in aggregate demand that took place in this period shifted a large part of owner-occupied required additions to the rental market and a large part of rental required additions to converted units.

The Post–World War II Boom

The period after World War II is more interesting for what did not happen than for what did. In many ways it repeats the experience leading from boom to depression following World War I, but the outcome was entirely different. Ignoring the effects of the war on the housing population, the 1945-50 period contained the basis for a sales boom (see Table 23). Owner-occupied required additions increased at the third, fifth, and sixth life-cycle stages in both 1940-45 and 1945-50. However, without the war the boom would have been different from the one that occurred, because the large increase in low-quality sales housing that characterized suburban development in 1945-50 would not have met the needs of the previously mentioned age classes. The population base for the market for this type of sales housing can readily be seen if account is taken of the movement of the housing population into and out of the armed forces.

With this adjustment, sales required additions for Stage 2 in 1945-50 were greater than in any *decade* covered in the study with the exception of 1900-1910. For Stage 1 they exceeded those for all decades, and for Stage 3 they were greater than in any prior half-decade.

Even more important was the increase in rental demand at the first two life-cycle stages that resulted from demobilization. The level of rental required additions for Stages 1 and 2 in 1945-50 exceeded the level reached in any decade from the 1870's to the 1950's, and the increase from 1940-45 to 1945-50 was over four times the largest increase in any other quinquennium. In fact, the increase in rental required additions for the 25-34 age class in the second half of the 1940's was greater than the largest increase in rental required additions for *all* age classes in any other decade or half-decade covered in the study.

The resulting shortage of rental units, together with considerations of equity for returning veterans, led to the extension of wartime rent controls into the postwar years. Thus, new construction was diverted from rental to sales units, and this led to a major sales housing boom concentrated in the production of relatively low-cost tract units. To some extent, this shift was possible only because of the availability of funds for government-insured mortgages, making potential owners of the large proportion of the population unable to meet the higher down and monthly payments required under conventional mortgage terms. The availability of such funds was one result of the decision to peg United States government bond rates at a low level. In retrospect, given our experience with a speculative rental boom in the 1920's, it seems that the diversion of

TABLE 23. TENURE COMPOSITION OF REQUIRED ADDITIONS DURING
WORLD WAR II AND THE POST–WORLD WAR II BOOM BY AGE CLASS,
BY QUINQUENNIAL PERIOD
(Thousands of dwelling units)

Quinquennial period	Age class						Total
	15-24	25-34	35-44	45-54	55-64	65-and-up	
Number, owner-occupied							
A. 1940-45..........	−49	−65	207	267	388	495	1,243
1945-50..........	46	243	304	189	433	600	1,815
B. 1940-45..........	6	100	225	267	388	495	1,481
1945-50..........	−9	79	287	189	433	600	1,579
1950-55..........	−53	38	327	397	373	778	1,860
1955-60..........	31	−200	375	616	400	789	2,011
Change from preceding period							
A. 1940-45..........	−53	−148	96	−63	102	76	10
1945-50..........	95	308	97	−78	45	105	572
B. 1940-45..........	2	17	114	−63	102	76	248
1945-50..........	−15	−21	62	−78	45	105	98
1950-55..........	−44	−41	40	208	−60	178	281
1955-60..........	84	−238	48	219	27	11	151
Number, renter-occupied							
A. 1940-45..........	−380	−224	354	285	308	286	629
1945-50..........	354	841	521	202	344	347	2,609
B. 1940-45..........	39	342	384	285	308	286	1,644
1945-50..........	−65	274	490	202	344	347	1,592
1950-55..........	−152	67	266	250	219	402	1,052
1955-60..........	137	−259	252	318	182	336	966
Change from preceding period							
A. 1940-45..........	−412	−511	163	−66	81	45	−700
1945-50..........	734	1,065	167	−83	36	61	1,980
B. 1940-45..........	7	55	193	−66	81	45	315
1945-50..........	−104	−68	106	−83	36	61	−52
1950-55..........	−87	−207	−234	48	−125	55	−540
1955-60..........	289	−326	−14	68	−37	−66	−86

ª Part A gives the estimates adjusted for the effect of World War II — see Appendix E.
Sources: Part A — Table 18, p. 132; Part B — Tables 18 and 19, pp. 132 and 134.

demand from rental to sales markets may have been the best possible solution to the postwar growth in housing demand.

Sales required additions decreased in 1950-55 relative to the war-adjusted 1945-50 level, producing in some ways a pattern of changes similar to those in 1930-35. The decreases were largest at the first and second life-cycle stages but also occurred at the fifth stage and remained about the same at the second stage. Despite these declines, the largest gain that ever occurred in the United States in the production of sales units took place in this quinquennium. Only a large shift in the tenure composition of demand, a large increase in headship rates, or a significant relocation of the housing population (all three of which did occur) could have explained this boom. Behind the changes that kept the sales boom going, the following factors were most important: (1) the quality back-log resulting from the war, (2) the increase in real income continued by the Korean episode, and (3) the government's mortgage insurance programs. The last factor, together with the fact that the adverse change in age composition came only five years after the end of the war instead of ten years after as in the 1930-35 period, seems most important in explaining the completely different response of the sales market in 1950-55 to the same change in sales required additions by age classes that led to collapse in 1930-35.

The change in the tenure composition of demand that took place in 1950-55 added to the decline in rental required additions, instead of off-setting it as in sales markets. The decrease was particularly large at the second and third life-cycle stages, which had already felt an abrupt drop because of population changes.

In 1955-60, the decline in sales required additions continued at the second life-cycle stage and wiped out the entire increase in demand for sales units that had taken place in this age class from 1945 to 1955, but the bottom was reached or passed at the other stages. With sales required additions concentrated at Stages 4 and 6 and with negative required additions at Stage 2, the shift away from tract building toward contract construction and the reduced responsiveness to credit policy in the last five years of the decade are both easily explained.

The continued boom in sales markets must have resulted from non-population factors — particularly the continued high level of income. The continuance of this boom far after the war backlog wore off and into the postpeak period in which the sales market had collapsed following World War I simply cannot be explained by population factors.

Some Conclusions

Wide shifts in the age composition of required additions over time have led to similarly wide shifts in the tenure composition of demand. The latter required reallocations of the building industry's resources among tenure classes that were difficult to bring about, especially given the lagged response of rental projects to increases in demand and the difficulty of halting such projects, once they were under way, when demand decreased. Moreover, shifts in the age composition of required additions within tenure classes were constantly calling for adjustment of the location, quality, and style of dwelling units required at different stages of the population cycle.

The pattern of these changes in age composition has tended to accentuate the cycles in total required additions by emphasizing the types of dwelling units most susceptible to speculative excesses in the upswing and reducing demand most rapidly for the same types in the downswing. The single bright spot is that changes in age composition have served to stabilize the average value relative to the number of additional dwelling units required.

The shifts in age composition of demand by tenure class followed a relatively regular pattern in the 1920's and 1940's (also between 1905 and 1915), leading to the conclusion that a repetitive population cycle has determined the tenure composition of required additions in the past. The pattern of shifts in age composition by tenure class in the 1930's and the 1950's is slightly less similar but still supports this hypothesis. However, the population cycle only controlled the production of dwelling units by tenure class through the early years of the Depression, after which its effects were far outweighed by changes in economic conditions and tastes.

IX. REQUIRED ADDITIONS, HOUSEHOLD FORMATIONS, AND HOUSING STARTS IN THE FUTURE: 1960's TO 1980's

The end of immigration as a major factor determining population changes, the decline in birth rates and births in the late twenties and during the Depression, and the baby boom during and following World War II have all left their marks on the long swing in population growth, especially in the striking changes in age composition that will take place in the next several decades. How required additions will reflect these new relationships and what sort of long swings in household formations and housing starts may result will be investigated in the present chapter, along with prospective strengths and weaknesses in different sectors of the housing market.

The break with all past experience in the 1950's — when headship rates changed to more than offset the contemporary decline in required additions — greatly increases the uncertainty involved in basing forecasts of housing starts or household formations on population factors, even for the time intervals used in this study. Much depends on whether this break was a temporary phenomenon or will prove to be a continuing feature of housing markets. That headship rates cannot increase indefinitely would seem certain, if only by definition.

Although projections of household formations are on a somewhat insecure basis until the sources of headship-rate changes and the effective rather than definitional "ceilings" on headship rates are better understood, it is possible to measure the effect on housing demand of population changes at a constant set of headship rates. The resulting quinquennial and decadal projections of required additions can then be compared with required additions over the last century and with household formations and housing starts in the 1950's. In this manner, the relative magnitude of population changes in the future can be placed in historical perspective and the potential for population changes alone leading to a residential construction boom in the 1960's or 1970's can be properly evaluated. The obvious conclusion, that the well-publicized acceleration in the rate of growth of the labor force must also mean increasing household formations and housing starts, is not so obviously correct when the age composition of future population changes and the determinants of household formations and residential construction in the recent past are considered. Doing so will make it clear that further changes in headship rates are absolutely necessary if the United States is to have the looked-for residential building boom. For this reason, forecasts based on the assumption that headship rates will increase by age class in the future at the same rate as in the second half of the 1950's will be presented, but no attempt will be made to predict the exact change in headship rates.

Estimates of required additions will be based on census projections of the age composition of the population by five-year intervals, weighted by 1960 headship rates for similar age intervals.[71] The use of population projections of any sort to estimate future demand might be questioned. However, most disillusionment with such projections stems from attempts to anticipate future birth rates. Until 1975-80, the population projections to be used are not based on birth rate projections for any age class and so are not subject to this criticism. In fact, until 1985-90, because of the relatively low headship rates for the 15-19 and 20-24 age classes, birth rate projections remain unimportant in determining required additions. Only in 1985-90 could a significant difference arise, depending on which of the birth rate projections presented by the Bureau of the Census is used. Consequently, the estimates made in this study will terminate in 1990.

With the population projections used largely independent of birth rate projections, possibilities for error could arise from changes in net immigration or mortality rates. For immigration to become important once again would require a major and unlikely change in our immigration policy. Mortality rate changes have not been important (within the time

---

[71] For the census estimates, see U.S. Bureau of the Census, *Current Population Reports,* Series P-25, 286 (July, 1964), pp. 41ff. Four different assumptions about birth rates are presented. Since the series differ only in terms of the future birth rates used, it is not until 1980 that the differences affect the housing population, and then they affect only the 15-19 age class. Series B — the second-highest, but in most ways a "middle" forecast — was used in making the estimates of required additions presented in this chapter. These will differ from estimates made by the U.S. Bureau of the Census (*Current Population Reports,* Series P-20, No. 123) from the same population projections, because each of the latter estimates is based on a different assumption about marriage rates, age of marriage, and so forth. For purposes of continuity with the estimates presented in earlier chapters and because of the close correspondence between required additions and household formations prior to the 1950's, beginning (1960 or estimated 1965) headship rates are used for basic estimates of required additions in the future given in this chapter.

intervals used) in the past, and, in the absence of war or epidemic, they have had their major impact on the last two life-cycle stages. There is little room for improvement at the first two life-cycle stages where the weight of population changes would give mortality rates their greatest leverage in the next two decades.[72]

Total and Tenure Composition of Required Additions: 1860-1990

Required additions in the 1960's will exceed any past level. However, despite the higher beginning headship rate and the acceleration in the rate of growth of the adult population, the increase in required additions from the 1940's to the 1960's was smaller than that between any past pairs of decadal peaks. Moreover, the increment from the 1950's to the 1960's was less than the comparable interdecade increases in 1900-1910, the 1920's, and the 1940's. In terms of population pressures then, the impetus to increased residential construction in the 1960's will be weaker than in any other long swing expansion during this century.

During the 1960's, the effect of shifts in age composition will be to reduce required additions for the first time (see Table 24), decreasing required additions for a given housing population (1960 level) by 2,234,-000 units and so offsetting to a great extent the increase — which will be the largest ever in the United States — in the size of the housing population. In fact, changes in age composition will be important in this negative sense at least through the 1980's, reversing the trend maintained through the first 60 years of this century.

Turning to the tenure composition of demand during the 1960's, sales required additions will actually fall, reflecting the current decline in the population increment at the middle life-cycle stages. Thus, population changes offer little basis for optimism about sales markets in this decade. In fact, if one-family housing starts were limited to sales required additions in the 1960's (as they were not in the 1950's), the resulting decline in sales starts would far exceed that of the 1930's.

Rental required additions will rise sharply in the 1960's. Unlike the even larger gain that could have been possible in the 1940's, the present increase should lead to a substantial expansion in the renter-occupied

---

[72] In testing the influence of different mortality rate assumptions on its population projections, the Bureau of the Census (*Current Population Reports,* Series P-25, No. 286, pp. 24-27) found that only small differences resulted in population totals and most of these appeared in the 65-and-up age class. If the most optimistic Census Bureau assumption is correct, then the estimates presented of household formations for the 65-and-up age class will prove too low, but only slightly so in any one quinquennial period, and those which involve the first four life-cycle stages will remain unchanged.

TABLE 24. TOTAL AND TENURE COMPOSITION OF REQUIRED
ADDITIONS FROM 1940-50 TO 1980-90, BY DECADE[a]
(Millions of dwelling units)

Decade	Required additions	Sales required additions	Rental required additions	Required additions due to Δ's in age composition/ Col. 1
	(1)	(2)	(3)	(4)
1940-50....................	6,146	3,008	3,138	32.0%
1950-60....................	5,619	3,607	2,012	6.1
1960-70....................	6,399	3,548	2,851	−34.9
1970-80....................	9,490	4,998	4,492	−3.2
1980-90....................	10,948	6,560	4,388	−3.0

[a] The estimates of required additions in this and subsequent tables in this chapter are based on changes in the total population rather than on changes in the continental population. Thus, the estimates will differ slightly in the 1940's and 1950's from those already presented. Population projections are available only for the total population.
    Sources: Based on the sources of total population data given in Appendix A and on 1940, 1950, and 1960 headship rates and on 1940, 1949, and 1959 tenure rates as shown in Appendix B.

housing stock. Idle resources, the absence of materials shortages and price and allocation controls (especially rent controls), and the relative availability of mortgage funds for apartment projects all differentiate the 1960's from the postwar years when the large potential increase in rental demand was siphoned off into sales markets. Given the nature of rental production, the results are more likely to be overproduction and increasing vacancies than shortages and waiting lists, but population growth in the next decade should more than compensate for any present mistakes.

The increase in required additions in the 1970's will be two to three times greater than in any past decade, leading to a level of required additions almost 50 percent greater than ever before, as shown on Chart 17. However, before deciding whether the population change alone will be sufficient to raise residential construction to equally unprecedented levels, it will be necessary to look at the relationship between population changes and residential construction in the recent past.

Unlike what is happening in the 1960's, the increase in required additions in the 1970's will be reflected in both sales and rental markets, with rental required additions almost 50 percent above the prior peak in the 1940's and sales required additions almost one-third greater than in the 1950's. In both tenure classes, the 1970-80 increase in required additions will be far greater than that in any past decade.

This expansion will continue through the 1980's, even if a reduced

CHART 17. TOTAL, SALES, AND RENTAL REQUIRED ADDITIONS:
1860-1990

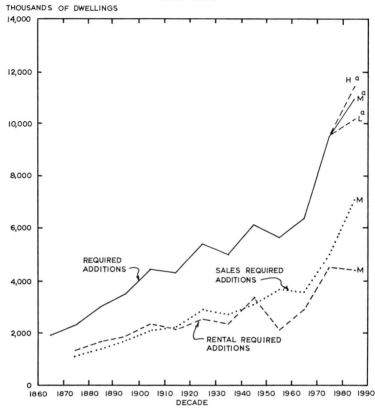

ᵃ *H, L,* and *M* refer to the high, low, and middle population projections discussed in the text, p. 151, and in fn. 71, p. 145; $H = 11,500,000$ and $L = 10,100,000$.
    Sources: Required additions, 1860's to 1930's, Table 1, p. 60, and 1940's to 1980's, Table 24, p. 147; sales and rental required additions, 1870's to 1930's, Table 4, p. 75, and 1940's to 1980's, Table 24, p. 147.

birth rate should take its toll in the second half of the decade. The increase, however, although large by past standards, will be less than one-half the size of that in the 1970's. This deceleration in required additions will tend to reduce the need for additional capacity in the residential building industry and to raise the possibility of overbuilding, should demand projections become tied to the rate of growth in the 1970's.

On the other hand, sales required additions will increase even more rapidly in the 1980's than in the 1970's, reaching a level higher than that of total required additions in the 1960's. At the same time, rental required additions will fall, but they will still be above the level of any

TABLE 25. TOTAL AND TENURE COMPOSITION OF REQUIRED
ADDITIONS FROM 1945-50 TO 1985-90, BY QUINQUENNIAL PERIOD
(Millions of dwelling units)

Quinquennial period	Required additions (1)	Sales required additions (2)	Rental required additions (3)	Required additions due to Δ's in age composition/ Col. 1 (4)
1945-50.	4,424	1,815	2,609	....
1950-55.	3,073	1,933	1,140	24.6%
1955-60.	2,738	1,898	840	−16.2
1960-65.	2,811	1,712	1,099	−49.2
1965-70.	3,588	1,836	1,752	−27.7
1970-75.	4,449	2,268	2,181	−10.7
1975-80.	5,041	2,730	2,311	2.7
1980-85.	5,334	3,184	2,150	2.4
1985-90.	5,614	3,376	2,238	9.6

Sources: From 1950-55 on, see Appendix A for the sources of the population data used and Appendix B for the headship and tenure rates used; 1945-50 required additions are adjusted for the effects of World War II on population changes (see Appendix E).

past decade except the 1970's. The diverse movement of sales and rental required additions can be traced respectively to the arrival of the population wave associated with the baby boom at the life-cycle stages where owner-occupancy rates are increasing most rapidly and to the second-generation effects of the decline in births during the Depression.

In general, the long-established pattern of alternating decadal peaks and troughs will be broken in the 1970's and 1980's. Instead, the long swing in required additions will show up only in absolute or percentage increments and so will resemble the long swing from the 1860's to the 1890's. In rate-of-growth terms, required additions will increase for two decades (rather than for one, as throughout the first half of the century) to a peak in the 1970's and then decline in the 1980's. Whatever population projection is used, required additions will grow more rapidly again in the 1990's.

Turning now to the long swing by quinquennial periods, in the first half of the 1960's required additions increased slightly (see Table 25) but remained below the 1950-55 level. Not until the next five years will population changes exert a considerable upward pressure on residential construction. But, although required additions will reach their highest peace-time level in 1965-70, they will remain far below the war-adjusted 1945-50 level and the increase will be about as large as the one in 1920-25 (see Chart 18).

CHART 18. REQUIRED ADDITIONS AND CHANGES, BY QUINQUENNIAL
PERIODS, 1900-1905 TO 1985-90[a]

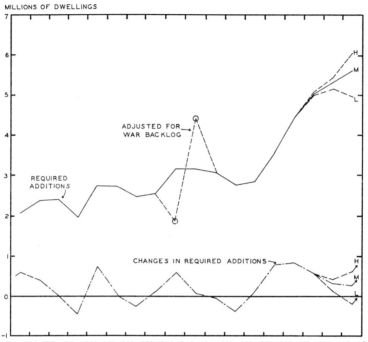

[a] H, L, and M refer to the high, low, and middle population projections discussed
in the text on p. 151, and in fn. 71, p. 145.
    Sources: Required additions, 1900-1905 to 1945-50 — Table 3, p. 71, and 1950-55 on,
Table 25, p. 149; changes, 1900-1905 and 1895-1900, based on estimates of the required
stock in 1895 derived by interpolating decadal population data (1890 and 1900) and adjusting for quinquennial changes in immigration; and changes, 1905-10 to 1945-50, based on
Table 2, p. 65, and from 1950-55 on, based on Table 25, p. 149.

Thus, population changes alone are not likely to bring about an expansion in housing starts at any time during the 1960's that would be
comparable with either of the major residential building booms experienced earlier in this century. The 1965-70 rise in required additions trans-
lated into housing starts valued at constant prices will offer a relatively
much weaker stimulus to economic expansion in 1965-70 than in either
the 1920's or the post–World War II decade.

Sales required additions will fall in 1960-65 and then increase slightly
in 1965-70, but they will remain below the level reached in the 1950's
throughout the decade. The relative weakness of population factors in
this sector of the housing market has generally been overlooked in most
discussions of housing market prospects for the remainder of the 1960's.

Instead, attention has been concentrated on the population changes that will raise rental required additions to an all-time high in 1965-70, involving much the largest increase in rental required additions in our history and accounting for almost 90 percent of the increase in total required additions. The peak effect of the baby boom on the rate of growth in rental demand will occur in the next five years.

However, a balanced picture must take account of the relative weakness in sales markets and of the present high level of rental vacancies in many metropolitan areas. Rental required additions increased in 1960-65 but by fewer than in many past quinquenniums and to a level below those in 8 of the last 12 quinquenniums. Ignoring as it did this historical perspective, the discussion of a rental boom in the early sixties was somewhat premature. In any event, the increase in rental vacancies in 1960-65 will serve to reduce the effect of the large increase in rental required additions on rental construction in 1965-70.

By 1970-75, required additions will finally top the adjusted 1945-50 level. In this half-decade there will occur the largest peacetime increment in required additions and the highest rate of growth in required additions that will take place in the next 25 years. If population changes alone can still lead to boom conditions, this is the period when they will be most likely to do so. However, it is worth noting that relative to the size of the economy the spurt in required additions following World War II was much more spectacular.

In the second half of the 1970's, required additions will continue upward, but the gain will be much smaller than in the first half. This trend will continue through the first half of the 1980's. By this time the increment in required additions will be far below the levels achieved in past expansion periods and comparable to the increase in 1960-65. A forecast for 1985-90 depends (for the first time) on the particular population extrapolation used; the "middle" series suggests about the same increase as in the first half of the 1980's, the "top" series implies more rapid expansion, and the "bottom" series shows required additions declining for the first time in 30 years. What will actually occur depends on what happens to birth rates in the next five to ten years. In this manner, the present rate of economic growth, present unemployment rates for young people, and present mores will determine the course of housing demand 20 to 30 years in the future.

Sales required additions will move with total required additions through the 1970's and 1980's but will achieve a peak increase one half-decade later than total required additions (in 1975-80, rather than in 1970-75). Rental required additions, on the other hand, will increase less rapidly in 1970-75 than in the next five years, continue to increase (by a still smaller amount) through 1975-80, then decline in the first half of the 1980's. Thus, the past lead of rental required additions over both total and sales required additions will be maintained, but it will be in terms of first differences instead of the level of required additions.

The quinquennial long swing in required additions has disappeared in absolute terms and will not reappear in the next 25 years unless birth rates fall abruptly from their present levels. On the other hand, the long swing marked off by first differences in required additions will continue as the age composition of the housing population continues to change.

The next first-difference peak will come in 1970-75, 30 years after the last peak. Thus, the peak-to-peak duration of the long swing seems to be lengthening. The next trough will come in 1980-85 or 1985-90, depending on the population projection used — 30 to 35 years after the last trough, compared with the 15- to 25-year periods between the three prior pairs of troughs. Most of the increase in the duration of the long swing is accounted for by the lengthening expansion phase. All four contractions shown on the lower part of Chart 18, including the one ahead, are 10 to 15 years in length.

The source of the increased duration of the long swing in required additions is the shift from immigration-based population changes, which tended to reverse the increments in required additions every decade, to housing population changes determined by past births. A period of falling births, 1925-35, was followed by a 15-year period of increasing births, 1935-50. Since that period of accelerating births was longer than most past periods of expanding population changes based on immigration, the duration of the expansion phase of the long swing has been increased. But, because the preceding period of falling births corresponded in length to earlier periods of declining immigration, the contraction phase has not been similarly lengthened.

Required Additions by Age Class in the Future

The wide swings that will occur in the age composition of required additions in the next 25 years will be at least as important as changes in total required additions in determining the influence of population changes on household formations and residential construction. The offsetting movements in required additions by age class will be unprecedented in magnitude, and the strengths and weaknesses of the market for different types of housing during the next five quinquenniums will vary with these wide fluctuations in age composition.

The lagged effects of the baby boom, following through the housing

TABLE 26. FUTURE DECADAL REQUIRED ADDITIONS,
BY AGE CLASS
(Millions of dwelling units)

Decade	Age class						Total
	15-24	25-34	35-44	45-54	55-64	65-and-up	
Number							
Prior peak[a] (date)	225 (1920's)	1,013 (1900's)	1,430 (1940's)		1,473 (1940's)		6,296 (1940's)
1950-60..........	−62	−357	1,135	1,522	1,132	2,249	5,619
1960-70..........	1,429	886	−577	1,467	1,616	1,578	6,399
1970-80..........	817	4,791	1,068	−600	1,440	1,974	9,490
1980-90..........	988	2,339	5,386	1,160	−554	2,182	10,948
Change from preceding decade							
Prior peak[b] (date)	174 (1930's)	258 (1920's)	874 (1940's)		313 (1930's)		1,268 (1940's)
1950-60..........	−48	−921	−295	557	−341	521	−527
1960-70..........	1,491	1,243	−1,712	−55	484	−671	780
1970-80..........	−612	3,905	1,645	−2,067	−176	396	3,091
1980-90..........	171	−2,452	4,318	1,760	−1,994	208	1,458

[a] If not 1950's.
[b] If prior peak change not in 1950's.
Sources: For prior peaks see Chapter VII (if before the 1950's). The data shown for prior peaks are based on the continental rather than the total housing population. But, before the 1940's, the total and continental population were almost identical. For the population data and the headship rates used in estimating the data from 1950 on, see Appendixes A and B.

life cycle just after the negative population increments based on the drop in births that occurred in the period 1925-35, will establish a pattern of negative changes (for the first time) in required additions followed by positive increments raising required additions to an all-time high in each age class.

By decades, the result is that required additions for the 15-24 age class will reach an all-time peak in the 1960's (see Table 26), with the increase several times as large as any past increment. They will fall in the 1970's and then recover in the 1980's (but remain far below the peak level of the 1960's).

Required additions for the 25-34 age class will also rise in the present decade. The increase will be the second largest ever to occur in the United States, exceeded only by the immigration-swollen increment in the 1900's. However, it will be small compared with the increase in required additions for the 25-34 age class in the 1970's. In fact, required additions for this one age class will be greater than those for *all* age classes in any decade prior to the 1940's. This single age class will account for almost one-half of the record level of required additions in the 1970's (a level 50 percent greater than in the 1960's). Then, in the 1980's, required additions for the 25-34 age class will be cut in half.

As the baby boom makes itself felt at the first two life-cycle stages in the present decade, there will be an equally significant decline in required additions for the key 35-44 age class to the point where, at beginning headship rates, fewer dwelling units will be required for this age class in 1970 than were required in 1960. However, in the next two decades required additions for this age class will rise, with most of the gain coming in the 1980's, when required additions for this single age class will reach a level just slightly below the total for all age classes in the 1950's.

Required additions for the 45-54 age class will fall slightly in the present decade and then receive the full impact of the Depression's decline in birth rates in the 1970's, when required additions for this age class will be negative and over two million units fewer than the number required in the 1960's. Finally, in the 1980's required additions for the 45-54 age class will increase, marking the final effect of the baby boom on required additions by age class in the period covered in this study.

The additional dwelling units required for the 55-64 age class will reflect past swings in immigration until the 1980's, when the negative change in required additions will reach this life-cycle stage. For this reason, the 55-64 age class is the only age class beside the first two in which required additions will increase significantly in the present decade. For the 65-and-up age class they will fall sharply in the 1960's and, while increasing in the next two decades, will never reach the all-time high in the 1950's.[73]

By quinquennial periods, the twin effects of the baby boom and the Depression can be even more clearly seen. Most of the record expansion in demand for the first life-cycle stage will be concentrated in the present half-decade (see Table 27). Required additions for this age class will account for two-thirds of the positive changes by age class in 1960-65 (but, it is worth noting, the increment will be less than the adjusted 1945-50 change). Then in the next five years, as required additions for Stage 1 move on to an all-time peak, the increase will be less than half

---

[73] This conclusion is based on the assumption (shared by the Census Bureau in their population forecasts) that the lower mortality rates at the late life-cycle stages, which accounted for much of the increase in required additions at these stages in the 1950's (see Chapter VI, Table 11, p. 104), will not continue.

TABLE 27. FUTURE QUINQUENNIAL REQUIRED ADDITIONS,
BY AGE CLASS
(Millions of dwelling units)

Quinquennial period	Age class						Total
	15-24	25-34	35-44	45-54	55-64	65-and-up	
Number							
Prior peak[a] (date)	400[a] (1945-49)	1,084[a] (1945-49)	825[a] (1945-50)	908 (1955-60)	777 (1945-50)	1,234 (1950-55)	4,424[a] (1945-50)
1955-60	108	−522	570	908	558	1,116	2,738
1960-65	621	−262	129	787	757	779	2,811
1965-70	808	1,148	−706	680	859	799	3,588
1970-75	462	2,476	−273	124	759	901	4,449
1975-80	355	2,315	1,341	−724	681	1,073	5,041
1980-85	110	1,485	2,811	−262	122	1,068	5,334
1985-90	325	854	2,575	1,422	−676	1,114	5,614
Change from preceding quinquennial period							
Prior peak (date)	829[a] (1945-50)	1,373[a] (1945-50)	307 (1940-45)	297 (1925-30)	206 (1930-35)	233 (1950-55)	2,552[a] (1945-50)
1955-60	262	−659	−43	257	−34	−118	−335
1960-65	513	260	−441	−121	199	−337	73
1965-70	187	1,410	−835	−107	102	20	777
1970-75	−346	1,328	433	−556	−100	102	861
1975-80	−107	−161	1,614	−848	−78	172	592
1980-85	−245	−830	1,470	462	−559	−5	293
1985-90	215	−631	−236	1,684	−798	46	280

[a] Adjusted for the war backlog.
Sources: Prior peaks (before 1945-50) — Ch. VIII; adjusted 1945-50 estimates — Appendix E; 1950-55-on estimates — Table 26; 1985-90 — data based on the "middle" projection of population by age class made by the Bureau of the Census (see Appendix A).

the increase in the present quinquennium. Required additions for Stage 1 will then fall through 1970-85, with the major decline coming in the first half of the 1970's, and will increase once more in 1985-90.

The pattern of required additions for Stage 2 will simply lag the changes at Stage 1 by one half-decade. In the present quinquennium, required additions for this important age class will be negative. Then, in the next five years, this age class will begin to take over the housing market, accounting for almost one-third of all required additions and for almost all of the positive change in required additions; the increase will even exceed the adjusted increase following World War II. By 1970-75, required additions for this single age class will dominate the population pressure for residential construction in a manner that is completely unprecedented, requiring over 2,400,000 additional dwelling units (over 50 percent of total required additions), or over twice as many as required for *any* age class in any earlier period. In 1975-80, required additions for this age class will fall slightly but still remain far above any past level, and then in 1980-85 and 1985-90 they will fall sharply.

In the present quinquennium, required additions for the 35-44 age class will be positive but far below the 1955-60 level. It is in the next five years that the negative change (noted previously for the decade as a whole) will be concentrated. Required additions for Stage 3 have only once before fallen by a large amount (in 1930-35), and they have never before been negative. This key age class, the one assigned the highest weight in the housing life cycle in the discussion of feedbacks, extent of postponement, income elasticity, and so forth, in the preceding chapter, will be negative for the next two quinquenniums. It may be significant that a major expansion in residential construction has never occurred when the levels of required additions for the two middle life-cycle stages (35-44 and 45-54) were falling or relatively low. By 1975-80, the population pressure for additions to the housing stock for the 35-44 age class will begin to increase rapidly, reaching an all-time peak in 1980-85 when this age class will account for over 50 percent of the total.

The performance of required additions for the 45-54 age class will lag the foregoing pattern by 10 years, falling in the next quinquennium, falling even more in 1970-75, reaching a negative level in the second half of the 1970's, and finally increasing and becoming positive once more in 1885-90. On the other hand, for the 55-64 age class required additions will increase in 1965-70, before starting to decline in each ensuing half-decade until a negative level is reached in 1985-90.

The 65-and-up age class will, of course, be unaffected by the major population waves starting in the late 1920's. In this age class, required additions will fall in the present quinquennium by about 25 percent. They will then slowly recover (except for a minor decrease in 1980-85) until they reach the 1955-60 level once again in 1985-90.

In sum, it is apparent that there was no reason for expectations that the much publicized population explosion would lead to a major residential building boom in the present quinquennium. In total and for the key age classes, required additions have been far below the level attained in 1945-50 (or in 1950-55).

In the next two quinquenniums, population changes at the first and second life-cycle stages will account for the major portion of the additional dwelling units required. Then, in 1975-80, the second and third stages will be most important, and in the 1980's, Stages 3 and 4 will dominate the housing market. At no time in the next five quinquenniums will the last two stages attain either the absolute or the relative importance that they held in the 1950's.

The Tenure Composition of Required Additions by Age Class

The very low ownership rate at the first life-cycle stage means that the expansion at this stage through 1965-70 and the subsequent decline will be felt primarily in rental markets. Rental required additions for this age class are particularly important in the present quinquennium, accounting for almost one-fourth of all additional dwellings required by population changes. They will increase still further in the next five years — but will be relatively less important — and then fall sharply through 1980-85 (see Table 28). With the decline following immediately after the all-time peak is reached in 1965-70 and with rental units for the 15-24 age class ordinarily designed to meet the needs of nonnormal families, a strong possibility exists for overbuilding unless investors correctly foresee the falling rate of growth in rental demand in this specialized market.

At present, both sales and rental required additions for the 25-34 age class are negative. In rental markets, the high level of required additions at Stage 1 more than compensates for the negative level at Stage 2. But sales required additions for the first two stages together are presently negative, and therefore the market for low-cost, speculatively built tract housing has a weak base in present population changes.

The concentration of required additions in the rental sector and for young households will be impressive in the next five years, when Stage 2 will account for most of the increase in rental demand. Over one-third of all required additions will be rental units meeting the specific location, style, and size needs of people under 35 years of age. The increasing population at Stage 2 will also be felt in sales markets, where the 1945-50 peak will be exceeded for the 25-34 age class.

One result of these developments will be the concentration of required additions in the sub-sector of the housing market (rental units for young people) where the average value of dwelling unit occupied is at its lowest level over the housing life cycle. Thus, the expansion in required additions in 1965-70 will require a less than proportionate increase in construction outlays.

TABLE 28. FUTURE QUINQUENNIAL SALES AND RENTAL REQUIRED ADDITIONS, BY AGE CLASS[a]
(Thousands of dwelling units)

Quinquennial period	Number by age class							Change from preceding period by age class						
	15-24	25-34	35-44	45-54	55-64	65-and-up	Total	15-24	25-34	35-44	45-54	55-64	65-and-up	Total
Prior peak (date)	46[b] (45-50)	243[b] (45-50)	341 (55-60)	598 (55-60)	441 (30-35)	813 (50-55)	1,933 (50-55)	95[b] (45-50)	308[b] (45-50)	97[b] (45-50)	199 (55-60)	134 (30-35)	178 (50-55)	572[b] (45-50)
						Sales required additions								
1955-60	20	-227	341	598	384	782	1,898	60	-277	3	199	11	-31	-35
1960-65	107	-115	84	527	547	562	1,712	87	112	-257	-71	163	-220	-186
1965-70	140	503	-460	456	621	576	1,836	33	618	-544	-71	74	14	124
1970-75	80	1,084	-178	83	549	650	2,268	-60	581	282	-373	-72	74	432
1975-80	61[c]	1,014	874	-485	492	774	2,730	-19[c]	70	1,052	-568	-57	124	462
1980-85	19[c]	650	1,833	-176	88	770	3,184	-42[c]	-364	959	309	-404	-4	454
1985-90	56[c]	374[c]	1,679	953	-489	803	3,376	37[c]	-276[c]	-154	1,129	-577	33	192
Prior peak (date)	354[b] (45-50)	841[b] (45-50)	521[b] (45-50)	366 (25-30)	344 (45-50)	421 (50-55)	2,609[b] (45-50)	734[b] (45-50)	1,065[b] (45-50)	167[b] (45-50)	131 (25-30)	81 (40-45)	82 (35-40)	1,980[b] (45-50)
						Rental required additions								
1955-60	88	-295	229	310	174	334	840	202	-382	-46	58	-45	-87	-300
1960-65	514	-147	45	260	210	217	1,099	426	148	-184	-50	36	117	259
1965-70	668	645	-246	224	238	223	1,752	154	792	-291	-36	28	6	653
1970-75	382	1,392	-95	41	210	251	2,181	-286	747	151	-183	-28	28	429
1975-80	294[c]	1,301	467	-239	189	299	2,311	-88[c]	-91	562	-280	-21	48	130
1980-85	91[c]	835	978	-86	34	298	2,150	-203[c]	-466	511	153	-155	-1	-161
1985-90	269[c]	480[c]	896	469	-187	311	2,238	178	-355[c]	-82	555	-221	13	88

[a] From the 1960's on, decadal totals are simply the sum of the two quinquennial periods in the decade, since 1960 headship and 1959 tenure rates are used in calculating required additions from 1960-65 to 1985-90.
[b] Adjusted for the war backlog.
[c] Based on estimated birth rates; the "middle" series was used (see Appendix A).
Sources: Prior peaks — Chapter VIII (if before 1940-45); 1945-50 war-adjusted estimates and 1940-45 data — Appendix E; 1950-55 on — required additions from Table 27 and tenure rates for 1949, 1954, and 1959 from Appendix B.

By 1970-75, Stage 2 will dominate both rental and sales markets to an extent never before experienced for one age class. Required additions will reach an all-time peak in both tenure classes (although the increase in rental required additions will be smaller than the increase just after World War II) for the 25-34 age group. With almost half of all sales required additions (and almost two-thirds of all rental required additions) for this single age class, the ability of builders and investors to anticipate the needs of young people just starting families will be put to the test. Once again, the increase in sales demand will be highly income elastic and dependent on credit conditions. However, there will be less chance of postponement than in 1965-70 as nonnormal families or families without children become relatively less important.[74]

During the second half of the 1970's, sales and rental required additions for Stage 2 will fall slightly but remain far above any level reached prior to 1970-75. Then in the 1980's, the growth in demand for low-cost sales units and rentals catering to the needs of families with small children will fall sharply, raising the specter — especially in rental markets — of overbuilding.

During the present quinquennium and through the first half of the 1970's, sales required additions will be falling or negative at Stages 3 and 4. The same pattern will occur in the rental market, but, because most households are owners by the middle life-cycle stages, the effect will be less important. This decline will reach its lowest level in the next five years. In that quinquennium, the absolute reduction in the stock of sales units required for the 35-44 age class could provide most of the sales units required by the rise in demand at Stage 2. Thus, the increase in demand for tract housing may not be so large as the population changes at Stage 2 suggest, leaving the construction of additional sales units primarily for the late life-cycle stages.

In both of the next two quinquenniums, but especially in the immediately following one, the growth in the population base ordinarily associated with the demand for larger, family-sized sales units and with the peak increase in the average value of sales units over the housing life cycle will be weaker than ever before and far below the 1955-60 level. At the same time that the market for tract units will be expanding rapidly,

---

[74] Because of the changes in headship and tenure rates during the 1950's, both the ratio of new household formations to total household formations and the ratio of first-time owners to total owner household formations now reach their peaks at Stage 2. Thus, the side effects of the age composition of required additions (e.g., through increased demand for consumer durables) should be relatively large in 1970-75.

the market for middle- and higher-priced sales units will face many problems if population changes do determine the path of sales demand. These trends will come close to offsetting one another in the next five years, but by the first half of the 1970's the rise in sales demand for the early life-cycle stages will be far greater than the decline at the middle life-cycle stages. However, the net effect of the population changes at the early and middle life-cycle stages will be to further reduce the average value of sales required additions in 1970-75.

Then, beginning at Stage 3 in 1975-80 and including both Stages 3 and 4 by 1985-90, sales required additions for the middle life-cycle stages will increase to an all-time high. Even the rental market will be dominated by required additions for the 35-44 age class in the 1980's.

In 1975-80, the two key life-cycle stages in terms of first-time ownership — the second and third — will account for over two-thirds of sales required additions. With the expenditures associated with first-time ownership at a maximum and the average value of sales required additions increasing once again, population changes in 1975-80 should have their major impact on economic growth through increased housing demand.

By 1980-85, one of every three additional dwellings required will be a sales unit for the 35-44 age class, and the average value of sales required additions will be increasing rapidly at the same time that the growth in sales demand becomes more and more insulated from the effects of income fluctuations. However, the composition of demand will be shifting away from units tailored to the needs of the early life-cycle stages (where both sales and rental required additions will be falling sharply) to the less-standardized and larger units required at the middle life-cycle stages. It is doubtful, judging from the record, that the building industry can make the shift without also making major mistakes along the way.

Sales (but not rental) required additions for the 55-64 age class will reach a peak in the next five years and then fall off through 1985-90. At the last life-cycle stage, population changes alone will not raise either sales or rental required additions to past peak levels at any time in the next 25 years. Thus, as sales and rental required additions continue to increase in the future, the relative importance of "retirement" housing in both tenure classes will become smaller and smaller.

In sum, from a population standpoint, the 1970's and perhaps the early 1980's should see a major residential construction boom — a boom that will first involve construction of dwelling units almost entirely for people under 35 and that will have to adjust successfully from rental to sales orientation in the mid-seventies.

Future Required Additions and Household Formations
in the Postwar Period

To this point, the population pressures for additions to the housing stock in the next 25 years have been compared with the influence of population changes in the past. Until the 1950's little more than this comparison would have been necessary to evaluate the strengths and weaknesses in housing markets and to forecast what the future had in store. In the 1950's, however, housing starts and household formations far exceeded required additions, both for total and for sales required additions. Thus, to put the population changes ahead in proper perspective, required additions in the next decade must be compared with housing starts and household formations in the recent past.

Required additions in the 1960's will be 6,399,000 compared with household formations of 9,990,000 and housing starts of 14,729,000 in the 1950's. It is clear that if housing starts are limited to the same excess over household formations in the future as in the fifties and household formations are equal to required additions, then, despite the large increase in required additions from the 1950's to the 1960's, there will be a major collapse in residential construction in the present decade.

The experience so far in the 1960's does not suggest that a collapse of the magnitude indicated will occur. In fact, on a quinquennial basis it appears that housing starts will rise in 1960-65 to a level just over 70 percent of the level that would take place in the entire decade if the above supposition held. This does not rule out the possibility of a major decline in housing starts in the next five years, especially if the rise in housing starts in 1960-65 over the level estimated from required additions happens to lead to a comparable gain in vacancies. Vacancies have increased, but net withdrawals have apparently remained at the high levels reached during the 1950's, which helps to justify the continued excess of housing starts over household formations. More important in the present context, household formations have once again exceeded required additions in the early 1960's. Thus, headship rates have continued to increase.

For this reason, it is necessary to make some adjustment for the increase in headship rates during the present quinquennium before comparing the effect of population changes in the future with the total change in households in the recent past. In the absence of detailed information on households by age class in 1964, the simplest procedure is to assume that headship rates increased — by age class — in 1960-65 as they did in the second half of the 1950's. Since the excess of household formations over required additions was somewhat smaller in the first four years of the 1960's than it would have been if headship rates actually had increased at the 1955-60 pace, this assumption contributes a slight upward bias to the adjusted estimates of required additions presented in Table 29.[75]

To give some indication of what the resulting series of quinquennial and decadal household formations might mean for housing starts in the future relative to the postwar period, estimates of housing starts based on the assumption that the excess of housing starts over household formations in 1955-60 will be repeated in each future five-year period are also presented in Table 29.

Even though the excess of housing starts over household formations in 1960-65 was greater than that in 1955-60, treating the difference between starts and household formations in 1955-60 as normal is clearly an optimistic assumption. The revised series for housing starts suggests that, at least from 1945 on, the old BLS series badly undercounted actual housing starts. Thus, long-run comparisons must be made with care. However, a large part of the undercount probably resulted from factors indigenous to the postwar era (e.g., urban sprawl). If so, then the 20-year period following World War II stands out as by far the longest in which housing starts exceeded household formations. In fact, for the decades in which both household formation and housing starts data are available, housing starts were greater than household formations only twice before: in the 1890's and 1920's.[76]

It is just possible that it has become normal for housing starts to exceed household formations — perhaps because of increased geographic mobility or increased withdrawals (resulting from "face-lifting" in our major metropolitan areas or from industrial expansion) or because of the reduced relative importance of net conversions resulting from higher real incomes — but it is optimistic to assume so in view of the past record. If such an excess has become normal (which amounts to assuming that "good times" have become normal so that geographic mobility will remain high and conversions low), then it would seem that of the last four quinquennia the 1955-60 period would be closest to the norm. In both

---

[75] From March, 1960, to March, 1964, the number of households increased by 3,386,000 (U.S. Bureau of the Census, *Current Population Reports*, Series P-20, No. 130) or at an annual rate of 846,500. Assuming the same annual rate for 1965, household formations would be 4,232,000 in 1960-65, which is comparable to the 4,830,000 households that would be formed in the same period if headship rates increased at the 1955-60 pace by age class and to required additions of 2,811,000 for this period.

[76] With data for periods prior to the 1940's, it is possible to compare only the old series nonfarm starts with nonfarm household formations (see Chapter IV, Table 2, p. 65).

TABLE 29. FUTURE HOUSEHOLD FORMATIONS AND HOUSING STARTS, IN
TOTAL AND BY TENURE CLASS, COMPARED WITH THE 1940-45 TO 1960-65
PERIODS, ASSUMING NO CHANGES IN HEADSHIP RATES AFTER 1965
(Thousands of dwelling units)

Period	Housing starts[a] (1)	House-hold for-mations (2)	One-family housing starts[a] (3)	Owner household for-mations (4)	Multi-family housing starts[a] (5)	Renter household for-mations (6)
1940-50	8,713	7,971	7,029	8,364	1,176	−393
1950-60	14,729	9,990	12,282	9,399	2,447	591
1960-70	12,558	8,718	7,572	4,690	4,986	4,028
1970-80	13,750	9,910	8,016	5,134	5,734	4,776
1980-90	15,153	11,313	9,626	6,744	5,527	4,569
1940-45	2,633	2,103	1,975	1,328	658	775
1945-50	6,258	5,868	5,194	7,036	1,064	−1,168
1950-55	7,783	4,964	6,600	5,158	1,183	−194
1955-60	6,946	5,026	5,682	4,241	1,264	785
1960-65	7,465	4,830	4,936	2,724	2,529	2,106
1965-70	5,808	3,888	3,407	1,966	2,401	1,922
1970-75	6,700	4,780	3,856	2,415	2,844	2,365
1975-80	7,051	5,130	4,160	2,719	2,890	2,411
1980-85	7,439	5,519	4,716	3,275	2,723	2,244
1985-90	7,714	5,794	4,910	3,469	2,804	2,325

[a] For the nonfarm area only until the 1960's and national data thereafter.

Sources: Col. 1 — 1945-50 to 1955-60 from Bureau of the Census new series housing starts (U.S. Department of Commerce, *Construction Review*, July 1964); 1940-45 old series housing starts (see Table 2, p. 65) blown up by the ratio of the new to the old series in 1945-50; 1960-65 estimated from the second half of 1960 plus 1961 to 1964 and a projection of housing starts (about equal to the first half of 1964) for the first half of 1965; 1965-70 on, see text pp. 162-5; 1960's housing starts are the sum of 1965-70 housing starts as given in Col. 1 plus 1960-65 housing starts estimated in the same manner as 1965-70 housing starts.

Col. 3 and Col. 5 — 1940-45 to 1955-60, new series total starts allocated between tenure classes on the basis of the ratio of one-family to total starts for the old series estimates by quinquennial period (see Council of Economic Advisors, *Economic Report of the President, 1964*) — this procedure probably underestimates one-family starts since the difference between the new and old series is entirely due to undercounting conventionally financed starts; 1960-65, estimated in the same manner as total starts (see Col. 1); 1965-70 — see text, pp. 162-5; 1960-70 — Col. 1.

Col. 2, Col. 4, and Col. 6 — based on Census counts of households by age class in 1940, 1950, and 1960 (see Appendix B). The Census count in 1950 by age class (based on a 20 percent sample) was adjusted up to the total returns count in 1950 (see Table 31 for procedure). Households by age class in 1945 estimated by multiplying 1940 headship rates times the 1945 population adjusted for mobilization (see Appendix E). Households by age class in 1955 from U.S. Bureau of the Census, *Current Population Reports, Series P-20, No. 67*). Households in 1965 estimated from projections of total population by age class in 1965 multiplied by 1965 headship rates. Latter estimated by adding the change by age class in headship rates from 1955-60 to the 1960 headship rates (see Appendix B). Households by age class from 1970 on based on 1965 headship rates and Census population projections (see Appendix A). Household formations are then the difference between households at five- or ten-year intervals. Owner and renter households were estimated by taking households by age class in 1940 and 1945 times the tenure rates in 1940, households by age class in 1950 times the tenure rates in 1949, households by age class in 1955 times the tenure rates in 1954, households by age class in 1960 and thereafter times the tenure rates in 1959. These procedures mean the entire change in tenure rates in the 1940's is assigned to the second half and that tenure rates are assumed to remain constant in the present quinquennium. Again, owner and renter household formations are differences between the estimates of owner and renter households for five- and ten-year periods.

the 1945-50 and 1950-55 periods, the backlog resulting from the war kept vacancy rates abnormally low as new construction replaced the makeshift arrangements used to meet the housing requirements of the returning veterans and others brought into the housing market by the postwar boom. This backlog was largely worked off by 1955-60 and vacancy rates rose relative to those of the first half of the 1950's as housing starts continued to exceed household formations. Since 1960 vacancy rates have risen still further (especially in the sales sector) and of late the increase has been most rapid where the population has been growing the most. This suggests that the excess of housing starts over household formations in the present quinquennium is above normal.[77]

Finding a suitable basis for relating one-family and multi-family housing starts to owner and renter household formations is even more difficult (witness the experience during the 1930's) than relating total starts to household formations. Recent developments have made ownership of units in large multi-unit structures common in many metropolitan areas, thus increasing the problem. Because of the difficulty, but in order that some indication of the possible influence of population changes on one-family and multi-family housing starts could be given, estimates of housing starts are presented, based on the simple assumption that the excesses in 1955-60 of one-family and multi-family starts over owner and renter household formations, respectively, will be achieved in each future quinquennium.

Obviously, the estimates of housing starts given in Table 29 and subsequent tables — particularly, the breakdown between single- and multi-family starts — must not be taken too seriously. They are based on a relatively optimistic assumption about the relationship between housing starts and household formations and thus contain an upward bias. Whether or not they will prove too low or too high will depend on whether or not the estimates of household formations presented also prove too low or too high. In fact, the chance of the estimates of housing starts presented being too low seems almost entirely dependent on what happens to household formations.

---

[77] For vacancy-rate data see, U.S. Department of Commerce, *Construction Review*, Vol. 11, No. 1 (January, 1965), and earlier issues. Vacant units for rent or sale were about 1.6 percent of the housing stock in 1950. This proportion had increased to 2.3 percent by 1955 and averaged about 3 percent for 1955-60. In the last four years it has averaged about 4 percent. More important is the fact that vacancy rates have increased most rapidly in the Western region — the region where the population is growing most rapidly. This suggests overbuilding in the West in response to population growth and will tend to dampen the effect of geographic mobility on the excess of housing starts over household formations.

Turning to the comparison of the future with the recent past, it is obvious that despite the rise in headship rates in the first half of the 1960's and the very large increase in required additions expected in the 1970's, household formations and housing starts will still fall in the 1960's and will remain below the level of the 1950's in the 1970's if headship rates do not increase after 1965.[78]

Under the assumed circumstances, residential construction would fall sharply in the next five years, as both housing starts and the average value of housing starts would be falling. Household formations and housing starts would then increase in 1970-75 and 1975-80 but would not reach the 1955-60 level until 1975-80. Unless the large excess of housing starts over household formations achieved in the present quinquennium reflects more than a temporary relationship, housing starts would not reach the 1960-65 level until the last half of the 1980's.

The lesson is clear: the expected residential building boom and the expected side effects of an increasing level of household formations will not materialize on the basis of population changes alone, the usual explanation of both forecasts. Instead, headship rates will have to continue to rise in order to keep household formations, and probably housing starts, from falling abruptly in the next five years and from remaining below past peak levels in the next 20 years.

It is only proper to note that the same statement could have been made about the last three quinquenniums. Once headship rate changes become an important source of increased households, further increases in

---

[78] This does not take account of the high level of housing starts already accomplished in the 1960's (or of the possible depressing effects of the increasing level of vacancies). Adding housing starts in total and by tenure-class in 1960-65 to the estimates presented for 1965-70 yields housing starts of 13,273,000, one-family starts of 8,343,000, and multi-family starts of 4,930,000. Thus, even if the present large excess of housing starts over household formations should have no depressing effect on starts in the next five years, housing starts would still fall in the 1960's relative to the 1950's as the decline in single-family starts would more than offset the increase in multi-family starts. One possible measure of the excess production of dwelling units in 1960-65 is given by comparing actual housing starts with the level consistent with the 1955-60 excess of housing starts over household formations. On this basis, housing starts should have been 6,750,00, or 715,000 less than they were; one-family starts should have been 4,165,000, or 771,000 less than they were; and multi-family starts should have been 56,000 greater than they were. How much of this excess has led to unwanted vacancies is impossible to determine, but unless net withdrawals have increased substantially or the excess is located in areas where the population is declining, such as rural areas (data for the Western region would suggest the opposite), the supposition must be that the residential construction "cobweb" has been at work and present overbuilding will substitute to some extent for future new construction.

headship rates may become necessary — even when required additions are increasing rapidly, as they will in the next two quinquenniums — to prevent a large decrease in household formations and consequently in housing starts. However, in both halves of the 1950's and in 1960-65, headship rates did increase sufficiently to prevent a major drop in household formations and housing starts.

Of course, in 1950-55, it was the increase in housing starts relative to household formations that prevented a decline in the former, since despite the increase in headship rates, household formations did fall. It is apparent that only a similiar increase in this ratio prevented a decline in housing starts in the first half of the 1960's, as once again the increase in headship rates did not prevent a drop in household formations. However, the fact that housing starts increased despite lower household formations in the present quinquennium is not much cause for optimism, especially considering the associated increase in vacancy rates.

Making a similar comparison for sales and rental markets, it is clear that without further changes in headship or tenure rates, owner household formations and presumably one-family construction would suffer the most, falling to the lowest level since the 1930's in the present decade, recovering only slightly in the 1970's, and remaining far below past peak levels in the 1980's. Since one-family starts in the present quinquennium are almost 60 percent of the level shown for the decade, it is unlikely that there will be a collapse of the magnitude suggested in Chart 19. However, even assuming that headship rates do increase in 1960-65 as much as they did in 1955-60, owner household formations would fall in the present quinquennium and then, in the absence of further changes in headship rates, would decrease further to less than one-half the level reached in 1955-60 in the next five years. Population changes alone will not bring sales starts up to the 1955-60 level in the next five quinquenniums. In this context, it is significant that one-family starts did fall in the present quinquennium relative to 1955-60, although the decline was far smaller than indicated by the decline in owner-occupied household formations.

On the other hand, without further changes in headship or tenure rates, rental household formations (and multi-family housing starts) would still increase by the largest amount ever in the 1960's and then increase again to an all-time high in the 1970's. However, if headship rates do advance as suggested in 1960-65, then further headship-rate changes will be necessary to prevent a decline in rental household formations in the next five years. But, no additional changes would be neces-

CHART 19. One-family and Multi-family Housing
Starts Through 1990[a]

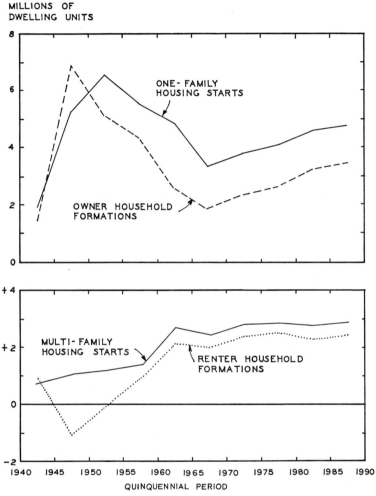

MILLIONS OF
DWELLING UNITS

ONE- FAMILY
HOUSING STARTS

OWNER HOUSEHOLD
FORMATIONS

MULTI- FAMILY
HOUSING STARTS

RENTER HOUSEHOLD
FORMATIONS

1940 1945 1950 1955 1960 1965 1970 1975 1980 1985 1990
QUINQUENNIAL PERIOD

[a] Assuming no changes in headship rates after 1965.
Source: Table 29, p. 163.

sary to bring the increase in rental demand to a new all-time high in
1970-75.[79]

[79] These conclusions about household formations and housing starts by tenure-
class depend on the assumed constancy of tenure rates after 1959. In 1954-59,
the only significant increases in ownership rates were for the 35-44 and 55-64 age
classes (see Appendix B). Thus, owner-occupancy rates have not been increasing
in the age-classes in which most of the population growth will occur. Further,

Whether or not a rental boom will develop in the next five years will depend on the inroads made into rental markets by the apparent over-production of sales units in the present quinquennium at starting tenure (but not headship) rates. It seems likely that in large part the excess supply of sales units was either offered on the rental market or offered for sale on terms which led to a further increase in owner-occupancy rates. In either event, the end result would be increased competition (and vacancies) for multi-unit rentals.

Increasing Headship Rates and Housing Demand in the Next Decade

The somewhat pessimistic conclusions to this point depend on the assumption that headship rates will not continue to rise, at least after 1965. But what if they do? Specifically, what if headship rates increase in each of the next two quinquennia at the 1955-60 pace? The changes in household formations and housing starts that would result are given in Table 30. After falling in the present quinquennium, household formation would rise in 1965-70 to the highest level ever and by an even larger amount in 1970-75. However, it is worth noting that the total increase in household formations over the decade beginning in 1965 and ending in 1975 would still be less than that in the single quinquennium following World War II.

Converting the projected changes in the number of households into housing starts (using the same assumptions as before) shows that housing starts would increase in 1965-70 if headship rates should rise as assumed. However, the increase would be only slightly larger than that in the present quinquennium and only about 20 percent of the peak increase in 1945-50. This suggests, contrary to much present opinion, that residential construction will offer no more stimulus to economic expansion in the last

---

much of the increase in the late fifties for the 35-44 age class can be explained as a lagged response to increased ownership rates at earlier life-cycle stages between 1945 and 1954. With ownership rates no longer increasing at the early stages, this lagged increase at the 35-44 stage will not continue. Moreover, the lagged increase at the 35-44 stage does not imply a similar, subsequent increase at the later stages, since a substantial majority of households have always been owners at those stages. Some effect beyond the mere pushing forward in time of first-time ownership may be felt, but the lagged effect of past increases in ownership rates will be greatly reduced from the fourth life-cycle stage on. Further increases in ownership rates at the late life-cycle stages must come primarily because of continued lowering of mortality rates or because of larger and more certain retirement incomes. For these reasons, the assumption of stable tenure rates seems credible. If anything, the attempts to revitalize the central areas of our major metropolitan complexes and to reverse the trend of migration to the suburbs may decrease owner-occupancy rates (or at least the relative demand for single-family dwellings) in the future.

TABLE 30. HOUSEHOLD FORMATIONS AND HOUSING STARTS IN THE NEXT
TWO QUINQUENNIAL PERIODS, IN TOTAL AND BY TENURE CLASS,
WITH HEADSHIP RATES INCREASING AT THE 1955-60 PACE
(Thousands of dwelling units)

Quinquennial period	Housing starts (1)	House-hold for-mations (2)	One-family housing starts (3)	Owner household for-mations (4)	Multi-family housing starts (5)	Renter household for-mations (6)
1950-55	7,783	4,964	6,600	5,158	1,183	−194
1955-60	6,946	5,026	5,682	4,241	1,264	785
1960-65	7,465	4,830	4,936	2,724	2,529	2,106
1965-70	8,172	6,252	4,581	3,140	3,591	3,112
1970-75	9,725	7,805	5,322	3,881	4,403	3,924

Sources: See Table 29 for the sources of the 1950-55 to 1960-65 data. The procedures used to estimate future housing starts are discussed in the text, pp. 162-5. Cols. 2, 4, and 6 from 1965-70 on — based on headship rates derived by adding the 1955-60 change in headship rates by age class to the 1965 headship rates (see Table 29). Cols. 4 and 6 from 1965-70 on — based on 1959 tenure rates applied to the household formations by age class summed in Col. 2.

half of the 1960's than in the first.[80] Moreover, this degree of optimism depends on the twin assumptions that headship rate will continue to rise and that the present high level of vacancies will not depress housing starts in the future.

However, with continued increments in headship rates, the level of housing starts would reach an all-time peak in 1970-75 (25 percent above any prior level and 30 percent greater than at present), and the gain in housing starts would be second only to the 1945-50 change. Thus, continued headship-rate increases should lead (along with the underlying population changes) to a sustained boom in residential construction by the first half of the 1970's, but one in which, because of the contemporary changes in age composition, the real expenditure per dwelling unit started will be falling and the increase in housing starts will be far smaller relative to GNP than in either 1945-50 or 1950-55. Moreover, it should be emphasized that if headship rates rise through the 1960's but then stop

[80] Quinquennial estimates cannot be used to pin-point annual turning points, but the annual projections of the population by age-class presented by the Bureau of the Census (Current Population Reports, Series P-25, No. 286) suggest that the large expansion in household formations at the early life-cycle stages which is behind the 1970-75 record increase will begin about 1968 with another major step-up in 1972. These annual population projections also suggest that very little additional stimulus to residential construction will come from household formations between 1964 and 1967.

advancing, despite the largest decadal or quinquennial growth in the age-standardized population base ever, household formations will fall.[81]

Translating these relationships into household formations by tenure class (assuming tenure rates unchanged) and into one-family and multi-family starts yields some surprising results. Owner-occupied household formations would expand again in 1970-75. But, the number of additional sales units required in the next two quinquenniums would remain far below the level reached in either half of the 1950's or in 1945-50, and the increase in 1970-75 would be about one-eighth of that after World War II. In fact, if the 1955-60 excess of one-family starts over owner-occupied household formations is taken as the norm, then one-family starts would be expected to fall in the next five years and to remain below the level reached in both halves of the 1950's and in 1960-65 through the first half of the 1970's.

Compared with recent rates of production, it looks as if relatively poor times are ahead for sales markets, even if headship rates increase. The boom in the construction of sales units and the rise in owner-occupancy were truly exceptional following World War II, and short of another large increase in ownership rates, this boom is not likely to be matched for some time to come.

For sales construction to expand in the next quinquennium, either the huge excess of sales starts over the change in the owner-occupied housing stock in the present half-decade must be maintained or tenure rates must shift significantly toward ownership. The first condition seems unlikely, since (1) the 1960-65 ratio of one-family starts to sales household formations is far above any in the past and (2) one-family starts fell in 1964 to their lowest level since 1958, at the same time that the rate of economic growth was greater than in any year since 1959. For ownership rates to rise at the early life-cycle stages (the key stages in this sense, because they contain most of the forthcoming population growth and have the lowest present ownership rates), at least the following conditions will have to be met: low unemployment rates — lower than at present — for young people, increasing per capita real income for young people, and no rise in long-term interest rates (a proxy for mortgage terms). Of course, if ownership rates do change to expand sales demand, then rental markets will suffer.

---

[81] Even the more optimistic assumption that headship rates will increase at the 1950-60 pace instead of as they did in 1955-60 would leave the increase in housing starts in the 1960's below that of the last two decades and the increase in 1965-70 below either the 1950-55 or 1945-50 increases. However, with this sequence of headship rate changes, housing starts in 1970-75 would be almost one-third greater than in the present quinquennium.

Turning to rental markets and assuming that tenure rates do not change but headship rates do, the number of additional households renting their dwellings would increase in 1965-70 and then again in 1970-75. By 1970-75, the number of additional rental units needed would be double the present peak rate, and the change in renter-occupancy would exceed the change in owner-occupancy for the first time since the 1920's.

Estimating multi-family starts in the manner described yields a level in the next five years that would be 42 percent higher than in the present quinquennium and far above any previous level. Then, in 1970-75 the number of multi-family starts would be larger than total starts in any quinquennium prior to 1945-50 (running at an annual rate of almost 900,000 units) and 75 percent above the present high rate.

Thus, if headship rates continue to increase, it seems clear that a rental construction boom of unparalleled proportions will occur by 1970-75. What happens in the next five years will be influenced by the present, relatively high level of vacancies in multi-family units. If it is assumed that the current excess of housing starts over the level justified by the 1955-60 ratio of housing starts to household formations will compete with multi-family rental units in the future, then the increase in multi-family starts in 1965-70 would be very small. But, with the vacancy problem thus accounted for, the increase in rental starts in 1970-75 would be even larger and far greater than in any past period.

The only other factors that could dampen the forthcoming rental boom are, first, the high income elasticity of nonnormal household formations (accounting for most of the rental household formations at Stage 1) if unemployment increases and, second, the possibility of credit policy shifting a major portion of the rise in demand for rental units to sales markets — an important possibility only because of the age composition of rental household formations in 1965-70 and 1970-75.

Apparently the prospects for residential construction in the next five to ten years depend on what happens to headship rates over this period. Apart from relatively minor demographic factors (e.g., the male/female ratio by age class), headship rates may be expected to vary primarily with tastes and such economic factors as unemployment rates and per capita real incomes within age classes. In the absence of some widely felt social experience, such as another world war, tastes can be expected to change slowly. This leaves the economic factors as the major determinants of short-run variations in headship rates.

For headship rates to remain at present levels, it will be necessary to achieve rates of growth rapid enough to absorb an accelerating increment in the number of job-seekers — especially at the first two life-cycle stages.

Simply to hold the line on headship rates will require more rapid economic growth that we have attained in the last 10 years. But more than this will be required to raise headship rates. To that end, unemployment rates must be reduced (at present real wage rates) and real incomes must rise for those already employed, again with primary emphasis on the early life-cycle stages. Even if unemployment rates are reduced and real incomes are increased, there is no guarantee that headship rates will continue to rise. At some point, demographic limits will intervene to slow down or halt the increase in headship rates. For example, in an age class evenly divided between males and females, if all were married to a member of the same age class, the maximum headship rate would be 50 percent. In this context, it is interesting to look at headship rates in selected age classes in the year 2000, assuming that headship rates continue to rise at the 1955-60 pace. This rate of increase would imply a headship rate of 41 percent (up from 22 percent), in the 20-24 age class, of 72 percent (up from 42 percent) in the 25-34 age class, of 67 percent (up from 53 percent) in the 45-54 age class, and of 72 percent (up from 58 percent, the 1960 peak rate) in the 65-74 age class. Unless there is a major change in marriage patterns or unmarried people all learn to "live alone and like it," these headship rates do not seem very likely. Sometime before the start of the next century, headship rates — at least in the above age classes — will probably stop increasing, and when they do there will be trouble in housing markets.

One other possibility deserves brief mention. Past headship-rate changes may have a lagged effect on headship rates at the middle and late life-cycle stages even if real incomes do not rise. The experienced increases in headship rates at the early life-cycle stages may have brought some people into the housing market as household heads who would never have entered at any life-cycle stage under pre–World War II conditions. If so, then the effects of headship rates changes in the 1950's will have been greater than simply pushing forward in time household formations that would have taken place at a later date anyway, and headship rates will continue to increase at the middle and late life-cycle stages for some time to come. The increments would be small but they would add to housing demand.

Headship Rate Changes and the Age Composition of Household Formations

Assuming that headship rates rise by age class in the present quinquennium as they did in 1955-60, the decline in household formations in the first half of the 1960's would be concentrated (see Table 31) at the

TABLE 31. AGE COMPOSITION OF TOTAL, OWNER, AND RENTER
HOUSEHOLD FORMATIONS IN THE NEXT TWO QUINQUENNIAL
PERIODS COMPARED WITH THE RECENT PAST, ASSUMING
NO CHANGES IN HEADSHIP RATES AFTER 1965
(Thousands of dwelling units)

Quinquennial period	Age class						Total
	15-24	25-34	35-44	45-54	55-64	65- and-up	
Total household formations							
1945-50.........	1,094	2,057	951	203	752	811	5,868
1950-55.........	94	515	1,286	934	694	1,441	4,964
1955-60.........	538	400	663	1,204	828	1,392	5,026
1960-65.........	964	579	88	1,160	848	1,191	4,830
1965-70.........	895	1,272	−708	703	868	859	3,888
1970-75.........	509	2,706	−260	116	763	946	4,780
Owner household formations							
1945-50.........	417	1,684	2,116	1,211	932	676	7,036
1950-55.........	−128	858	1,225	1,012	910	1,281	5,158
1955-60.........	65	203	1,025	912	875	1,161	4,251
1960-65.........	166	253	57	777	613	858	2,724
1965-70.........	154	557	−461	471	626	619	1,966
1970-75.........	88	1,185	−170	78	552	682	2,415
Renter household formations							
1945-50.........	677	373	−1,165	−1,008	−180	135	−1,168
1950-55.........	222	−343	61	−78	−216	160	−194
1955-60.........	473	197	−362	292	−47	231	784
1960-65.........	798	326	31	383	235	333	2,106
1965-70.........	741	715	−247	232	241	240	1,922
1970-75.........	421	1,521	−90	38	211	264	2,365

Sources: See Table 29, Cols. 2, 4, and 6, for the procedures used to estimate total, owner, and renter household formations. 1950 Census data giving households by age class were based on a 20 percent sample and sum to about 575,000 less than the total returns count; the total count of the Census, in turn, was about 700,000 less than the sum of households by age class reported for the 1950's in *Current Population Report* (U.S. Bureau of the Census, Series P-20, No. 33). The 1950 Census data by age class were blown up to the census total count on the basis of the difference between the census and the *Current Population Report* estimates by age class, which, it was assumed, gives some idea of where the sample fell short. Most of this difference is accounted for by the 55-64 age class. If the *Current Population Report* data had been used in 1950, then household formations in 1945-50 would have been 6,598,000 rather than 5,868,000 and in 1950-55 they would have been 4,234,000 instead of 4,964,000. The general pattern of changes would have been the same.

third and sixth life-cycle stage. A significant increase in construction would be necessary only for the first and second stages, with most of it for the 15-24 age class. Because of the differences in ownership rates between the first two and subsequent life-cycle stages, this would mean a major drop in owner-household formations and the demand for the larger, family-sized, one-family dwellings, for middle- and higher-priced sales units, and for single-family units tailored to the needs of retired people would grow less rapidly than at any time since World War II.

Rental household formations, on the other hand, would spurt ahead of the 1955-60 total change, increasing in every age class, but with over one-half for the population under 35 years of age.

Assuming no further headship-rate changes after 1965, the difference between the performances of the early and the middle life-cycle stages would become even more striking than in 1960-65. Together, household formations at Stages 1 and 2 would double their present level, but they would fall sharply at Stages 3, 4, and 6, reaching a negative level at Stage 3. The result would be a large decline in total household formations accompanied by a drop in the average value of the dwelling units required to satisfy the remaining increase in demand. The decline would be concentrated in sales markets, especially in the construction of larger, middle-priced units intended for households with school-age children. In fact, much of the potential increase in the demand for tract housing at Stage 2 could be diverted into the units released at Stage 3 by the excess of the number of households leaving over the number entering.

Even rental household formations would fall in the next five years if headship rates should fail to rise after 1965. The large increase in rental household formations at Stage 2 would be more than offset by the decreases at all other life-cycle stages. Adding to the uncertainty would be the fact that an increase in rental demand at Stage 2 is likely to shift to ownership markets if conditions warrant. Clearly, upward changes in headship rates are necessary for expansion in either sector of the housing market in 1965-70. But, if they do not materialize, it seems probable that sales markets will suffer more than rental markets.

If such advances do take place, the increase in household formations would still occur almost entirely at Stages 1 and 2 (see Table 32). At Stage 2, household formations would be almost four times the present level and would exceed the 1945-50 peak. However, household formations at Stage 3 would remain negative (not even the 1950-60 rate of increase in headship rates would change this) and far below any past level. From Stage 4 on, household formations would about hold their own or increase slightly. Thus, expansion in residential construction, if it is to

Table 32. Age Composition of Total, Owner, and Renter
Household Formations in the Next Two Quinquennial
Periods Compared with the Recent Past,
with Headship Rates Increasing
at the 1955-60 Pace

(Thousands of dwelling units)

Quinquennial period	Age class						Total
	15-24	25-34	35-44	45-54	55-64	65-and-up	
Total household formations							
1945-50	1,094	2,057	951	203	752	811	5,868
1955-60	538	400	663	1,204	828	1,392	5,026
1960-65	964	579	88	1,160	848	1,191	4,830
1965-70	1,324	2,238	−731	1,170	960	1,291	6,252
1970-75	1,035	4,133	−282	592	869	1,458	7,805
Owner household formations							
1945-50	417	1,684	2,116	1,211	932	676	7,036
1955-60	65	203	1,025	912	875	1,161	4,241
1960-65	166	253	57	777	613	858	2,724
1965-70	229	980	−477	784	694	930	3,140
1970-75	179	1,810	−183	396	628	1,051	3,881
Renter household formations							
1945-50	677	373	−1,165	−1,008	−180	135	−1,168
1955-60	473	197	−362	292	−47	231	784
1960-65	798	326	31	383	235	333	2,106
1965-70	1,095	1,258	−254	386	266	361	3,112
1970-75	856	2,323	−99	196	241	407	3,924

Source: Table 30, p. 169.

come in the next five years, must result because the increase in household formations at the first two stages more than compensates for the decrease at Stage 3. It will do so in numbers, but with the average value of dwelling units occupied higher at Stage 3 than at Stages 1 and 2, it is not clear that the increase in household formations will be reflected in an increase in expenditures. Certainly, expenditures can be expected to increase (in real terms) less than proportionately with housing starts.

The importance of the first two life-cycle stages in the next five years is shown by the fact that if headship rates do continue to rise from Stage 3 on but not for the first two life-cycle stages, then household formations will not expand over the present quinquennium and will remain below the level of the last three quinquenniums in 1965-70. Obviously, the key to housing market prospects — so far as they are determined by household formations — will be what happens to headship rates for the population under 35 years of age. Achieving increased residential construction is thus linked directly to the problem of finding jobs for a rapidly expanding number of young people.

Turning to the tenure composition of household formations, neither the 1955-60 nor the 1950-60 rate of increase in headship rates can bring the growth in demand for sales units up to the 1955-60 level in the next five years. Sales demand could rise more rapidly than in the present quinquennium mostly because of the gain at Stage 2; but even continued positive increments in headship rates cannot raise the increase in sales demand by our senior citizens back to the level attained in either half of the 1950's. What will happen could depend largely on whether the increase at Stage 2, offset by half by the negative change in sales demand at Stage 3, would be sufficient to raise construction expenditures much above the present level.

In the rental sector, the 1965-70 growth in demand for both Stages 1 and 2 would be several times greater than the 1955-60 level and far above that for 1960-65. In addition, the gain in renter-occupancy at the last three life-cycle stages would be greater in the second than in the first half of the 1960's. However, some difficulty might arise because of the smaller increase in rental demand at Stage 1, where requirements are highly specialized and recent rates of increase may contribute to mistaken estimates of the future growth in rental demand. It is also possible that the additional vacancies arising from the huge excess of housing starts over household formations in the present quinquennium will substitute for part of the increase in rental construction required by the growth in demand at Stage 2.

In sum, if headship rates do increase, 3,562,000, or over one-half of the additional dwelling units required, would be for the very young or for households just starting families (Stages 1 and 2) and 2,353,000, or over one-third of these, would be rental units — a concentration of increased demand within two consecutive age classes unlike any ever experienced before.

Only 439,000 (slightly over 6 percent of all household formations) additional households would be formed at the middle life-cycle stages (35-54), compared with 1,867,000 (or 37 percent) in 1955-60. Thus, the increase — in both absolute and relative terms — in the demand for larger family homes and for medium- to higher-priced rentals would be very low compared with recent levels, even if the favorable assumption of continued increases in headship rates turns out to be correct.

Looking even further ahead, if no headship rate changes should occur after 1965, then household formations in 1970-75 would be far below the present quinquennium in total. However, a huge increase would still occur at Stage 2, raising household formations for this age class to a level far above the earlier peak in 1945-50. With headship rates increasing at the 1955-60 pace, more household formations than in any full decade prior to the 1940's would be squeezed into the first half of the 1970's.

At Stage 1, household formations would decline. The number at Stage 3 would continue to fall and the increase at Stage 4 would be only one-half the increase in 1965-70 and far below that of 1955-60. Thus, the market for middle- and higher-priced dwellings would tend to remain relatively depressed, even if headship rates should continue to rise. At Stage 5, household formations would drop to slightly above the 1955-60 level, and at Stage 6 they would finally increase again to about the 1950-55 level.

Nothing so far discussed suggests a boom or even an increase in household formations in 1970-75. But household formations in this quinquennium will be 25 percent greater than in 1965-70 (and 33 percent greater than the highest level experienced previously) as a result of the increase in household formations for one age class, the 25-34 age class. For the other five life-cycle stages combined, household formations will fall by 342,000 in the first half of the 1970's even with continuous headship rate changes, but household formations for Stage 2 will increase by 1,895,000 to the astounding total of 4,133,000, or over 80 percent of all household formations and more than required additions for all age classes in all quinquenniums prior to 1970-75.

A tremendous boom, primarily felt in the production of low-cost tract units and rental units with some provision for young children, would seem certain. However, household formations at Stage 2 are relatively income elastic compared with later stages, and a slowdown in economic growth or an increase in unemployment rates in the 25-34 age class could cut the ground from under the potential boom. In fact, since the boom is predicated on continued increments in headship rates at Stage 2 (without such an increase, even if headship rates should increase at the other five stages, household formations would fall abruptly in 1970-75), more rapid economic growth and lower unemployment rates than in the next five years would be required.

Despite the magnitude of the prospective 1970-75 increase in household formations at Stage 2 (and in total, for that matter), owner household formations would still be considerably below the 1955-60 level and less than one-half the 1945-50 level. For Stages 3 to 5, only 1,301,000 additional sales units would be required, compared with 4,259,000 in 1945-50; 2,812,000 in 1950-55; or even 1,938,000 in the present half-decade. Thus, more than continued changes in headship rates will be necessary to revitalize sales markets and bring the increase in owner-occupancy up to recent peak levels. Except for the tract component of sales production in 1970-75, there will not be a sales market comparable with the one following World War II in the next two quinquennial periods without further increases in owner-occupancy rates.

This means that the expansion in household formations beyond past peak levels would be concentrated in the rental sector of the housing market and, within that sector, in rental units meeting the specialized needs of young married couples, often with young children, and of a relatively large number of nonnormal families.

Some Major Conclusions

(1) Further increases in headship rates are necessary if household formations are to rise rather than fall in the next five years. Continued increases at the 1955-60 rates (after a 1965-70 increase at the same pace) would raise household formations above past peak levels in 1970-75. The resulting increase over the preceding quinquennial period would be the second largest ever, exceeded only by the 1945-50 increment.

(2) The predicted acceleration in the growth of demand for housing by people under 35 years of age does not depend on increased headship rates. Without any further changes in headship rates, household formations for the 15-34 age class will reach an all-time high in 1970-75. However, the equally well-publicized increase in our older population will not raise household formations for people over 55 above past peak levels unless headship rates do continue to rise.

(3) If headship rates increase from life-cycle Stage 3 on, but not at the first two stages, then household formations will still fall in 1965-70. If, after increasing in 1965-70, headship rates continue to rise in 1970-75 at all but the second life-cycle stage, then household formations will decrease sharply in the first half of the 1970's.

(4) Point three suggests that the prospects for household formations and presumably for residential construction in the next two quinquennial periods will depend on what happens to headship rates at the first two life-cycle stages.

(5) Thus, the prospects for increased household formations and housing starts over the next 10 years depend on what happens to employ-

ment opportunities and the real incomes of young people. To raise headship rates, unemployment rates would have to be reduced and real incomes increased or stabilized at present levels.

(6) Because of the declining proportion of household formations accounted for by the middle life-cycle stages at which the average value of dwelling unit required is highest, the average value of the dwellings required will be falling in both of the next two quinquennial periods, regardless of what happens to the number of households formed. Thus, if housing starts increase in the next five years or in 1970-75, it is very likely that residential construction expenditures will increase less than proportionately, and this will be especially true of one-family construction.

(7) A sales boom in 1965-70 is almost out of the question. The recent trend in ownership rates (no increases in 1955-60 at the first two life-cycle stages) and the population mix as it will be in the next five years suggest that an increase in ownership rates will not occur in the age classes where it must for a sales boom to materialize. Even with headship rates increasing, the demand for sales units (except for tract housing) will not rise so rapidly in 1970-75 as in either half of the 1950's or in 1945-50.

(8) Continued increases in headship rates could lead in 1965-70 to a boom in the construction of rental units specialized to the needs of households headed by people under the age of 35 and then in the first half of the 1970's to a tract-housing boom for the same age group. In both of the next two quinquennial periods, the market for other types and price ranges of dwelling units would expand by much less than in the recent past. However, the large increase in household formations at Stage 2 in 1965-70 and the extreme concentration of household formations at this stage in 1970-75 indicate that a relatively large and growing number of new households and first-time owners (and consequently a relatively sizable rise in associated expenditures) will accompany the population changes in the next two quinquennial periods.

(9) At least within the next five years, when the emphasis will be on large-scale rental projects, the resources freed from other sectors of the housing market may be unneeded in the expanding sector. In any event, the increase in housing starts in both of the coming quinquennial periods will not match the effect on the economy (either relatively or absolutely) of the increase that immediately followed World War II. For the same reason, it is unlikely that construction costs or property values will rise as rapidly in the future as they did in the first decade following World War II.

APPENDIX A

Sources of Basic Population Data

With one exception, from 1850 to 1960 estimates of the national required housing stock presented in this study were based on continental population (excluding the armed forces overseas) data by age class on July 1 of each year. The one exception was in 1945 when civilian population data by age class were used (see Appendix E). In 1850 and 1860, these data were available for the 15-19, 20-29, 30-39, 40-49, 50-59, and 60-and-up age classes. In 1870, 1880, and 1890, they were available by five-year intervals from the 15-19 age class to the 60-64 age class and for the 65-and-up age class. From 1900 on, continental population data were available by five-year intervals from the 15-19 age class at least through the 70-74 age class.

From 1940 through 1990, estimates of the required housing stock based on the total population (including the armed forces overseas) by age class were presented. From 1940 to 1960 these estimates excluded Hawaii and Alaska, and from 1965 on they included Hawaii and Alaska; 1960 data including Hawaii and Alaska were also presented. The total population data were available for five-year age intervals from the 15-19 age class at least through the 70-74 age class.

All of the population data used were published by the United States Bureau of the Census. The sources by year follow:

	Years	
Sources	Continental population	Total population
1. *Historical Statistics of the United States, 1789–1941*, Table B81-144, p. 28.	1850,1860,1870, 1880,1890	
2. *Current Population Reports*, Series P-25, No. 114.	1900,1905,1910, 1915,1920,1925, 1930,1935,1940	1940
3. *Current Population Reports*, Series P-25, No. 265.	1950,1955,1960[1]	1950,1955,1960[1]
4. *Current Population Reports*, Series P-25, No. 286.		1960,1965,1970 1975,1980,1985, 1990

[1] The 1960 total and continental population data to July 1 were adjusted to exclude Hawaii and Alaska by subtracting census-date (April 1) estimates of the population by age class in these states (U.S. Bureau of the Census, *U.S. Census of Population, 1960* [Washington: U.S. Government Printing Office, 1964], Vol. 1, *Characteristics of the Population,* Pt. 3, Table 96 and Pt. 13, Table 96) from the July 1 estimates of the total population including Hawaii and Alaska.

The population data for 1905 and 1915 were based on interpolation between census years. All other mid-decade data were based on a combination of the age-cohort method of estimating population changes by age class and on census data (see the sources listed above for a detailed discussion). The result is that the decadal estimates of required additions (based on census data adjusted to July 1) are somewhat more reliable — at least through the 1950's — than the quinquennial estimates, and that small differences in required additions (particularly for specific age classes) cannot be given much weight.

APPENDIX B

Headship and Tenure-Rate Data

Headship Rates

Except for the 1890 headship-rate data, which is the work of Ned Shilling, all the headship rates used in estimating required additions in this study were derived from estimates of the number of household heads in different age classes prepared by the United States Bureau of the Census.

In 1930, data were available only for the number of male household heads by age class. To include the number of female heads by age class (about 13 percent of all household heads in 1930), the percentage distribution of female heads in 1940 between age classes was first calculated and then used to distribute the total number of female heads in 1930 among age classes. The number of female heads by age class so derived was then added to the number of male heads to obtain the total number of household heads by age class.

In 1940, 1950, and 1960, total household heads by age class as reported in the decennial censuses of those years were used in calculating headship rates. In 1955, the estimate of headship rates was based on the number of household heads by age class reported in the current population survey of that year.

The population data used in computing the total population headship rates in 1940, 1950, and 1955 and the continental population headship rate in 1955 were the same as those used in estimating the required housing stock for the same years. This means that March or April 1 estimates of households by age class were divided by July 1 estimates of the population by age class to compute the headship rates for the population totals in 1940, 1950, and 1955. As a result, the estimates of headship rates in these years will be slightly too high in the age classes in which the population was falling and slightly too low in the other age classes. However, a comparison of headship rates in 1960 based on the same dates and on the previously mentioned differences in dates suggests that the error introduced by comparing March 1 households with July 1 population totals is very small.

In 1930, 1940, 1950, and 1960 the continental population headship rates were based on household heads and the population by age class at census dates, as were the total population headship rates (including and excluding Hawaii and Alaska) in 1960.

Another problem was introduced by the fact that headship rates could not be calculated for the same age intervals at all dates. When comparing two periods using headship rates for different age intervals, an error may result if the larger interval includes smaller intervals for which the headship rates differ by a substantial amount.[1] Comparison of two periods using the headship rate based on the larger interval in both may also lead to an error under these circumstances. In both cases, the extent of the error will depend on the extent of the variation in headship rates among the smaller intervals and on the extent of the variation in the distribution of the housing population among the smaller intervals. Only in using the 1930 headship rate for the 25-34 age class would one expect to find a relatively large error of this sort.[2]

The headship rates used in making the estimates of required additions and the changes in headship rates from one date to the next are given in Table B1.

As would be expected, the headship rates for 1960 based on the current population survey (in March) estimates of households and the July 1 total population estimates are lower than the headship rates for the same year based on data at the census date for the several age classes. The difference between the two sets of headship rate estimates also arises from the differences in age intervals from the 35-39 age class on and from differences in survey or sample methods (especially in the degree of training of personnel — on this score, the current population survey is superior).[3] For purposes of comparing the changes in headship rates between

---

[1] Of course, any age interval may lead to some error of this sort. However, as was noted in the text, this error can only be substantial when the differences in headship rates within the age intervals are substantial, and, even then, the error will only be substantial if the relative size of the population weights for the different headship rates shifts widely over time.

[2] Using the 1940 headship rates for the 25-29 and 30-34 age classes rather than the 1930 headship rate for the 25-34 age class lowers required additions for the 25-34 age class in 1930-35 and raises required additions for this age class in 1935-40, but the extent of each of the changes is so small that is can be assumed that more detailed information on headship rates in 1930 would not change the estimates in any significant manner.

[3] For the same reason, the 1950-55, 1955-60, and 1950-60 data showing changes in headship rates for the continental population and the 1950-60 total population headship rate changes based on census data contain an undetermined bias. The 1950 and 1960 estimates are based on the census enumeration of households and population by age class, whereas the 1955 estimates are based on the *Current Population Survey* of that year. Since households as reported in the 1950

halves of the 1950's or for projecting changes in headship rates, the current population survey data must be used.

Tenure Rates

Estimates of the age-tenure distribution of households with male heads from the 1930 and 1940 censuses were used to calculate the 1930 and 1940 tenure rates. The use of tenure rates based on male heads alone might be expected to overstate the number of owner-occupied units required at the early life-cycle stages and to under-state the number required at the late life-cycle stages. However, the estimates of the owner-occupied housing stock in 1930 and 1940 based on the tenure rates used are practically identical to the number of owner-occupied units reported in the 1940 census for these years.

After 1940, estimates of the percentages of spending units that own and rent were used to calculate tenure rates for 1949, 1954, and 1959. Unlike the 1930 and 1940 tenure rates, which were based on continental population totals, these tenure rates were based on data collected for the nonfarm sector only.

All the tenure rate data were available only for 10-year intervals, and intervals of this size may cover up rather wide shifts in the proportions of owner-occupied units required at Stages 2 and 3 of the housing life cycle. Again, the extent of the resulting error will depend on the extent of the changes in the distribution of the population between the smaller intervals within the 10-year intervals.[4] The tenure rates used are presented in Table B2.

Current Population Survey were 1,275,000 (see Table 31) more than reported in the 1950 census (by age class), it seems likely that the census data involve a substantial undercount. As a result, the changes in headship rates shown from 1950-55 and 1950-60 probably overstate the actual change (and thus the change shown from 1940-50 probably understates the actual change). To some extent this bias is offset in 1950-55 by the opposite bias introduced by relating March households to July population totals. Despite the apparent census undercount of households by age class in 1950, both to preserve continuity with earlier headship rate estimates based on census data and the 1960 census estimates and because of the finer age breakdown available in the census, the 1950 census data were used to calculate 1950 headship rates. However, as was noted in the text, for comparisons of headship rate changes within the 1950's and as a base for projections of headship rate changes, the 1950, 1955, and 1960 headship rate estimates based on the *Current Population Surveys* are most reliable.

[4] The fact that the negative change in the entering population (15-19 age class) in 1945-50 will be followed by a series of increased required additions for the entering population (beginning in 1950-55) means that the use of 10-year age intervals for tenure rates is more likely to result in errors in the next 20 years than in any past period. Never before have the population increments by age class for 5-year intervals varied so widely relative to one another.

TABLE B1. HEADSHIP RATE ESTIMATES

Part A. Continental population

Age class	Date					
	1890	1930	1940	1950	1955	1960
15-19...................	0.6%	0.7%	0.6%	1.2%	1.5%	1.8%
20-24...................	10.7	11.7	11.3	16.4	19.5	22.8
25-29...................	27.3	} 32.8	28.3	33.2	35.3	40.1
30-34...................	38.5		37.8	40.1	42.4	45.3
35-39...................	45.1	} 44.9	42.7	43.4	} 48.2	47.7
40-44...................	47.9		46.4	46.2		49.6
45-49...................	51.6	} 50.4	49.5	48.4	} 51.0	51.8
50-54...................	53.4		51.8	50.1		53.7
55-59...................	56.0	} 53.7	53.6	51.9	} 54.4	55.9
60-64...................			54.3	53.1		56.7
65-69...................	} 51.8		55.6	54.2	} 55.8	58.2
70-74...................		53.2	55.6	54.3		58.8
75-and-up...............			59.2	47.8	50.6	51.6

Change from preceding date[a]

Age class	Date					
	1930	1940	1950	1955	1960	1950-60
15-19...................	0.1%	−0.1%	0.6%	0.3%	0.3%	0.6%
20-24...................	1.0	−0.4	5.1	3.1	3.3	6.4
25-29...................	} 0.3	} 0.1	3.9	2.1	4.8	6.9
30-34...................			2.3	2.3	2.9	5.2
35-39...................	} −1.5	} −0.4	0.7	} 3.4	} 0.5	4.3
40-44...................			−0.2			3.4
45-59...................	} −2.0	} 0.2	−1.1	} 1.7	} 1.7	3.4
50-54...................			−1.7			3.6
55-59...................	} −0.3	} −0.1	−1.7	} 1.9	} 1.9	4.0
60-64...................			−1.2			3.6
65-69...................			−1.4	} 1.5	} 2.5	4.0
70-74...................	} 1.4	} 0.6	−1.3			4.5
75-and-up...............			−1.4	2.8	1.0	3.8

[a] Where applicable, changes are based on averages of smaller intervals; see footnote 3, p. 184.
Sources: 1890 — Louis Winnick, *American Housing and Its Use* (New York: Wiley, 1960), Table 31, p. 81.
1930 — Estimated (see text) from data given in U.S. Bureau of the Census, *U.S. Census of Population, 1930*, Vol. 6 (Washington: U.S. Government Printing Office, 1933), Table 35, p. 28, and *U.S. Census of Population, 1950*, Vol. 2 (Washington: U.S. Government Printing Office, 1954), Table 107, p. 1-192 ff. Population data from the U.S. Bureau of the Census, *U.S. Census of Population, 1930*, Vol. 2 (Washington: U.S. Government Printing Office, 1933), Vol. 2, Table 16, p. 587.
1940 — Households from the U.S. Bureau of the Census, *U.S. Census of Population, 1950* (Washington: U.S. Government Printing Office, 1954), Table 38, p. 1-90. Population data from the same source, Table 107, p. 1-192 ff.
1950 — Same sources as 1940.
1955 — Households from U.S. Bureau of the Census, *Current Population Reports, Series P-20*, No. 67. For population data see Appendix A, source of 1955 continental population data.
1960 — Households from U.S. Bureau of the Census, *U.S. Census of Population, 1960*, Vol. 1 (*Characteristics of the Population*, Pt. 1.), *United States Summary* (Washington: U.S. Government Printing Office, 1964), Table 181, p. 444 ff.
Population data from the same source, Table 45, p. 146.

Table B1. (Continued)

Part B. Total population

Age class	Date								
	1940[a]	1950[a]	1960[a]	1960[b]	1955[c]	1960[c]	1965[b]	1970[b]	1975[b]
15-19...	0.6%	1.2%	1.8%	1.8%	1.5%	1.6%	1.9%	2.0%	2.1%
20-24...	11.2	16.1	22.2	22.2	18.6	21.0	24.6	27.0	29.4
25-29...	28.2	32.9	39.6	39.6	34.8	39.4	44.2	48.8	53.4
30-34...	37.7	39.9	45.0	45.0	42.1	45.0	47.9	50.8	53.7
35-39...	42.7	43.4	47.5	47.5	} 47.9	47.8	48.3	48.2	48.1
40-44...	*	46.1	49.4	49.4					
45-49...		48.3	51.7	51.8	} 51.0	52.7	54.4	56.4	58.4
50-54...		*	*	53.7					
55-59...				55.9	} 54.3	54.8	56.8	57.3	57.8
60-64...				56.7					
65-69...				58.1	} 55.9	57.6	60.1	61.8	63.5
70-74...				58.8					
75-and-up...				51.6	50.6	53.9	54.9	58.2	61.5

Change from preceding date

Age class	Date							
	1950[a]	1960[a]	1960[d]	1955[c]	1960[c]	1965[d]	1970[d]	1975[d]
15-19.........	0.6%	0.6%	....	0.3%	0.1%	....	....	....
20-24.........	4.9	6.7	....	2.5	2.4	....	....	....
25-29.........	4.7	5.1	....	1.8	4.6	....	....	....
30-34.........	2.2	4.1	....	2.3	2.9	....	....	....
35-39.........	0.7	3.3	....	} 3.4	−0.1 {	....	....	....
40-44.........	−0.3	3.4	....			....	....	....
45-49.........	−1.2	*	....	} 2.0	1.7 {	....	....	....
50-54.........	*		....			....	....	....
55-59.........			....	} 2.3	0.5 {	....	....	....
60-64.........			....			....	....	....
65-69.........			....	} 1.5	1.7 {	....	....	....
70-74.........			....			....	....	....
75-and-up.....			....	3.3	3.3	....	....	....

[a] Excluding Hawaii and Alaska.
[b] Including Hawaii and Alaska.
[c] Based on current population survey households data instead of census data.
[d] Not applicable.
* Remainder the same as for the continental population.
Sources: 1940, 1950, and 1955 — data for households from the same sources as those for continental population headship rates and population data taken from the same sources as the total population data for these years given in Appendix A;
1960[a] and 1960[b] — same sources as 1960 continental population headship rates;
1960[c] — households from U.S. Bureau of the Census, *Current Population Reports*, Series P-20, No. 105, and population data from the same source as 1960[a] and 1960[b]; 1965, 1970, and 1975 — estimated by adding the 1955-60 change in Table B1, Part B, to 1960[b] headship rates for 1965, to 1965 headship rates for 1970, and to 1970 headship rates for 1975; and change to 1955[c] — based on 1950 headship rates derived from households as reported in *Current Population Reports*, Series P-20, No. 33, for 1950 and the total population in 1950 by age class (see Appendix A).

TABLE B2. TENURE RATE ESTIMATES

Age class	Tenure rate					Change from preceding period			
	1930 (1)	1940 (2)	1949 (3)	1954 (4)	1959 (5)	1940 (6)	1949 (7)	1954 (8)	1959 (9)
Owner-occupied									
15-24[a]	9.6%	11.5%	25.7%	18.6%	17.3%	1.9	12.2	-7.1	-1.3
25-34	24.8	22.4	36.3	43.5	43.8	-2.4	13.9	7.2	0.3
35-44	44.2	36.9	55.1	59.8	65.2	-7.3	18.2	4.7	5.4
45-54	55.9	48.4	61.3	65.9	67.0	-7.5	12.9	4.6	1.1
55-64	65.3	55.7	63.0	68.8	72.3	-9.6	7.3	5.8	3.5
65-and-up	72.9	63.4	65.9	70.1	72.1	-9.5	2.5	4.2	2.0
Renter-occupied									
15-24[a]	90.4%	88.5%	74.3%	81.4%	82.7%	…	…	…	…
25-34	75.2	77.6	63.7	56.5	56.2	…	…	…	…
35-44	55.8	63.1	44.9	40.2	34.8	…	…	…	…
45-54	44.1	51.6	38.7	34.1	33.0	…	…	…	…
55-64	34.7	44.3	37.0	31.2	27.7	…	…	…	…
65-and-up	27.1	36.6	34.1	29.9	27.9	…	…	…	…

[a] In 1949, 1954, and 1959 the estimates for this age class are actually for the 18-24 age class; assuming that no one under 18 owns a home and including the population between 15 and 17 years of age in the base yields an estimate of 23.7 percent for the owner-occupancy rate in 1949.

Sources: Cols. 1 and 2 — data based on the age-tenure distribution of male heads of households presented in U.S. Bureau of the Census, *U.S. Census of Population: 1940, Population and Housing, General Characteristics* (Washington: U.S. Government Printing Office, 1943), Table 12, p. 32, with percentage distribution of households among tenure classes by age class calculated from these data by dividing the number of male heads owning their homes by the total number (farm and nonfarm) of households with male heads; Cols. 3, 4, and 5 — data based on "The Survey of Consumer Finances, Housing of Non-Farm Families," *Federal Reserve Bulletin*, Vol. 45, No. 9 (September, 1959), Supplementary Table 2, p. 1107.

APPENDIX C

The Treatment of Immigration

Annual data on immigration were available only for three broad age classes for most of the period covered in the study. To make these annual data comparable with the data on population changes used to estimate required additions, they were converted to estimates of the quinquennial changes in population due to immigration, which were then allocated among the smaller age intervals used in this paper.[1]

[1] Through 1866, the annual data included a small number of immigrants not reporting their age. The "no reports" were allocated to the three age classes (less than 15, 15-40, 41 and over) for which age data were shown in this period on the basis of the ratios of the number reporting their age in each age class to the total number reporting their age.

The age classes for which immigration data were available differed over time as follows: 1850 to 1899 (less than 15, 15-40, 41 and over); 1900 to 1917 (less than 14, 14-44, 45 and over); 1918 to 1952 (less than 16, 16-44, 45 and over); and 1953 to 1960 (five-year intervals, 15-19 to 75-79). Single-year age differences were ignored. Adjusting so that the first year in the second age class was always 15 would lower required additions due to immigration slightly in 1900-1905 to 1915-20 and raise required additions due to immigration slightly from 1920-25 to 1945-50. However, given the allocation procedure used (see the text, pp. 190-3), the fact that prior to 1900 the second age class terminated at 40 rather than 44 years of age could not be ignored without distorting the allocation of immigrants to the 15-24, 25-34, 35-44, and 45-64 age classes prior to 1900. The pre-1900 data were adjusted to a 15-44 basis as follows. The ratios (see text, p. 192) used to allocate the 15-44 age class from 1900 on among the 15-19, 20-24, 25-34, and 35-44 age classes were divided by the ratio of immigrants in the 15-40 age class to immigrants in the 15-44 age class in order to convert them to proportions of the 15-40 age class. The latter ratio was estimated by taking the proportion of the 15-34 age class in the 15-44 age class (76 percent) and adding one-half the remainder (or 12 percent), which serves as an estimate of the proportion in the 35-39 age class. The 40-44 age class was then determined by taking the average for 1900-1905, 1905-10, 1910-15 of the ratio of one-half the 35-44 age class as estimated to the 45-and-up age class plus one-half the 35-44 age class and using it to determine the number of immigrants in the 40-44 age class prior to 1900. The remaining immigrants in the 40-and-up age class were then allocated to the 45-64 and 65-and-up age classes as described in the text, p. 192. After 1910-15, the ratio of the 40-44 age class to the 40-and-up age class began to fall, but to allocate the pre-1900 data it seemed best to use this ratio based on periods in which war or legis-

189

The first step involved simply summing the number of immigrants in each of the three age classes over a five-year period (e.g., for the year ending June 30, 1901, to the year ending June 30, 1905). Since some of the immigrants in the first two age classes would enter the next age class and since some of the immigrants in all age classes would die or would return to the country of their origin, the resulting estimates of the population changes due to immigration will not be the same as the true changes. However, estimates of the age composition of interstate migrants in the years since World War II suggest that the procedure outlined will not involve any major errors.[2]

The second step involved allocating the estimates of population changes due to immigration among age intervals more similar to those used in this study. There were three kinds of data available for this purpose, (1) annual data on the age composition of interstate migrants from 1947 to 1958, (2) estimates made in 1940 and 1947 of the number of persons in different age classes that had made an interstate move since 1935 and 1940 respectively, and (3) data on immigration from 1955 to date for the same five-year age intervals as those used in computing required additions.[3]

The latter data were ruled out because they reflected the constraints placed on immigration by legislation rather than the response of immigration to changes in economic conditions and tastes. However, if one assumes that the forces leading to immigration in the relatively distant past are similar to the forces leading to interstate migration and determining the age-composition of interstate migration in the United States since 1935, then either of the first two kinds of data might be used to allocate changes in the housing population due to immigration between 5- or 10-year age intervals.[4]

lation were not determining immigration. The bias would be (if the later data are more nearly correct for the pre-1900 period) a slight understatement of required additions due to immigration before 1900.

[2] The sources of data on interstate migration are, US Bureau of the Census, *Current Population Reports,* Series P-20, Nos. 22, 28, 36, 39, 47, 49, 57, 61, 73, 82, and 85.

[3] For the end-of-period data see *Current Population Reports,* Series P-20, No. 14. For the 1953-62 age distribution of immigrants see, US Department of Justice, *1962 Annual Report of the Immigration and Naturalization Service,* p. 36.

[4] This assumption is made with more confidence for the allocation of the 15-44 age class among its component parts than for the 45-and-up age class. One could derive the actual distribution of interstate migrants within the 15-44 age class on a priori considerations of the stage of life when a person's employment and family position and his willingness to accept change are most likely to make him a migrant. There is no reason why the same determinants would not apply to the immigrant population, but there is no proof that they do, and so one cannot

As might have been expected, the percentage distributions of the inter-state migrant population in the 15-44 age class among the 15-24, 25-34, and 35-44 subclasses based on the annual postwar data and on the end-of-period data were not the same. The difference was not large, but for the purpose in mind the end-of-period distribution seemed clearly superior. This percentage distribution reflects the movement of migrants out of the age class they were in at the time of migration and therefore gives a better estimate of the distribution of the migrant population between age classes at the end of a five-year period than does the distribution based on the age composition of migrants in the year they moved. Unless the actual change in the population in the 15-44 age class due to immigration differed widely from the change estimated by the sum of the number of immigrants over five years (which seems unlikely), the allocation procedure used should come close to correctly estimating the population changes due to immigration in the 15-24, 25-34, and 35-44 subclasses, always assuming that interstate migration provides a suitable base for this allocation.[5]

Because of the large difference in the proportions of the migrant population in the first and second halves of the 15-24 age class in the postwar period, and because of the equally large difference in the headship rates between the 15-19 and 20-24 age classes, the estimate of the change in the population due to immigration in the 15-24 age class was further divided between the first and second halves of this age class. This division was accomplished on the basis of the distribution of the interstate migrant population in the postwar period between the 15-19 and 20-24 age classes (adjusted to an end-of-period basis).

The estimated change in the population over 45 due to immigration was also distributed between the 45-64 and 65-and-up age classes on the

---

establish empirically that most immigrants were between 18 and 34 years of age (with the peak within this age class coming in the early 20's), even though a priori considerations suggest that this is correct, and immigration in the 1950's followed this age pattern. On the other hand, the basic reasons for interstate migration at the later life-cycle stages probably differ from the motivation for immigration at these stages. This is reflected in the larger proportion of all inter-state migrants in the 45-and-up age class than of all immigrants in this age class in the 1950's.

[5] An independent check of the allocation procedure used is provided by actual changes in population increments by age class as immigration moves up or down in total. The population changes at the first two life-cycle stages clearly move with immigration. The change at the third stage tends to move with immigration but much more sluggishly, and the change at the fourth stage tends to lag behind immigration. If immigrants were distributed among age classes in the manner the allocation procedure used suggests, this is exactly the pattern of population increments one would expect to find in response to swings in immigration.

basis of the annual data on interstate migration in the postwar period.[6] No attempt was made to further subdivide the 45-64 age class, since the variation in headship rates within this age class is very small.

These procedures led to the following percentage distribution of the age classes for which immigration data were available among the smaller age classes used in computing required additions resulting from immigration.[7]

15-44 age class	*45-and-up age class*
10%.....15–19	75%.....45–64
26.......20–24	25.......65-and-up
40.......25–34	
24.......35–44	

Except for the 65-and-up age class, it was assumed that the headship rates calculated for the total population in each age class also applied to the change in the population in the age class due to immigration. Because of the concentration of recent immigrants in low-income groups and because of the social and cultural differences between recent immigrants and the rest of the housing population, one would expect that this assumption would tend to overestimate the immediate impact of immigration on total and sales required additions. However, as the immigrant population is assimilated, a lagged impact on required additions would be expected as the applicable headship rates adjust toward the norm of the nonimmigrant population.

---

[6] This procedure probably underestimates the change in the population in the 45-64 age class because the relative importance of interstate migrants in the 65-and-over age class probably overstates the relative number of immigrants in this age class. However, the lag of changes in immigration for the 45-64 age class behind changes at the earlier stages suggests that some of the immigrants in this age class came over to join children who had immigrated in the past. The resulting lower headship rate would tend to compensate for the underestimate of the population change due to immigration in this age class.

[7] The result differs remarkably little from the age composition of postwar immigration, suggesting that economic and life-cycle factors still play an important part in determining the age composition of immigration despite the effect of legislation. This is particularly true for the 15-44 age class. The percentage distribution of both the 15-44 and the 45-and-up age classes for immigration between 1953 and 1962 is given below along with the percentage distribution used in this paper to allocate past immigration within the same age classes.

	1953–62	*Text (above) allocation*	
15–19.................	14%	10%	
20–24.................	26	26	15–44
25–34.................	41	40	
35–44.................	20	24	
45–64.................	87	75	45-and-up
65-and-up.............	13	25	

TABLE C1. CHANGE IN POPULATION BY AGE CLASS DUE
TO IMMIGRATION, BY QUINQUENNIAL PERIOD
(Thousands of people)

Quinquennial period	Age class							Total
	0-14	15-19	20-24	25-34	35-44	45-64	65-and-up	
1850-55.........	428	139	380	569	310	54	19	1,899
1855-60.........	178	77	210	318	160	25	9	977
1860-65.........	172	72	197	295	162	28	10	936
1865-70.........	350	125	342	513	293	53	18	1,694
1870-75.........	374	123	335	502	309	62	21	1,727
1875-80.........	198	85	231	346	185	31	11	1,085
1880-85.........	685	218	594	891	479	81	28	2,975
1885-90.........	436	175	478	717	380	63	22	2,270
1890-95.........	317	199	543	815	354	40	14	2,282
1895-1900.......	230	132	361	541	253	35	12	1,563
1900-1905.......	463	316	822	1,265	759	155	52	3,833
1905-10.........	595	414	1,076	1,655	993	172	57	4,962
1910-15.........	691	360	936	1,440	864	198	67	4,460
1915-20.........	223	92	238	366	220	104	34	1,276
1920-25.........	486	191	497	764	458	182	61	2,639
1925-30.........	238	110	286	440	264	90	30	1,458
1930-35.........	40	15	38	59	35	25	8	220
1935-40.........	47	20	53	81	49	44	14	308
1940-45.........	26	11	28	43	26	29	10	172
1945-50.........	137	58	149	230	138	113	38	864
1950-55.........	232	93	159	287	158	131	29	1,088
1955-60.........	318	133	240	375	180	159	23	1,428

Sources: 1850-55 to 1935-40 — U.S. Bureau of the Census, *Historical Statistics of the United States, 1789-1945* (Washington: U.S. Government Printing Office, 1949), Table B331-336, p. 37 (see text for the method of allocation used to distribute the reported data among the age intervals); 1940-45 to 1945-50, 1951, and 1952 — U.S. Bureau of the Census, *Statistical Abstract of the United States: 1960* (Washington: U.S. Government Printing Office, 1960), Table 118, p. 96, with data for the reported age intervals distributed among the various age classes in the same manner as for the pre-1940 data; and 1953 to 1960 — U.S. Department of Justice, *Annual Report of the Immigration and Naturalization Service* (Washington: U.S. Government Printing Office, 1962), p. 36.

Because most of the people over 65 arriving in this country probably came as members of family groups, the immigrant population over 65 was disregarded in estimating the effect of immigration on required additions.[8] The double counting of the number of households formed by immigrants is thus largely avoided.

Using these assumptions and procedures, it was possible to estimate the effect of immigration on housing markets. Confidence in the results

---

[8] However, in Table C2, required additions for the 65-and-up age class are shown (but not included in total required additions due to immigration). If they were included, the difference would be insignificant.

TABLE C2. CHANGE IN REQUIRED ADDITIONS BY AGE CLASS
DUE TO IMMIGRATION, BY QUINQUENNIAL PERIOD
(Thousands of dwelling units)

Quinquennial period	Age class						
	15-19	20-24	25-34	35-44	45-64	Total Cols. 1-5	65- and- up
	(1)	(2)	(3)	(4)	(5)	(6)	(7)
1850-55.................	1	42	187	144	29	403	10
1855-60.................	1	22	104	74	13	214	5
1860-65.................	..	21	97	75	15	208	5
1865-70.................	1	37	169	136	29	372	10
1870-75.................	1	36	165	147	34	383	12
1875-80.................	1	25	114	86	17	243	6
1880-85.................	1	64	293	223	44	625	15
1885-90.................	1	51	236	177	34	499	12
1890-95.................	1	58	268	165	21	513	7
1895-1900..............	1	39	178	118	19	355	6
1900-1905..............	3	88	411	352	82	936	28
1905-10.................	4	115	538	461	92	1,209	30
1910-15.................	3	100	468	401	105	1,077	36
1915-20.................	1	25	119	102	55	302	18
1920-25.................	2	53	248	213	97	613	32
1925-30.................	1	31	143	122	48	345	16
1930-35.................	..	3	19	16	13	51	4
1935-40.................	..	6	27	22	23	78	7
1940-45.................	..	2	14	12	15	44	5
1945-50.................	1	24	84	62	57	228	20
1950-55.................	1	30	112	76	69	288	15
1955-60.................	2	39	138	81	81	341	13

Sources: Population data — Table C1; headship rate data — Table B1, Appendix B, as follows: 1890 headship rates through 1925-30, 1930 headship rates in the 1930's, 1940 headship rates in the 1940's, 1950 headship rates for 1950-55, and 1955 headship rates for 1955-60.

is increased by the fact that most of the conclusions derived from the estimates of required additions due to immigration and presented in Chapter VII depend on the concentration of most immigrants in the early life-cycle stages and not on the precise distribution of immigrants between age classes. The estimates of population change and required additions due to immigration by age class are shown in Table C1 and Table C2, respectively.

APPENDIX D

Mortality Rate Changes

To trace precisely the impact of changes in mortality rates on the housing population in a given age class one would need to calculate the change in the number of people in each age class using two sets of mortality rates, and these mortality rates and the age distribution for single years of age at different dates would also be needed. Both data and time limitation precluded this sort of calculation for this study, so another method was developed to rough in the effect of changing mortality rates on required additions. This method was based on death rates per annum (expressed as a percentage) for 10-year age intervals at different dates.[1]

To find the number surviving from, for example, the 25-34 age class to the 35-44 age class at a given mortality rate over a decade, it was assumed that everyone in the 25-34 age class was 30 years of age at the beginning of the decade. Then the number of people was multiplied by one less the percentage of deaths per annum (the survivor rate) for the 25-34 age class raised to fifth power. The product was the estimate of the number surviving to enter the 35-44 age class (to reach 35) at the middle of the decade. This number was then multiplied by the survivor rate per annum for the 35-44 age class raised to the fifth power to find the population in the 35-44 age class at the end of the decade.

To find the population base for estimates of the impact of changes in mortality rates on required additions, first the above calculation was made for each age class using survivor rates at the beginning of each decade, and then the same calculation was made using survivor rates at the end of the decade. The difference between the resulting estimates of the housing population at each life-cycle stage when multiplied by the headship rate in each age class is the estimate of the impact of mortality rate changes on required additions.

[1] See US Bureau of the Census, *Statistical Abstract of the United States, 1960* (Washington: U.S. Government Printing Office, 1960), Table 67, p. 62.

195

Of course, the procedure followed does no more than provide an index of the relative impact of changes in life expectancy in different decades and give some idea of the number of dwelling units likely to be involved. To compensate for the fact that the above procedure assumes that the improved death rates (as reported at the end of a decade) applied throughout the decade, the initial estimates of the effect of mortality rate changes on required additions was divided by two. The result may be in error because the population in an age class was not evenly distributed through the age class or because the change from beginning to end-of-period death rates occurred in one jump near either end of the decade and not evenly throughout the decade (as dividing by two implies).

APPENDIX E

Adjustment for the War Backlog

The change in the continental population from 1940 to 1945 clearly overstates the effect of population changes on housing demand. A large proportion of the population (especially of males at the early life-cycle stages) was in the armed forces and had delayed forming a family or heading a nonnormal household. Or, if a family was left behind or the individual entering the service headed a nonnormal household, the household existing in 1940 may have been dissolved and the remaining members (if any) doubled up with other households. For similar reasons, the population changes from 1945-50 would understate the level of required additions, since changes in the continental population would not account for the effect of demobilization (except for the portion of the armed forces overseas in 1945).

Thus, to even roughly measure the effect of mobilization and demobilization on housing demand, the 1945 continental population data must be adjusted in some manner. The following assumptions and calculation were made to adjust the 1945 housing population by age class and to estimate the required housing stock in 1945.

(1) For the 15-19 and 20-24 age classes, it was assumed that no one in these age classes who was in the armed forces in 1945 headed a household. This implies that the small number of households headed by those in the 20-24 age class in 1940 when they were in the 15-19 age class were dissolved when the heads entered the armed forces. Thus, the civilian population in 1945 was the base for the required housing stock in these age classes in 1945.

(2) For the 25-29, 30-34, and 35-39 age classes it was assumed that no households in existence in 1940 (at the 20-24, 25-29, and 30-34 age classes, respectively) were dissolved, but that no additional households were formed by members of these age classes entering the armed forces. Thus, the required housing stock in 1945 for these age classes, using the

197

30-34 age class as an example, was estimated as follows. First, the civilian population in the 30-34 age class in 1945 was subtracted from the continental population in the 25-29 age class in 1940 to estimate mobilization. Actually, the resulting difference would equal mobilization plus civilian deaths plus the number in the armed forces in the United States in 1940. For the age classes under consideration, natural deaths are relatively unimportant and the number in the armed forces in 1940 was a very small proportion of the continental population. The number mobilized so estimated was then multiplied by the headship rate for the 25-29 age class in 1940 to determine the number of households in existence in 1945 with heads in the armed forces. This total was then added to the required stock derived by multiplying the 1945 civilian population by the 1940 headship rate to obtain the total required stock for these age classes.

(3) For the 40-44-and-up age classes it was assumed that mobilization had no effect on the number of households. The difference between the total and the civilian population in these age classes in 1945 was very small, and it seems reasonable to assume that most of the household heads mobilized did not dissolve their households. However, the required stock was based on the total rather than the continental population in 1945 to account for the fact that some part of the population in these age classes was in the armed forces.

The bias introduced by this adjustment procedure should be clarified. For the 15-19 and 20-24 age classes, the approach used would tend to overstate the effect of mobilization (and so of demobilization), since some small part of the households formed in 1940 by those between 15-19 years of age would not be dissolved — a minor error, since the original number would be small and heavily weighted with nonnormal households likely to be dissolved — and because some small part of the population entering the armed forces would form and maintain a household. This bias is partly offset by the fact that applying total headship rates to the civilian population disregards both the difference in headship rates between males and females by age class and the large change in the sex composition of the civilian population in 1945 in the 15-19 and 20-24 age classes. However, in this period (1940-45) there was a substantial increase in the number of female heads relative to the female population, and the use of total headship rates probably does not overestimate the number of dwelling units required by the civilian population in 1945 by much.

On the other hand, the procedure used for the remaining age classes would tend to understate the effects of mobilization. In the first place, even if not wholly correct, the assumption that no additional households were formed by individuals entering the armed services has little effect beyond the 30-34 age class (and a rapidly declining effect from the 25-29 to 30-34 age class) because, mobilized or not, few additional households are formed by individuals in these age classes. However, some households whose heads were inducted into the service, especially the non-normal households, certainly were dissolved between 1940 and 1945.

The net effect is that the procedures used may tend to overestimate the effect of mobilization and, consequently, to overestimate the impact of demobilization at the first life-cycle stage, while having the opposite bias at the second and third life-cycle stages.

Once the required stock in 1945 was estimated in the above manner, then required additions were calculated by taking the differences between the required stock in 1940 and in 1945 by age class and between 1945 and 1950 by age class. Since the 1945 required stock is based on 1940 head-ship rates, this approach implicitly assumes that all of the relatively large increase in headship rates during the 1940's occurred in the second half of the decade.

The circumstances that accounted for the increase in headship rates between 1940 and 1950 (decreasing unemployment, increasing real incomes, the changing size of family groups, earlier marriages, and motherhood) may have been at work in the 1940-45 period, but most of the effective changes must have taken place in the second half of the 1940's, simply because the housing units required were not available before the end of the war.